How to Talk to Children About Food

How to Talk to Children About Food

A New Approach to Managing Food Issues, Fussiness and Eating Disorders, for Ages 0-16

Dr Anna Colton

LEAP

First published in the UK in 2025 by LEAP
An imprint of Bonnier Books UK
5th Floor, HYLO,
103–105 Bunhill Row,
London,
EC1Y 8LZ

Owned by Bonnier Books
Sveavägen 56, Stockholm, Sweden

Trade Paperback – 978-1-785120-55-8
Ebook – 978-1-785120-56-5
Audio – 978-1-785123-68-9

All rights reserved. No part of the publication may be reproduced, stored in a retrieval system, transmitted or circulated in any form or by any means, electronic, mechanical, photocopying, recording or otherwise, without prior permission in writing of the publisher.

A CIP catalogue of this book is available from the British Library.

Design and Typeset by Envy Design Ltd
Illustrations by Jake Cook
Printed and bound by Clays Ltd, Elcograf S.p.A

3 5 7 9 10 8 6 4 2

Copyright © Dr Anna Colton, 2025

Dr Anna Colton has asserted her moral right to be identified as the author of this work in accordance with the Copyright, Designs and Patents Act 1988.

Every reasonable effort has been made to trace copyright holders of material reproduced in this book, but if any have been inadvertently overlooked the publishers would be glad to hear from them.

LEAP is an imprint of Bonnier Books UK
www.bonnierbooks.co.uk

*To the young people and families with whom
I have worked, who have trusted me through the
most difficult times in their lives.*

This book is for information or educational purposes only and is not intended to act as a substitute for medical advice or treatment. Any person with a condition requiring medical attention should consult a qualified medical practitioner or suitable therapist.

All names and personal details have been changed to protect the identity and privacy of patients and their parents and carers.

Contents

Dear Reader — 1
   Note to Parents and Carers — 7

Chapter 1: What Is Food? — 9
   A Game to Get Kids Having Fun Talking About Food — 16

Chapter 2: Your Family Food Legacy — 21
   Identity — 27
   Food Scarcity and Abundance — 30
   Culture — 36
   Religion — 40
   Screentime and Mealtimes — 46
   Table Manners — 49

Chapter 3: Feelings — 57
   Our Emotions — 61
      Emotional Vocabulary Exercise — 61
      The Emotion Wheels — 64
      Distress Tolerance — 74
   Thinking 'Errors' — 81
      Black-and-White Thinking — 82

Emotional Reasoning	83
Catastrophising	86
Comparisons	87

Chapter 4: Communication Through Food — 91
- Connection, Eating and Mental Health — 92
- Parental Love — 99
- Modelling — 101
- Methods of Communication — 109
  - A Note on Children's Behaviour — 109
  - Treats and Rewards — 111
  - Anger and Punishment — 115
- The Dessert Conundrum — 124

Chapter 5: Developmental Stages with Eating — 129
- Pregnancy and Birth — 130
- Infancy and Early Childhood — 133
  - From Birth to Three Months — 134
  - Two to Six Months — 138
  - Five to Nine Months — 139
  - Seven to 15 Months — 141
  - One to Three Years — 144
  - Starting School: Ages Three to Six — 148
  - Middle Childhood: Six to 12 Years — 152
- Allergies and Illnesses — 156
- How to Teach Your Kids to Recognise When They're Hungry — 162
- The Different Types of Hunger — 163
- So How Do You Educate Your Children About Nutrition? — 169

Chapter 6: Childhood — 179
- Picky Eating — 182

Chapter 7: Adolescence — 191
- Puberty — 197

Eating	198
Body Image and Communication	200

Chapter 8: Diet Culture — 215

Diet Rules and the Food Police	217
Diet Culture and Weight Loss	224
Ditch the Diets and Learn to Eat Intuitively:	
How to Do It Yourself	230
Reject the Diet Mentality	231
Honour Your Hunger	231
Make Peace with Food	231
Challenge the Food Police	232
Discover the Satisfaction Factor	232
Feel Your Fullness	232
Cope with Your Emotions with Kindness	232
Respect Your Body	233
Movement – Feel the Difference	233
Honour Your Health – Gentle Nutrition	233
Helping Your Kids to Ditch the Diets	234

Chapter 9: Disordered Eating and Eating Disorders — 241

Eating Disorders	248
Anorexia Nervosa (AN)	249
The Nature and Causes of AN	249
Signs and Symptoms of AN	253
Treatment of AN	254
Bulimia Nervosa (BN)	256
The Nature and Causes of BN	256
Signs and Symptoms of BN	258
Treatment of BN	260
Binge Eating Disorder (BED)	260
The Nature and Causes of BED	260
Signs and Symptoms of BED	262
Treatment of BED	263
Orthorexia	264

Signs and Symptoms of Orthorexia	266
Avoidant Restrictive Food Intake Disorder (ARFID)	267
The Nature and Causes of ARFID	267
Signs and Symptoms of ARFID	269
Treatment of ARFID	270
Please Remember	271

Chapter 10: Putting It All Together — 273
- Whose Baggage Is It? — 274
- Breaking the Cycle — 275

Resources and Further Reading — 289
- Weaning — 289
- Allergies — 289
- Diabetes — 290
- Religious Dietary Practices — 290
- Eating Disorders (General) — 290
- Anorexia — 290
- Bulimia — 291
- Feeding Your Children and Picky Eating — 291
- Health at Every Size (HAES) — 291
- Intuitive Eating & Diet Culture — 291
- Avoidant Restrictive Food Intake Disorder (ARFID) — 292
- General Parenting Books (Behaviour) — 292

Appendix: The Minnesota Starvation Experiment — 293
References — 299
Acknowledgements — 307
About the Author — 309

Dear Reader

Were you ever told that you had to 'finish everything on your plate because there are starving children in the world'? Or to be 'grateful for your meal because there are children who don't have enough food?' Or, 'you can't have dessert unless you eat all your vegetables'? Perhaps you've said, 'Mummy's on a diet, so she can't eat that', or, 'Daddy's fat, you don't want to be like me'.

We are fed from the moment we're conceived, and from the moment we're born we start receiving messages about eating, being fed, food, body shape and weight – what I call throughout this book 'all things food'. We may not realise it, but we're constantly communicating our thoughts on all things food to our children, partners, friends and families. We can easily think that our attitudes to eating are 'normal', and that we don't carry any baggage or deep-seated beliefs around food. But we do.

Everyone has their own particular relationship with food. Our upbringing and our parents' attitudes towards their and others' weight, shape, size and eating habits inform it. As do our own beliefs, societal norms, the media, social media, and experiences at school and in the workplace – it's multilayered and multifactorial. At the most fundamental level, food is a basic necessity but it is also so much more: a source of pleasure and joy; part of a culture that binds communities and families together; and something that nurtures us. And yet, over the last century in particular, food has become mired in anxiety, shame, conflict, confusion and despair.

Adults and children are confused about *what* to eat, *when* to eat and even *how* to eat. Responding to our body's hunger and satiety (fullness) cues has been replaced by prescriptive eating – meal plans with weighing, measuring and counting calories. We watch cooking shows, applauding the artistry of show-stopping desserts, and yet diet culture reigns and we are bombarded with messages about the evils of sugar, fat and highly palatable foods, the right and wrong way to eat, good and bad foods, 'perfect' bodies, new fads and powders that are supposedly better for us than real food. The diet and fitness industries are worth billions of dollars per year, selling quick fixes for a 'happier' life through altering our weight and shape, which we are told are solely the product of, and controllable via, what and how we eat and how much we exercise.

Why is something so basic to our survival so complicated? What is it about food and eating that can cause so much distress and confusion? How can eating and starvation both become addictions like drugs or alcohol? How can a necessity for sustaining life also be a vehicle for numbing emotion, for punishing, celebrating, sharing, depriving, nurturing, loving and hating?

Parents frequently ask me, as a clinical psychologist specialising in eating disorders, how they can prevent their child from developing an eating disorder and – in the same breath – how they can help their child lose weight or stop them gaining weight. These two questions are in direct conflict. I'm sure you can think of a friend or family member who was told they had 'puppy fat', 'legs like tree trunks' or needed to lose weight. Comments like these stick and shape young peoples' relationships with eating and with both their self-esteem (related to your attributes and confidence in relation to the world) and self-worth (a deeper belief in your intrinsic worth and value as a human being). So, how do we help our children develop and maintain a healthy relationship with food?

The language we use to talk about food is incredibly important. Through our communication on all things food, we teach kids what to think and how to feel about it, and our views and hang-ups become theirs. Is the language you use about food neutral? Is it loaded? Do you imply that food and eating are moral issues or that one's weight is a choice? Do you tell your kids that they need to eat healthily or that food can be harmful? Or, do you openly embrace all foods in your home with a food-neutral approach?

Communication not only comes from what we say, it's non-verbal too: the way we react to other people's weight or eating practices; our behaviour around food and exercise; even the way in which we dress ourselves and our kids. We send messages to our children through the food we buy, the meals we prepare and how we eat – whether we pick at our food or gorge on it. It can be a minefield to navigate how we communicate about all things food because it's so wrapped up in a multitude of influencing factors: the way we were brought up, our relationship with it, our beliefs about it and the external, unsolicited messages we constantly receive about healthy (and unhealthy) living. But here's the crux: what we communicate to our kids about food determines the relationship they form with it, and the relationship we form with food in childhood informs our relationship with it for the rest of our lives.

Remarks such as the ones at the start of this chapter are confusing to a child. Whilst it's true that there are starving children around the world, leftover food is not going to find its way to them. Similarly, linking food poverty in others to gratitude for your children's food can lead to guilt and shame in you or your kids around the food that they do have. So, teaching gratitude through food can breed confusion and resentment, which is an unhelpful foundation upon which to build. Educating around issues such as poverty and famine, and appreciating one's more privileged situation, are more helpfully taught and more easily heard away from the meal table. This minimises the drawing of connections between feelings like guilt, shame, embarrassment, resentment, sadness or anger with food and eating.

Common phrases such as 'you can't have dessert unless you eat all your vegetables' are unhelpful to children. They communicate that foods aren't equal; that vegetables are less tasty and dessert is a reward to be desired. It's up to parents to decide whether children can have pudding but to teach kids that vegetables are not delicious whilst sugar is sets up associations with different types of food that we then have to undo later when we want our kids to make sensible and healthy choices.

More phrases that make this unhelpful link include: 'you can't have chocolate today because you've been naughty'; 'you've been such a good girl today – here's a treat for you'; and, 'no pudding until you've done your homework'. These are all used to encourage certain behaviours and discourage others. It's understandable that adults use them because if certain foods are desirable, then it follows that children will be motivated to acquire them. But using food to train children can be problematic both in childhood and later life because it connects food with behaviour and morality which interferes with developing a good relationship with food. And that matters because a tricky relationship with food in childhood continues into adulthood: kids who grow up linking food with behaviour tend to become adults who continue to reward or punish themselves using food.

However, what kids usually want most is parental attention, so using language to praise them when they've done something well and giving them your time when they need you is enough. A cuddle or playing a game one-on-one will give children the positive attention they desire without linking their behaviour to food. Similarly, when a child falls over and grazes their knee, offering a kiss better, a plaster, and an acknowledgement that their knee is grazed gives them the care and recognition they need. This is better than chocolate buttons or a biscuit, which can be confusing because they have nothing to do with the source of distress and pain. The food is being used as a pacifier, to soothe or quieten crying, but it's illogical as it's unconnected to the sore knee. This is an example of linking feeling pain with using food to soothe: comfort eating. When we see children comforting each other, food is almost never involved because it's unavailable as an option. Kids use words, touch and distraction, and they work beautifully.

As we've seen from some of the examples so far, communication about all things food is commonly indirect. How we speak about food, ourselves and others says so much to our kids. To grow up with 'Mummy's on a diet, so she can't eat that' or 'Daddy's fat, you don't want to be like me' are about so much more than food. They're about aesthetics, worth and morals. But it is essential for good mental health to build a value system that is about personality, qualities and attributes, not looks. Kids learn by modelling parental behaviours, not by being told what to do. When children hear phrases like these and watch parents' diet, this is what they understand to be the norm and therefore the way to be, even if we tell them otherwise. It's inevitable that our children will learn that how they look is socially important, but the longer we can delay this the better.

Through this book, I aim to show how parents and carers can help their children to realise that no food is bad, to listen to their body's hunger signals, eat as broad a range of foods as possible and build their self-worth on their qualities as a human being rather than on their aesthetics. This is especially challenging today with the rolling images of stereotypical ideas of beauty and aspirational, 'perfect' bodies that bombard our teens and young adults in particular, on social media.

We have an epidemic of eating disorders of a previously unseen magnitude.[1] They are serious illnesses with severe psychological and physical consequences. Added to unhelpful beliefs about, and a complex relationship with food, these outcomes become even more entrenched and difficult to treat. Whilst having untroubled associations with food does not prevent eating disorders, it is a strong protective factor and one we should aspire to foster in children and young people.

This book is definitely *not* a diet book or a nutritional guide. It's not a 'how to' manual for healthy eating, intuitive eating or any other form of eating. Instead, it is a journey into the multiple meanings we ascribe to, relationships we have with, and ways in which we view and use food. It is a judgement-free conversation about how we develop beliefs about eating, feeding, weight and shape, as well as much else to do with this complex area. We need to change the narrative around food for our kids and ourselves, so that this life source and fount of pleasure and joy is no longer mired in anxiety and distress. I hope this book will help you understand how you developed your beliefs and attitudes towards food and eating, how that will have affected your relationship with food, and how this can impact your kids. I hope, too, to give you the tools and show you how to talk to children about food so that they can develop as good a relationship with it as possible.

Note to Parents and Carers

Throughout the book, I pose questions for you to consider that will help you to reflect – alone, or with your partner or kids – on your relationship with food. These are questions I ask my clients, to help them gauge their own influences and habits. I hope you will find them useful too.

I realise that this book may be deeply challenging for some of you. The pervasive nature of diet culture, and the systemic intertwining of all things food with moral values, reward structures, punishment, fear, celebration and every aspect of our lives means that we have a lot of unlearning to do. It is harder to disentangle our beliefs around food because messages about all things food are endemic in society and, however hard we try, it is impossible to escape them. Much of what I encourage you to examine about your beliefs and attitudes towards all things food may oppose societal norms. Take the chance and be interrogative of yourself and your values. I hope that thinking about these issues will be thought-provoking and helpful.

I want you to know that this isn't easy. I screw up with my kids too. I notice the wrong thing, make the wrong comment, get hooked on my own baggage, and catch myself doing or saying something I'd advise my clients against. Grim though I find it when this happens, I'm at least aware of my mistakes, which means that when I botch, I can attempt to repair it, and sometimes that's the best I can do. Only when we're aware can we notice how we're communicating, and only then can we change those communications. Without the awareness, we're doomed to repeat. My hope for you is that in reading this book, you will become aware of your own 'stuff' around food and eating, so that you can choose what parts you give to your kids and what you don't. And in the inevitable moments where you're running on autopilot, that you notice any errors you make giving you the opportunity to repair.

Finally, throughout this book I refer to mums, dads and parents. I know, of course, that many children are brought up by carers who are not their mums or dads, and that many parents or carers have sole responsibility for the children they bring up or share care amongst a number of caregivers. But for ease and readability, I have used these three terms.

CHAPTER 1

What Is Food?

'Now the first and greatest of necessities is food, which is the condition of life and existence.'

Plato, *The Republic*

Everyone needs to eat. Food is as necessary as water and air. No food and we die. It's as simple as that. So, what makes food such a troubled and often tortured part of life? We don't angst over whether or not to breathe. We don't have screaming rows about whether to drink water. We take these actions as we should – as essentials of life.

Often, arguments about food are over *which* foods are good for us, *what* we should eat and *when* we should eat. How many portions of fruit and veg should we eat in a day? What happens if we don't follow this guideline? Is breakfast actually the most important meal of the day? Is it better to eat an early supper or a late one? Three meals a day without any snacks or six smaller meals? The endless messages that we receive about the superpowers of some foods, the dangers of others, the best portion sizes, the optimal number of meals a day and whether we should be 'fasting' (restricting or starving ourselves) are confusing. As you will have experienced, you feel hungry before eating and full after. When the body needs food, it lets us know by making us feel hungry. When we eat, we begin to feel less hungry and depending on whether we are having a snack, a full meal or a binge, it determines how sated we feel.

The signals that communicate these states are natural. We experience them from the moment we're born; it's why babies cry when they're hungry and stop feeding when they've had enough. It's very important that we teach our children to listen to these cues, and to do so ourselves. When we diet, fast or overeat, we're overriding what our bodies want and the signals they're sending us. If we do this too often, it disconnects us from our bodies and the hunger and full signals we receive, leaving us unsure of what or when we need to eat.

There is an evolutionary component to eating. We evolved from hunting and seeking our food in the wild, where we depended on our senses to establish whether food was safe or not. The cost to our ancestors of foraging the wrong foods was significant. Sourcing food took much energy and so selecting incorrect foods was a waste of effort. For example, some plants were not nutrient-dense enough and so didn't provide sufficient energy (fuel); others could be poisonous and lead to illness or death. Each overarching flavour contains different nutritional elements, although these nutrients are not exclusively found in those flavour groups. Sweet foods were sought because they contain sugar, which is an efficient source of energy. Sour foods, such as lemons, contain vitamin C, which the body needs but does not make naturally, and salty foods contain magnesium and potassium, both essential minerals.[2] As we know, vitamin C can be found in many non-sour foods and a lot of non-salty foods contain magnesium, potassium and other vital nutrients. However, these broad flavour groupings indicate necessary nutrients. Furthermore, our ancestors knew to be cautious with bitter-tasting foods because the bitterness could indicate the food contained toxins or poison, so the ability to detect bitterness was protective of health and, ultimately, life.[3] Even today, these evolutionary preferences guide food choices: for the hundreds of millions of people living with food insecurity, these four broad taste groups help them to identify energy-dense foods. These tastes with their acquired knowledge may also help to explain why we respond to sweet, salty, sour and bitter tastes as we do – particularly sweet foods, which many berate themselves for liking and craving. It makes sense that that evolutionary learning remains. Once our ancestors discovered how to create fire, they were able to change the nature, texture and taste of foods by cooking them, and this is thought to be one of the reasons why we like complex flavours.[4]

Because we have evolved as a species to survive periods of famine, when the human body is deprived of food, it comes to a halt much more slowly than a battery or a car with an empty petrol tank. When a car runs out of fuel, it splutters, jerks briefly and stops. It won't work again until we put more fuel in it. Our bodies are different. We can continue to run without refuelling for a long time, using up our energy and fat stores. Initially, you might feel absolutely fine, but bit by bit you lose energy, feel tired and lethargic, your muscles become weaker as your body takes the additional energy it needs from them, and you find your normal daily routine harder. Focus and concentration wane and your motivation diminishes, along with your sense of humour and interest in others. You notice that your thoughts become increasingly about food and eating, body dysmorphia (being distressed by perceived, often imaginary or unreal, flaws in your appearance) sets in and your mood lowers. Social situations feel scary and you become more withdrawn. Your sex drive dwindles, then disappears. You feel increasingly cold and as your weight drops, a fine, downy hair called lanugo develops over your face and body in an attempt to keep you warm. Your immune system weakens, your hair falls out and your skin and nails become dry. If you are a woman, your ovaries shrink and your periods become patchy and then stop. If you are a man, your testosterone decreases. Essentially, when the body is being starved, all energy gets directed to the essential organs like the heart to keep you alive, leaving nothing for other bodily functions. Eventually, your vital organs start to fail and at the most extreme end, starvation is fatal.

Whilst the body's ability to continue with insufficient food is an amazing survival tool, it is also a cause of complacency and disrespect around eating and fuelling ourselves. Children need to know that food is fuel – that eating is imperative for survival and for life. When you start with this, there is a foundation upon which to build; communication around food and eating which is layered upon this foundation will be more easily understood as nuanced. Without this underpinning to replace foundation, kids can believe that all food is bad, or that it's just easier or safer not to eat.

Sophie came to see me with her seven-year-old son, Josh. She was worried because Josh was a picky eater and often would prefer not to eat. Josh frequently felt lethargic and low in energy and mood. He seemed uninterested in food and indifferent to its importance. Here's the conversation I had with him:

Me: 'Why do you think we need to eat?'
Josh: 'I don't know … because Mummy says so.'
Me: 'Do you like eating food?'
Josh: 'Some foods.'

Me: 'Why do you think that Mummy really wants you to eat?'
Josh: 'I don't know.'
Me: 'Do you think that you need to eat?'
Josh: 'No.'

At this point, I explained to Josh that everybody has to eat. I do, he does, his parents and friends do because eating helps us to live and keeps us alive. Josh looked at me, suddenly more engaged than he had been since entering the room.

'Really?' he asked.

'Really,' I replied. Then we went on to talk about putting fuel in a car, and how our bodies are like the car, and food is the fuel that makes them go.

When I next saw Sophie and Josh, eating had become less fraught because Josh understood that he had to eat every day. There was still work to be done around likes and dislikes, but the initial barrier to eating had been removed with this very simple understanding.

Within the context of teaching kids to respect their body and its hunger and full signals, help them notice how they feel when they're hungry and how they feel when they've eaten. Just think about your child for a moment and how they are when hungry. It's likely that they become lethargic or bad-tempered. Your child might cry or throw a tantrum. Now think about how they are when they have just eaten. I expect they're happier, have energy and want to go and play, or run around. With their playfulness and interest in things having returned, they also chatter away and smile more. Gently highlighting these changes to your child is a great way of helping them tune into their body: to notice when they are hungry and to understand and appreciate how eating enough makes them feel.

Yuli brought her seven-year-old son, Arthur, to see me because he was having regular tantrums at home and school and, despite her best efforts, she couldn't work out what was going on. He often woke up angry, which meant that the whole morning routine was fraught. She always made sure that he had breakfast before going to school but even that was a battle. However, he liked school and so he went off happily, had friends and seemed fine. School reported that Arthur's mood seemed to fluctuate throughout the day. He was sometimes cheerful and playful, full of energy and seemed carefree, whilst at other times he was flat and seemingly more miserable. They, too, weren't sure why and couldn't find a common link. His teacher said he was often not hungry for lunch, though on the days when he ate well, he was happier during the afternoon. Yuli said that Arthur often wasn't hungry, rarely asked for food and had to be encouraged to eat.

I asked Arthur about this, and he said 'food was fine' but he didn't get hungry very much. I asked how he felt after eating and his reply was 'good'.

Before embarking on deeper work, I asked Yuli to give Arthur a cup of milk – more filling than water, but not too much more – as soon as he woke up in the morning so that he wasn't too hungry to eat breakfast. I also asked her to ensure Arthur had a mid-morning snack, to collect him from school with a snack and to avoid leaving more than a couple of hours between the times when he ate. I asked her to keep a diary of his mood and tantrums alongside this, as well as asking Arthur how he felt first thing in the morning, before and after eating.

When they came back a week later, life had changed. Arthur's mood was more stable, he had only had one tantrum, and school had reported he was consistently happier and less 'up and down' in mood. Yuli had discovered that Arthur didn't recognise when he felt hungry. We hypothesised that his body and brain didn't tolerate hunger for long, but that he felt it in his mood rather than as a physical feeling of hunger and that the solution was to make sure he ate every couple of hours until he learnt to notice the signs of hunger.

It's not unusual for kids to need more frequent snacks and meals than adults. We're all different irrespective of our age, but kids have small stomachs and they are doing loads of growing, so need regular fuelling. I'm sure you can think of a time when you were hungry and your mood was impacted. Recognising this for your kids (as well as yourself) is super helpful both for them and for you.

I'm sure it seems obvious to you that eating is essential to sustain life, but unless you tell your kids this, they may not know it. It doesn't need to be a deep and serious conversation; rather, a fact that is referenced from very early on in their childhood so that they grow up knowing it. The analogy I used with Josh about fuel in the tank of a car is a great one that kids tend to like and easily understand. You can also talk about everyone – not just them – needing to eat; they see you eat, their friends and family eat, and so on. In this context, it's easy to drop in comments like:

'Food gives us energy to do things.'

'Food makes us grow.'

'We need to eat to stay healthy, and without it we lose energy and stop working well – just like a car.'

'Food keeps us alive.' I would be very matter-of-fact about this because many children feel anxious about death. So, whilst this is correct, it's a message to deliver in a light and factual way.

A Game to Get Kids Having Fun Talking About Food

It's both important and fun to be playful with your kids around food. This can be through cooking or baking, by using your senses to test the smell of different foods, by doing experiments such as mixing bicarbonate of soda and vinegar and seeing the 'volcano' that erupts, and verbally. If your child struggles with eating, is anxious around food or is a bit picky, then it's particularly important that you find a way to expose them to talking and thinking about food playfully whilst remaining as relaxed as possible. If they are better eaters, then this will all be easier; however, it's still worth being curious with them about the many ways food crops up in our lives. The English language is littered with food-based expressions. For example:

'That was a piece of cake!'
'I'd been walking on eggshells.'
'I thought he'd be a hard nut to crack.'
'It was bananas!'
'I had to butter her up first.'
'Those two are like peas in a pod.'
'He's the apple of her eye.'
'She's a smart cookie.'
'She brings home the bacon.'
'I've got bigger fish to fry.'
'He put all his eggs in one basket.'
'I stayed cool as a cucumber.'
'That's it, in a nutshell.'

Let your kids have a go at working out the meaning of some of these sayings. Don't give them too much help initially – there's a lot of laughter to be had on hearing what they come up with. Once they've shared what they think, congratulate them if they deciphered the expression correctly or explain the meaning if they weren't sure.

There are more food-based idioms to decipher in Table 1.1 below. If your family likes a competition, you can keep a score of who can work out the meaning of the most sayings in a set time – this could be 30 seconds or one minute, depending on the ages of those playing. Or, keep the table hidden and race against the clock to see who can think of the most food idioms in the set time. Alternatively, you can just enjoy chatting about them.

Bringing in the dough	Earning the money
The breadwinner	The main earner in a household
Cheap as chips	Very cheap
Bun in the oven	Pregnant
Eat like a horse	Eat a large amount
As flat as a pancake	Totally flat with no undulation – often land
Egg someone on	Provoke or strongly encourage someone
Gravy train	Make a lot of money easily with little effort
Apples and oranges	Comparing two totally different things
Have your cake and eat it	Try to have, or do, two things simultaneously that are impossible to have, or do, together
Spill the beans	Reveal information / disclose a secret
Cool beans	Sounds good
Full of beans	Have lots of energy

That's the way the cookie crumbles	That's the way it goes
Take it with a pinch of salt	Don't take it seriously
Salt of the earth	Honest, humble, kind person or people
Worth your salt	Worth your pay / good at your job
Sugar-coat	Sweeten or gloss over bad news
Selling like hotcakes	Selling fast
Forbidden fruit	Something banned / forbidden
Bear fruit	Get favourable results
Rotten to the core	Very bad or corrupt
Life is a bowl of cherries	Life is good
In a pickle	In trouble
Top banana	The leader or boss
Low-hanging fruit	The easiest thing to get to
Pie in the sky	An empty / fictitious hope or dream
To have your fingers in lots of pies	To be involved in many things
Half-baked	Not thought through
Peanuts	Very cheap
Bite off more than you can chew	Take on more than you can manage
Bite the hand that feeds you	Hurt or dismiss someone who helps you

Eat humble pie	Apologise (humbly)
Eat like a bird	Eat very little
Food for thought	Something to think about carefully
Have a lot on your plate	Have a large amount to deal with
A bad egg	A bad or undesirable person
Egg on your face	Be embarrassed
Drop something like a hot potato	Immediately stop or abandon something
Couch potato	Someone who watches a lot of TV and does little else
Chew the fat	Chat in a leisurely way
Smells fishy	Seems suspicious
Packed like sardines	Extremely crowded
Toasty	Cosy, warm and comfortable
Bread and butter	Your job / how you earn money
Greatest thing since sliced bread	A new and exciting innovation
Not my cup of tea	Not to my liking
Cry over spilt milk	Fret over something that can't be fixed

Table 1.1. Food-based idioms.

Food is present in every area of our lives. In art galleries, we admire the still lifes of great artists — bowls of fruit or vases filled with flowers. We watch cookery shows on TV, hang posters of cans of Campbell's soup on our walls, arrange cookbooks on our shelves, or scroll through images of beautiful plates of food on social media. We connect with friends and family over meals. For some, food is a love language, whilst for others it's a method of reward or punishment. So yes, food is a life source, but it is also so much more. As we move through the chapters to come, we'll discuss these influences on you and your association with the many ways in which food and eating permeate your life and your children's lives.

CHAPTER TAKEAWAYS

- Food is fuel and essential to sustain life – kids need to know this.
- Much of how our sense of taste has developed is evolutionary.
- The language that we use about all things food is of foundational importance and will directly contribute to our children's relationship with food, eating and their body.
- Food idioms show just how much food permeates everyday language.
- Have a go at finding food idioms with your kids – it can be great fun.

CHAPTER 2

Your Family Food Legacy

'Food for us comes from our relatives, whether they have wings or fins or roots. Food has a culture. It has a history. It has a story. It has relationships.'

Winona LaDuke

What were the messages in your family around food, body image, shape, weight and eating during your childhood? How was your parents' relationship with their bodies? What was their relationship with food? What about with exercise and clothes? Were comments passed on your or others' appearance, shape and size? Was food scarce or plentiful? Did you have to finish everything on your plate whether or not you were hungry? Did your carers enjoy cooking and preparing food? Did you eat as a family? Were mealtimes fraught and stressful or happy and relaxed? Was it the same meal for everyone or did your parent make multiple meals according to people's individual likes and dislikes? Did you serve yourself your food, or did your parents determine your portion size?

Did you eat in front of the TV? Were there special traditions around certain foods or meals?

All of us have a food and eating legacy which significantly contributes to our relationship with food. Our legacy consists of beliefs and values that we acquired during childhood and adolescence. It comes from our parents, culture, religion and social contexts whilst we were growing up. The answers to the questions above will make up some of your family legacy, along with additional factors including your genetics and biology; whether you have health issues or allergies; any eating habits you formed, such as always leaving some food on your plate; your relationship with your body; social influences; and your psychological make-up. Any history of eating disorders – yours or within your family – and any trauma of your own, or intergenerational trauma in the family, can all contribute. In light of these, considering the questions asked in the previous paragraph may feel overwhelming and can take a long time to unpick, even with help. Nonetheless, it is worth taking the time to think them through, as reflecting on these questions is enlightening.

Our relationships with our bodies, with food and with eating do not emerge overnight. They develop subtly and iteratively over the course of our life, but with the most fundamental time being during childhood and adolescence. No single factor will determine your relationship with food – it is about the combination of, and the interplay between, all factors. Understanding your connections with these things is essential in order for you to be aware of what you might inadvertently pass onto your children. That awareness, in turn, gives you choices about how you communicate with your kids.

So, cast your mind back to your childhood. What are your first memories of food and eating? These will give you an indication of the general foundation of your relationship with them. What is the overriding mood of these memories? Was it warm and nurturing with pleasurable family meals filled with tasty food and enjoyable conversations, lingering over the food to prolong the enjoyment? If so, you will likely have positive associations with mealtimes and the sharing of meals. You are more likely to want to replicate these in your family, and to have an internal model that will enable you to do so. If, on the other hand, mealtimes were fraught or stressful, then the underpinning of your relationship with food will likely be associated with anxiety and tension. Passing this on to your own children is deleterious to them, and if they become anxious around food it will negatively impact you too.

Hayley came to see me because she was struggling with her two sons, particularly at dinner time. 'It is all so stressful,' she told me. 'Ben is a really slow eater, and it takes him more than double the time to eat the same amount as Max. Max doesn't want to wait for Ben; he wants to leave the table and so do I. We just sit waiting and watching. I try to cajole Ben but end up getting frustrated and cross with him. My husband, Cal, doesn't struggle with the boys. Ben still eats slowly but the three of them seem to manage to have a laugh whilst eating and Max doesn't complain about staying at the table whilst Ben finishes.'

Hayley's parents had not got along and had eventually separated when she was 14, but they had been keen for the family to eat dinner together. Unfortunately, they often argued during meals, and Hayley and her siblings felt anxious, angry and desperate to leave the table as quickly as possible. There were few fun conversations, and the general mood was tense with stilted questions at best. Hayley was now unwittingly engaging in a similar dynamic with her boys. Although she and her husband were in a secure and happy marriage, she didn't have a model of enjoyable mealtimes. Unlike Cal's family, she had no experience of banter, story-telling or games during meals, so she was unconsciously replicating a part of her upbringing that had been unhappy.

No one intends to make mealtimes stressful or unhappy, but until we unpick and understand what we are bringing into our families, we are destined to repeat patterns. The mind gravitates to whatever is familiar, as it associates familiarity with safety. It's not a choice that we make: it is primal and evolutionary. When we were cave dwellers, the cave was familiar and safe. It gave protection, shelter and warmth. When we left the cave to hunt for food we were in much greater danger; predators were lurking, ready to hunt us, just as we were hunting prey for ourselves. Consequently, being out on the plain was unsafe.

I'm going to take a moment to outline how our brain works when it comes to detecting and assessing danger because this is the root of anxiety. Broadly speaking, we can think of our brain as having two parts: our primal or chimp brain (I will use these interchangeably) and our highly evolved, intellectual, human brain. Our primal brain is a primitive system – the instinctive, reactive part of the brain that we do not control. It's emotional and responds to the world based on feelings. Survival is its sole focus and all of its impulses and responses are in aid of surviving. The human brain is the conscious, thinking part – the part that makes you you. It relies on facts and logic which take time to gather and piece together. These two parts of our brain coexist but our primal brain sometimes hijacks our thinking, human brain. Just as a chimpanzee is much stronger than a human, your chimp brain is much stronger than your human brain:[5] however rational and measured you are, your primal brain is nonetheless powerful and active because it is your threat detection system.

Over the course of the day, we receive masses of information from our environment, our interactions and daily events. All information comes into the amygdala (the home of our chimp brain) – a small, almond-shaped part of the brain that is most closely linked with emotion including fear. It is the threat-detection centre of the brain (our chimp), and when it detects danger, it alerts us by making us worried. If the threat is small, we use our rational, human brain to assess and dismiss the threat. When the danger is life-threatening, we don't have time to assess the threat and the primal brain responds automatically by flooding our body with adrenaline and cortisol, leading to a state of heightened arousal and the desire to fight, flee or freeze. You will have heard stories of people managing to run with a broken leg or survive a situation that sounds impossible. These happen when we are flooded with adrenaline and the primal brain is in full force and solely focused on survival. When we are in genuine danger, this instinctive response is an amazing survival system without which we would be at much greater risk, even though today we very rarely need the level of threat detection that our hunter-gatherer ancestors did. Our primal systems remain and operate as they did back then – and when we are in life-threatening danger, it is this primal, instinctive response that saves our life.

We are lucky, nowadays, that the dangers our ancestors faced hunting are largely non-existent. However, that doesn't mean that you haven't experienced other moments of threat around food. Anything that causes fear or significant anxiety will be responded to by a flood of adrenaline from your primal brain. Common examples are allergies, food poisoning and food insecurity, which all present genuine danger to health and life. Conflict around food at home and bullying about your eating or size can also be frightening and trigger similar reactions. Unless processed properly, these encounters stick in our brain and cause us to feel that they are still happening now, thereby shaping our perceptions of the world and our future experiences. This explains why you can be triggered by something that happened decades ago: it is stuck in your amygdala and your mind responds as if it were happening now.

The power of the primal brain and subconscious mind tells us what is and is not safe. The information upon which the primal brain runs is programmed into us from the moment we are born, by the experiences and interactions that we have. If our needs were predominantly met and we were nurtured in infancy and childhood, we grow up expecting this to happen and so having needs and asking for them to be met feels familiar and safe. If meals were enjoyable, they will feel safe, we will have positive memories and look forward to them. However, if family relationships with food were stressful or distressing, or mealtimes were a source of conflict, anger or shame, then that becomes familiar and the mind interprets these as unsafe, however much we rationally want a different experience. This is why we repeat patterns of relationships and behaviours even when we consciously want something different. Our mind is powerful and we are run much more by our primitive, subconscious brain than our rational, conscious one, however uncomfortable this is.

I hope that knowing how the mind reacts to threat, and that familiarity is interpreted as safety even if the situation is not objectively safe, helps you understand why I am asking you to consider your childhood and your parents' food legacy: they are probably still influencing you. How did your parents eat and what was their legacy from their parents? Did they prepare fresh food or did you have a diet of pre-packaged meals? This is not about right and wrong: the food and meals we have as children lay the foundations for later life. Watching parents preparing fresh food creates a belief that it is possible to use fresh ingredients and create your own meals. You will also have watched and learnt some of the skills that you need to cook. If there were only packaged foods and ready meals at home, you won't have had the learning and skills that come from a household that cooks. If your parent cooked but didn't enjoy it, you may learn cooking is a chore, a burden you don't want to impose on yourself or your family. Conversely, if cooking was a joyful and scrumptious experience, you know that food can be delicious and versatile, that flavours can vary with the addition of seasoning, and that preparing meals can be pleasurable, creative and fun.

Identity

What does the food that you put on your plate say about you? Are you what you eat, as the saying goes? What do your food choices and habits communicate? How do they contribute to your identity? You will have many parts of your identity, rather than just one. I think of everyone as a jigsaw: a picture comprising multiple pieces that interlink, and which, when pieced together, create a whole. Everyone has at least one piece of their identity jigsaw that contains food, and many of us have more.

We all have a human experience that is connected to food and the food choices that we make as individuals and as groups. These reveal beliefs, ideologies, passions, cultures, knowledge, assumptions and personalities. They tell stories of religions, traditions, families, migration, assimilation, connections and journeys travelled.

As the anthropologist Claude Fischler wrote, 'Food is central to our sense of identity in that any given human individual is constructed, biologically, psychologically and socially by the foods he/she chooses to incorporate.'[6] Take a moment to consider the different components that create your identity. These might include your family (immediate and extended), your work (past and present), your geographic identity (national and local), your background, religion, heritage and culture. Consider your hobbies and the groups and institutions of which you are a part. Now add in your own personality: do you feel that you're a good cook, terrible cook, foodie, someone who struggles with food, baker, host, entertainer, party lover?

Many people have a symbiotic relationship with food, as highlighted by the food historian Sidney Mintz: 'On many occasions, people define themselves with food; at the same time, food consistently redefines *them*,'[7] emphasising how food both helps to maintain past identity and aids new forms of that same identity. We saw much of this during the Covid-19 lockdowns when people learnt to make sourdough. All over social media, people were posting beautiful photos of their latest loaf. This was a new skill, which quickly became part of their identity. Most of these people already had enough confidence in their culinary ability to attempt something new: bread is rarely the first thing that a non-cook learns. So, a part of their identity was likely as someone who could bake, and they had this self-definition and there began the iterative process. The very existence of this identity meant that, as Mintz described, food and identity then redefined them as they learnt a new skill within the domain.

Another expression of identity through food is your choice of restaurant. For example, when you go out for a meal with your young children, you want to go somewhere that is child-friendly, has quick service and simple foods on the menu. When having a business lunch, you choose somewhere different. For a romantic evening, your choice is elsewhere again. Restaurants do much more than only offer food, just as we do much more than simply feed ourselves. Restaurants aim to pair the emotional and physical needs of their diners with their food, ambience, service, location and price bracket. They have 'personalities' and target audiences to whom they cater.

It's easy to identify with something you love, so if you're a 'foodie', a passionate cook or baker, you will quickly appreciate its importance in who you are. If, on the other hand, you struggle with food, you eat to live and nothing more, you may not think that it forms part of who you are. But even then, food is an important piece of your identity because of the way it permeates our lives.

Excited to begin a new chapter in her life, Ellie headed off to university to study maths, full of optimism. She was a quiet but confident person with a love of baking. At home, she would bake cakes and biscuits for her friends and family, and she'd even been commissioned to make celebration cakes. When she talked about it, her face lit up and she became animated, describing the combination of science and artistry that great baking required. She knew that she was skilled and this was a part of her identity.

When she arrived at university, she was in catered halls of residence that didn't have a full kitchen. Unable to bake, she felt lost. She couldn't smell the aromas of her biscuits or feel the springy dough of her breads. She enjoyed her course and joined a couple of student societies, but she had no way of engaging this significant part of her identity and she experienced it as a loss. Her mood dipped, she felt low and was less able to put herself out there and find new friends. By chance, she saw a post on social media looking for people to help set up a new cooking society and although she preferred baking, she got involved. She was amazed at the difference it made to her – she found people with similar interests. She was able to bake as she had previously done, both to connect with others and as an outlet. Her mood lifted, she became happier and more sociable, and she quickly discovered there were many bakers and non-bakers who shared such a huge part of her identity.

When we find people with whom we click, it's because we identify with something in them. The shared interest brings a shared understanding. There will be an instant point of connection, though it doesn't mean that you'll necessarily become bosom buddies; rather, you'll have a greater chance of bonding over common interests and building a relationship.

Research into the psychological influences on people's food choices and habits[8] found that children tend to choose foods eaten by their older siblings, people they admire, and their favourite fictional characters: it is all part of modelling. Modelling describes the way in which children learn by watching and copying rather than by following verbal instructions. In keeping with this, researchers found that children looked up to their heroes and aspired to be similar through their food habits. (There is a reason why the popularity of the Popeye cartoon led to a dramatic spike in spinach eating in the US in the 1930s.[9]) When thinking about how to help your children to eat foods that they may not naturally choose, try invoking a character or a role model – asking what their teacher's favourite lunch is, for example, can be an extremely useful tool. It can be done with subtlety and without conflict.

Food Scarcity and Abundance

In some families, where parents or grandparents grew up with privations, the belief that one must 'clear one's plate', leaving nothing is deeply rooted. It is common to feel irritation or indignation if your children leave food or seem to take it for granted. There's nothing inherently wrong with this, but it's important to understand your reaction to your child's eating and food behaviours and to take responsibility for it as your issue, rooted in your childhood. Recognise this and it is much easier to talk to your children about food and eating in general. Without such understanding, conflict over meals develops and escalates quickly, often leading to negative associations with eating or food becoming the vehicle for asserting power. A child quickly learns what irks a parent and how to leverage that. When this is food, the child inextricably links conflict, anger and power to food, which is not the link we want to nurture.

My father was part of the post Second World War generation, for whom rationing was in place during his childhood and food wasn't freely available. He also went to boarding school from a very young age where he had to eat everything he was given. With these conditions, he learnt to disregard how he felt in terms of hunger and fullness and to eat what he was given when he was given it, knowing there'd be no more food, regardless of his hunger, until the next meal. This rationing legacy continued for the rest of his life as he finished our leftovers, ate food that he didn't like, and loathed seeing even the tiniest morsel of food wasted. This is a common experience for children of his generation, and growing up with rationing or at boarding school (or both) have lifelong impacts on peoples' relationship with food.

It isn't, of course, only rationing that can lead to a scarcity mindset (not believing or trusting that you will have enough food). If you grew up in a low-income home, it may be that food was not plentiful or readily available. What do you remember about this? Were your parents anxious about where the next meal would come from and was this passed on to you? Did your mum manage to magic up a meal when it seemed there had not been enough food to do so? Do you have memories of going to sleep hungry? Did your parents forego food so that you and your siblings could eat? The answers to these questions are important in terms of your relationship with food and how you

32 | HOW TO TALK TO CHILDREN ABOUT FOOD

impart it to your children, even if you now have ample food. And the pattern can repeat: many baby boomers, who grew up in an era of relative plenty but whose parents had suffered privations during the Second World War, had the ingrained habits of food insecurity. In turn, they passed these habits to their own children in the seventies and eighties – even when neither child nor parent had experienced hunger themselves. This is how intergenerational transmission occurs in all things food.

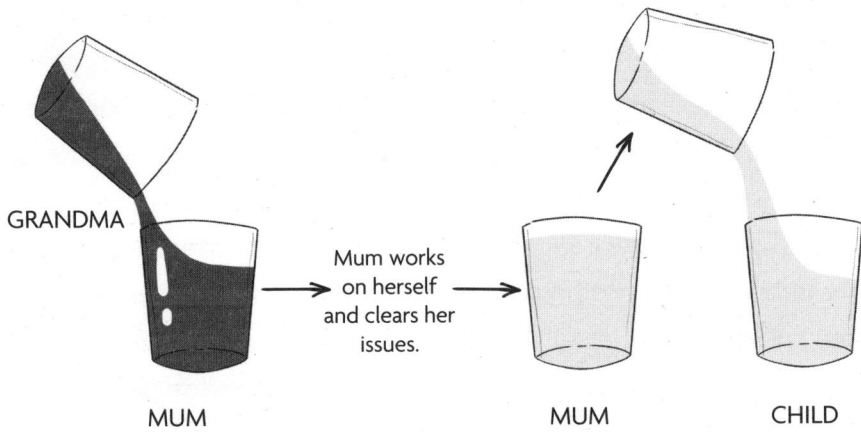

Figure 2.1 illustrates intergeneration transmission. The grandparent is pouring water muddied by their own issues with food into the parent (their child). This will continue generation to generation until someone works on their relationship with food. Once they've resolved their own issues, the water becomes clear and then unmuddied water is passed from parent to child.

If you or your parents had the experience or habits of food insecurity, you may have been brought up to clear your plate and not leave food. You may also have experienced stress and anxiety around food and whether you would eat, or eat enough, or shame about not having enough food or a choice of food.[10] You may hate or feel angry at seeing food left and require your child to clear their plate – or you may eat their leftovers serving the function of a 'food rubbish bin', whether or not you're hungry. You might go the other way and need to have cupboards that are fully stocked all the time, perhaps with much more food than you need, for fear of running short. You may experience marked anxiety if you're unable to find your staple foods or food that your children like. Or unwittingly communicate to them that food is a source of great stress, or something that they must not take for granted and you might struggle emotionally if they are not grateful.

Alisha found mealtimes with her husband, Graham, and their three children almost intolerable. She was deeply distressed as she told me that her children left food on their plates and Graham allowed it. She was furious and overwhelmed even thinking about mealtimes. Both she and Graham were doctors, and she knew rationally that she shouldn't make her children eat when they were already full, but she couldn't stop herself. If they refused to finish their food, Alisha found herself eating their leftovers even when she too was full, and she was also angry about this. She was enraged that they didn't express gratitude for their food and at times 'had the audacity to turn their noses up at the meal'. Graham didn't understand why she was so angry as the children were doing nothing wrong. 'They're typical kids,' he told me. Mealtimes were fractious and both Alisha and Graham were worried about the impact on the family.

Graham had come from a comfortably-off family. His parents were both doctors, too, and had always been in work. On the surface, Alisha's family was similar. Her mum was a radiographer and her father an optician. However, it transpired that for much of Alisha's childhood, her mum hadn't been working, so that she could look after her children, and her dad had struggled financially as he was out of work and then set up a business that went bankrupt. They had been through years of food insecurity, causing her parents much anguish. They had felt both guilty and ashamed that they were unable to feed their children enough, which meant that they did not seek support or get assistance. The girls were forbidden to tell anyone how bad things were and the whole family kept the secret of these food-insecure years – even Graham had not known until our sessions.

Alisha had memories of her parents not eating meals so that she and her sisters could eat. Her parents never blamed her, but she felt guilty about this, wrongly believing that if she were not there, they would be able to eat. Even when both her parents were working again and her dad's business became successful, Alisha remained ashamed of, and traumatised by, these years. Her history of food insecurity was activated when her kids left food on their plates. It was so ingrained and upsetting that she ate when she wasn't hungry, and she unconsciously resented her husband and children for having choices that she had not. She still carried her parents' shame and felt ashamed of how she was acting with her own young family. It was only by working through this that Alisha understood what was driving her overwhelming feelings and could eventually feel more relaxed around her kids at mealtimes.

The impact of food insecurity is not solely the 'complex mix of malnutrition and stress'.[11] Children who do not have enough food experience a myriad of detrimental physical, psychological and academic effects.[12] These include malnutrition, delayed or stunted growth, poor concentration leading to difficulties learning, muscle weakness and fatigue, making exercise and sport difficult. Food insecurity for children means getting used to hunger, stress and anxiety about when they can next eat, shame about not having enough food, and social consequences linked to humiliation, resentment, jealousy and potentially being unable to have reciprocal friendships.

Sadly, food poverty remains for many families today and being free to choose what and when you eat is a privilege. In the UK, food insecurity more than doubled between 2022 and 2023 with 17% of households being 'food insecure'[13] and with almost four million children experiencing food poverty.[14] In 2024, one in five UK households with children are unable to provide enough food to meet the needs of their children and themselves.[15] It's devastating that many children are currently learning to feel hungry, with its associated physical and emotional repercussions. It will leave a legacy that is likely to play out in their own children.

An abundance mindset with regards to food is the knowledge or belief that there will not only be enough food to feed you and your family, but that there will be more than enough. Consequently, food may be taken for granted, and in some people this manifests as entitlement or a lack of gratitude and appreciation for their own privilege. It's hard to feel concerned about wasting food or throwing away leftovers when food has always been plentiful and you've never considered the feelings or anxiety associated with scarcity.

Your experiences and your family's narrative about food and eating when you were growing up will have impacted you. They will likely affect your children, too, because you can't eradicate your experiences from your relationship with food. You have nothing to be ashamed of or to feel guilty about: if you have a troubled relationship with food or a tricky time around it with your kids, this is normal given your childhood circumstances. Take some time and space to work through your feelings so that, like Alisha, you can be freer and less activated by your kids. If you and your partner come from different mindsets or backgrounds it can be challenging, and cause conflict or resentment. You may benefit from outside help, as your children will receive mixed messages and pick up the tension between you.

Culture

Walk down almost any street and you will find a plethora of restaurants and cafés of every culture and cuisine adorning it. At a given moment you could eat whatever cultural fare you fancy: Japanese, Chinese, Lebanese, British, Indian, Greek, Italian and many more. Each country has its unique identifying foods. The great British sarnie or fish and chips; Italian pizza, pasta, tiramisu; Greek salad and baklava; Turkish donner kebab; Lebanese hummus, falafel, tabbouleh and pitta; Japanese sushi and teppanyaki; Chinese dim sum, spring rolls, and a more recent addition, Taiwanese bubble tea... The array is mind-boggling. We tend to take the choice for granted and pick according to the taste and our desire in that moment.

Food and culture are inextricably linked. By culture, I mean the shared beliefs, ideas, social behaviours, traditions and norms of a set of people. It is not biologically inherited, nor genetic. It's learnt by modelling behaviour and language, which begins at birth. Different cultures have different food choices and 'eating is a daily reaffirmation of cultural identity'.[16] From the moment your child comes into the world they acquire your family culture. It may also be part of a broader culture, ethnic group and religion which contain specific foods and food rituals too. The food is a part of us: who we were and who we become. Often the memories associated with it are ones of happiness, connectedness, warmth and family. It's no surprise therefore that as adults, the comfort foods that we often seek are those from both our childhood and our culture.

Take a minute to think about the foods and traditions around meals that you love and choose to continue with your family. Where did they come from? Did your mother or father start them, or do they go further back over generations? What are the images that come to mind and what's the meaning to you of those foods, meals and customs that you value? I imagine that this exercise will bring up memories of happy times, and maybe some of less cheerful periods in your life. Memory is not the domain of the verbal alone. Food contains the language of memory – the smell of a spice, the aroma of freshly baking bread, onions sweating in a pan – which instantly transport you back to your childhood, provoking emotions that are unexpected and memories that you didn't realise were there. Food brings stories, social connections, non-verbal, sensory, taste and smell associations. Cooking and eating Grandma's cakes, or the smell of boiled Brussels sprouts from school, takes you back to them and brings them to you, whether or not they are alive or present. Food and its associated memories link the past to the future and we're more likely to choose to eat foods for which we hold positive memories.[17]

Ava's grandma was 'eccentric' with food. She ate super slowly, telling Ava to chew each mouthful 33 times. She was fussy, and although she liked salads and her vegetables cooked al dente, she preferred most of her cooked food to be overcooked. She would dip dark chocolate discs in double cream accompanied by strong black coffee. Ava had memories of eating in smart restaurants with her grandmother because rather than enjoying the chef's culinary skill, her grandma would repeatedly send back her meal, asking for it to be cooked a bit more: 'Please could you ask the chef to burn it,' she would request, much to the horror of the waiters. Her grandmother was an excellent baker and dessert lover, and Ava had wonderful memories of making cakes and pancakes with her, and also of the home-baked goodies that were on offer when she was at her house.

Ava's face lit up as she relayed this to me, although restaurant meals with her grandma didn't evoke the same pleasure!

Think about a grandparent or family member who is no longer alive. What memories do you have of them? What meals or foods did you share with them? Did they have a favourite food or way of eating? Did they have a jar of sweets from which you could help yourself? Grandparents are often indulgent with their grandchildren's favourite foods as the relationship is special and doesn't usually involve parenting responsibilities. Notice how you feel. Are you smiling, frowning or tearing up reflecting back over these memories? They will give you lots of information on your associations with that person and their eating habits.

Often, we hold more than one culture within us, arising from the groups in which we mix. You have your family, work and religious culture, the culture of your friendship group(s) and those allied to your beliefs (for example, vegetarianism), education, leisure activities and so on. These different cultures coexist and sometimes overlap. Holding different cultures is particularly salient for families or peoples who have migrated. A family will move to a new country and immediately children begin to learn to speak the language of their new country, whilst parents and grandparents may not. With assimilation comes integration of absorbing the foods, customs, language, clothes and behaviours of the adopted country. Simultaneously, however, the customs of the native country or culture remain and food is one of its mainstays. The culinary heritage usually remains for generations after people leave their country of origin and assimilate into their new, adopted country, because food is such a strong part of personal and cultural identity. As the activist Norma Joseph says in her exploration of Iraqi Jewish identity through food, 'Many immigrant families lose their language of origin but food patterns, though often transformed, retain distinctively ethnic components.'[18]

We see this in the UK, where the diverse cuisines found in every city echo the range of nationalities and cultures that live here. There are many British-Indian or British-Asian restauranteurs whose heritage and culture remains strong and is honoured and continued through their food, from their country of origin, their family history and heritage.

Amy and Vijay came to see me over concerns about their sons, Jay and Hari, aged five and eight. Both boys were very fussy eaters but ate completely different foods. Amy and Vijay found themselves making two meals at every mealtime and polarising with the boys in terms of who ate what. Both were exhausted from the tears, upset and stress of mealtimes. They said it was even worse when the children went to their grandparents because neither set were accommodating, so they always had to take foods the boys would eat with them.

Vijay was of Indian origin and Amy white British. During our conversation, it emerged that although Amy liked to eat Indian food, she didn't want to learn to cook it and as Vijay was often not home in time to prepare dinner, most of the cooking fell to Amy. When he cooked, Vijay felt that he always had to cook Indian food, even when he wanted something else, because Amy didn't. He was frustrated by the boys' limited tastes, complaining that the food was bland and flavourless, and he was upset that Amy did not encourage more diverse seasonings. This is a common complaint about children and it's normal for their tastes to change throughout childhood, often seeming faddy in what they will eat. Amy, on the other hand, felt that their boys would acquire more 'exciting' tastes when they were older, and she thought that it was wrong to expose them to strong spices too young.

Vijay had been brought up eating spicy and flavour-rich Indian food from the moment he was weaned, whilst Amy had much more traditional English foods. Their expectations of what their boys could eat were mismatched and the cultural differences between them and their families played out through food, at mealtimes and via their sons' fussy eating. As soon as they realised this, they altered their approach to meals. They worked together to understand their different perspectives, had discussions about meals out of earshot of the boys, and helped their sons to understand that everyone has different likes and there is no right or wrong. They began to talk in front of Hari and Jay about the foods they had liked and disliked when they were children, and so their differences became interesting rather than a source of conflict. In addition, Jay and Hari started to hear stories about their parents' childhoods and they all began talking about food in a fun, relaxed, rather than fearful way.

Amy and Vijay involved the boys in meal preparation without feeling held hostage to their picky eating. Instead of plating the boys' meals they put selections of dishes on the table for them to taste and everyone ate from the same selection. There were always foods that were 'safe' for the boys, as well as new foods and flavours. Over the weeks and months that followed, Jay and Hari's repertoire of accepted foods increased, with some even being enjoyed by them both. Mealtimes became less fraught and rather than the polarisation of two parents and two cultures, a third way developed – a new approach to family meals with a novel fusion of flavours and a more cohesive family culture.

Religion

Culture and religion are often closely tied but whilst everyone has a relationship with a culture, religion is not universal in the same way. Feasting, fasting and dietary laws or practices are, to differing degrees, a part of every religion, deriving from the religious texts and ideals of each.

If you were brought up observing a religion, this will have impacted you and your relationship with food, eating, family meals, festive eating and fasting irrespective of whether or not you are currently observant. A number of religions have a doctrine of non-violence and so practise vegetarianism, such as Jainism, Hinduism, Buddhism and Sikhism. Jewish and Muslim food rules, for instance, can be complex and this might make it harder for your child to socialise with friends and groups from different religions. Observing religious dietary requirements in school can be difficult without help from teachers or lunch staff. To assist with this, the Public Health Agency (PHA) produced a guidance for schools on religious dietary laws, which can be found in the Resources and Further Reading section on page 290.

Such strong doctrines influence your beliefs about the consumption of animal products and other eating behaviours and, consciously or otherwise, you will communicate this to your children. It may be through the foods that you cook and eat at home, but it might be via the extrapolation of broader principles such as never harming an insect or feeding your pet before you feed yourself. If you were brought up as vegetarian for religious reasons and you have eschewed this, there will be meaning to that decision and, again, this will be transmitted to your children. You may choose not to discuss it until they're a certain age, but if your practices are different to those of your parents – their grandparents – they are likely to ask questions, and you will need to have thought through what you want to tell them. Even without strong views, if you observe dietary laws, you'll have thoughts and feelings about eating prohibited foods, even if it is just that you could not imagine doing so yourself, or the thought of eating a particular forbidden food turns your stomach.

If your children, when old enough, decide to follow a less observant path and eat foods that you have never allowed, you will feel an emotional response. You may feel angry, rejected or betrayed, or find it difficult to see them in the same way as you did previously, which might manifest in your interactions and relationship with them. Many adult children never tell their parents when they stop following the family food practises. Mimi told me it would be 'too difficult'. 'I get on well with my parents and they think that I still keep kosher at home and out, which I don't. My dad was furious when my brother stopped and my mum was really upset. I can't face causing them that much pain or having to deal with their reaction. It doesn't harm them, so they don't need to know … It's not a problem to continue as if nothing has changed. It's not like I have to eat meat or shellfish when I'm out with them.'

This argument makes sense and, given the reaction of Mimi's parents to her brother, avoids pain and conflict. However, as I discussed with Mimi, it would also require extra thought when with her parents. Furthermore, if she invited them to a meal or event with her friends, information could slip out in an unplanned way and cause distress based on perceived dishonesty. There is no right and wrong here, simply an illustration of how such issues can play out in families and within us individually.

As with Vijay and Amy, difficulties can also arise in a relationship when the couple have different religions, or one member has no religion. Couples in these situations must navigate whose dietary requirements and food customs will be observed at home, and once children arrive, how they will be brought up in terms of what they can and cannot eat. Such decisions, about what food is permitted in the house and what children are allowed to eat, can be extremely fractious and require significant negotiation and compromise, particularly to avoid distress and confusion to children.

And then there's alcohol. Buddhism, Islam and Mormonism forbid intoxication and the drinking of alcohol, but what then happens when your adolescent, as part of their adolescent developmental process, goes against this? How do you respond? They are behaving in a completely appropriate way developmentally, working out their identity and who they want to be, pushing boundaries and beginning the separation process. But rather than just breaking parental rules, they are breaking religious rules that carry a different weight and are often taken more seriously. Your reactions to all of this may be visceral and powerful, but I urge you to pause before responding. If you are overwhelmed by distress, you won't notice what is happening for your child, preventing you from seeing and listening properly, and potentially leading you to say and do things you later regret.

Food and religion are also about community – coming together to share festive meals, ritual foods, traditions and culture. Food is a language between people that allows communication where there is otherwise no shared language. Across the world on Diwali, Hindus, Sikhs and Jains will celebrate the festival of light, celebrating together and sharing *mithai*, the traditional Indian sweets and desserts. During Ramadan, Muslims will be partaking in *suhoor* before dawn, fasting during sunlight hours and sharing *iftar* after sunset. On Yom Kippur, Jews will be fasting together and on Passover will be participating in the Seder with the ritual and symbolic Passover foods. Arrive in any mosque, synagogue or community at these times with food to share, and you will be able to communicate that you are a member of that tribe and feel connected.

A further example of this is Christmas. Widely celebrated across the world, I imagine you may have somehow marked Christmas, even if only because it is a bank holiday in the UK and many other Western countries. You might also have memories of the numerous Christmas foods and drinks. Were there mince pies and mulled wine? Roast turkey and Brussels sprouts? If you marked Christmas, did you help cook, lay the table, decorate the house? Was it a time that was magical, filled with family, friends, joy and connection or was it stressful, anxious and a day you wished would pass as quickly as possible? What were your traditions? Did you meet other families? Did you give and receive gifts? Did you spend it helping at a care home or rough sleepers hostel? Did one of your parents work on Christmas Day? Were there tensions over food? How do you feel now, remembering what it was like for you as a child? These questions apply whatever religion you are, and no matter what it is that you celebrate – birthdays included. Every family that marks Christmas or any significant religious celebration has their own stories of it, and how you experienced it will inform how you approach it with your family and the atmosphere that you create.

'It's the most wonderful time of the year.' Only for many it's not. Christmas can bring with it an acute awareness of the difficulties in your life: loneliness, financial worries, family rifts, tricky relationships, anxiety, depression, bereavements and grief. If any of this has been your experience, then finding a way to create a meaningful Christmas, containing happiness for your children and loved ones, may be a challenge. The best way to navigate this is to be honest with your children. Tell them that Christmas brings up some difficult feelings for you, but those feelings are not about them and you want to create a different experience for them. Then, they will understand if they see or sense that you are not as happy as others. Without this explanation, they might feel anxious and worry that they are causing you distress somehow.

Lana was suffering with a severe eating disorder and found Christmas extremely difficult. As a child, she'd found it special and exciting. However, as her bulimia developed during her adolescence, Christmas became fraught: she feared the food on offer, knowing that she was likely to overeat and would then want to purge (vomit or exercise to get rid of food eaten). She tried to avoid going downstairs and became withdrawn, which caused ructions with her parents and grandparents. She recovered well, but her memories of Christmas remained tinged with sadness and regret about the years she had been unwell and the upset she felt she had caused to her family.

I cannot write about religion and food without talking about fasting. As an eating disorders specialist, I rebel against dieting, intermittent fasting (food restriction packaged as health enhancing) and food restriction generally. But religious fasting is different because it's a religious imperative similar to praying and feasting, and because the reason for fasting is not about weight, shape or size but about something more meaningful.

Understandably, many children want to join their family and community by trying to fast in the years running up to the required age. It is up to you, as parents, when to allow your children to fast and for how long. This needs to be a thoughtful decision involving your child, and also taking into account their age, physical and psychological health, tolerance for hunger and thirst, activity levels and nutritional needs. If your child needs to eat every two or three hours to maintain their energy, concentration and mood, they are probably not yet ready to fast. The fuelling and metabolic requirements of a child are very different to those of an adult, and they need more fluids and a source of energy to maintain a healthy body, especially for brain development.[19] If they have suffered from an eating disorder, I would strongly advise against letting your child fast until they are fully recovered and have maintained it for at least 12 months.

When explaining fasts to your children, place the emphasis on religious imperative, not on choice. I say this because with the notion of choice, they learn that they can potentially choose to fast any time, and you don't want them to make this choice. It is protective that the family and wider community are fasting at the same time for the same purpose. Talk to them, too, about the risk of feeling unwell and give them explicit permission and encourage-ment to stop fasting if this happens, ensuring that they let you know if they are feeling well. It may sound pedantic, but if they are stopping fasting before others, I would suggest referring to it as 'stopping' fasting rather than 'breaking' their fast as the word breaking can imply doing something wrong, like breaking a rule.

Screentime and Mealtimes

Popcorn at the cinema, toddlers and children with iPads during mealtimes, scrolling through your social media whilst snacking, dinner in front of the TV – eating with screens has become normalised over the past decade. Whilst common and with many understandable reasons, regularly eating with screens brings problems.

Have you found that if your child eats whilst watching their iPad or the TV they eat better? They are calmer, less fussy, more compliant, quieter, easier to manage and eat a bigger portion? Whilst distracted by a screen, they will engage less in what they are eating and more in what they're watching. This makes mealtimes easier, especially if you have a picky eater or you want them to be 'well behaved' in a restaurant or at an event. I completely understand the benefits in giving your child a screen to engage and distract them whilst they eat, and as an occasional one-off, it's not a problem. However, when this is a regular strategy, these benefits are outweighed by the problems they cause.

When we're focused on screens we disengage from eating. 'Yes, that's the point', I hear you say, and it is. It's why it is easier for your child to eat with a screen, but it also disconnects them from their body, its hunger and full signals, from noticing how their body feels whilst eating and from observing how different foods taste and feel. It inhibits interaction with you and the family during meals and the sharing of food, conversations and bonding that family meals bring. It also prevents them from learning by watching and modelling, which is the best form of learning.

We've all eaten popcorn whilst in the cinema or watching a film at home, and there's something enjoyable about it. But have you ever noticed that you eat the popcorn even once you are full or no longer want it, or that you leave the cinema feeling physically uncomfortable? In the cinema, we also sit in the dark and therefore barely notice what and how much we are eating. I really don't want to take away from any joy or bonding that munching in front of a film brings, so if that is a way that your family bonds, keep it up. Given that I'm writing about all things food, however, I want to bring your awareness to things I've seen over my career that can be problematic so that you can make conscious choices. Mindless eating (eating without paying attention to what and how much we're eating) has been shown to lead to overeating and bingeing in adults because they do not know or notice when they are full and they make poor choices about the types and portion of food they consume.[20]

Mealtimes are a great opportunity to sit with your child, eat together, share food and model a healthy relationship with it – kids learn by watching and copy what parents do. Parent and child sit on equal terms – no 'front seat' – and children try out, establish and assert their own character, personality and place in the family. It's a time to talk about the food, to socialise and enjoy each other's company; to chat, nurture your bond and the development of your child's relationship with food, eating and their body's communications. Children need to learn skills around eating, such as feeding themselves, noticing their hunger and full cues, and their flavour preferences. To understand which foods nourish them, learn to serve themselves and to eat independently. Although it can be tough and feel like it's lasting an eternity, we don't have many years to influence our children's eating habits. The early years are when our influence is greatest in terms of what, when, how, where and with whom they eat. It's during the early years that children learn to eat solids, sit at a table, explore food in taste, texture, colour, and to lay the foundations of sociable, enjoyable and healthy eating habits, which come from paying attention to the food they are eating.

Dad, Ken, found his daughter Molly's mealtimes boring and irritating. At three years old, she was old enough to feed herself but was 'whingey and demanding'. She wanted the iPad so that she could watch TV. Ken didn't want her to become 'one of those kids who needs a screen to eat'. However, when he said no, Molly wanted Ken to cut up her food, to play with her, to give her something different to what was on her plate, and meals became unpleasant. He adored his daughter but couldn't imagine ever enjoying mealtimes, so he either sat in frustrated silence or felt that he was giving in by letting her have the iPad to watch.

Ken came from a family where mealtimes were perfunctory. His family ate together in a transactional way: there was little humour or genuine connection and this dynamic was playing out with Molly. Over a number of weeks, Ken changed his approach. I urged him to take the focus off food and to chat to Molly about her day, to tell her stories about his childhood, to play some word games and when she whined, to use distraction by playing 'I spy' or similar. This transformed mealtimes for the two of them. Molly became engaged and smiley, loving the special time she got with Dad, and Ken felt connected to her, positively looking forward to meals. This was a virtuous cycle transforming a hard slog into a pleasure.

It is harder work to interact with your child during meals than to give them an iPad, but I promise you the time you invest will be well spent. When we rely on TV and distraction to get children to eat, they do not notice the meals, properly taste or familiarise themselves with the food. This is why it is an easier mealtime, but in the longer term it leads to children not developing a relationship with, or enjoyment of food. In the medium to long term, it can make picky eating, fussiness, tantrums and food refusal worse, in addition to their needing to be distracted to eat.

Table Manners

It is usual to want your child to be on their best behaviour when at someone else's house, in a restaurant or when you have guests. I wouldn't want my kids face-planting into their plate, being rude or running around shouting and disturbing the whole room – it's very stressful. By contrast, having well-behaved kids who eat beautifully, don't make too much noise, manage to get their food from their plate into their mouths without depositing half of it on their clothes and the table is lovely. It means that you're an easy family to entertain and invitations abound. Friends and family compliment you on your kids and praise them directly. It can be a rewarding and positive cycle. Between these extreme examples lies the normal, appropriate, imperfect behaviour. When nurturing a healthy relationship with food for your child, there are risks around focusing heavily on mealtime rules, manners, politeness and etiquette, as Sanjay and Jo's story illustrates.

Sanjay and Jo came to see me because one of their children was a very fussy eater. Lauren, aged eight, would only eat two vegetables. She liked desserts, biscuits and chocolate, but she was not allowed these until after she had cleared her plate. This meant that mealtimes were fraught with conflict, threats and tears. Jo was worried that Lauren was already on the road to developing an eating disorder.

Jo and Sanjay had had different upbringings and the attitudes to food and eating in their respective families were also significantly different. Where Jo wanted her children to eat and to enjoy eating and mealtimes, Sanjay had extremely high standards for table manners. Lauren and her six-year-old brother, Theo, had to use cutlery, never use their fingers, sit up 'properly' at the table, finish all their vegetables and talk politely throughout mealtimes. Jo had had a difficult relationship with food during her teenage years and wanted her children to have a good relationship with food. She wasn't concerned about table manners.

The opposing priorities of Sanjay and Jo created conflict between them, adding to the fraught atmosphere at meals. This caused significant stress as Lauren had a small appetite and did not always finish her vegetables or her meal. The stricter Sanjay was, the more distressed Lauren became, and the less she was able to eat; things frequently escalated. Torn between pleasing her father and listening to her body, Lauren became increasingly stuck at mealtimes.

Sanjay and Jo needed to work on this together and away from

the table. Helping Sanjay to relax his standards and Jo to support his request for some basic table manners eased the tension between them and the pressure and anxiety on Lauren was less. In response, Lauren relaxed, giving her brain more space to connect with her body and to enjoy family time at the table more.

In reality, if parents have conflicting views on table manners or other mealtime rules, they play out at every meal whether or not you are both present, and your kids notice it. They become confused and anxious and the potential pleasure and bonding that mealtimes can bring is lost.

Hannah, one of three children, was struggling. At the age of nine, she had changed from a child who was happy and relaxed around food to one who was anxious and at times would refuse to eat at all. She had been a 'good eater' since birth. Weaning was straightforward and she had had a very brief 'fussy phase' at the age of four. There was no specific trigger to the change, but Hannah had become, as her mum put it, 'more defiant' of the family mealtime rules: they had to clear their plates; they chatted through meals, but the children were not allowed to talk with their mouths full. Mum was aware that each of the children had different preferences, but she couldn't cater to them all each mealtime and everyone ate the same meal, which Mum portioned up.

When I met with Hannah alone, she was able to tell me that she found meals stressful. She knew it was rude to talk with food in her mouth, but she was so worried about getting into trouble that she felt it was easier not to talk at all. She wasn't always hungry and wished that she could leave food or eat less on a low appetite day, or when it was a meal she didn't like. She said that she used to find mealtimes fun but now just wanted to eat on her own.

Whilst it's lovely to have a well-mannered child at the dinner table, placing too great an emphasis on it causes significant stress. Instead of focusing on their body's cues, getting involved in the conversation and hubbub of a meal, your child worries about whether they're pleasing you, behaving well enough, finishing their plate and so on. Instead of trying new foods freely, they're anxious about saying that they don't like the taste. Rather than respond spontaneously and contribute to the conversation, they're concerned about speaking with food in their mouth or concentrating hard on their motor skills to use their cutlery correctly. We need to teach our children manners, simultaneously ensuring we maintain the positive benefits of shared meals discussed above.

But how to do this when you and your partner disagree on what's important? Start by discussing your views on table manners: how would you like your kids to behave and what table manners are important? Instead of challenging each other's views, listen carefully to one another. Be curious about where your partner's beliefs come from and talk about your own. It feels very different if the reason that you are not interested in manners is because you can't be bothered with the effort of teaching your kids versus because as a child you struggled with eating and you want to give your child a different experience. Once you've heard each other and understood where your beliefs come from, find common ground. One of you might have to accept requiring a little more discipline and the other less. If you have non-negotiables start with these – you'll both have to compromise.

Consider your attitudes towards and requirements for table manners. Do you expect your child to use cutlery in both hands, swallow their food before talking, sit without their elbows on the table, clear their plate, stay at the table for the duration of the meal and ask permission to leave? Or are you content with them leaning on the table, chatting whilst chewing, sometimes using their fingers and leaving when they have had enough? These, of course, are not the only options; there are many variations to expectations around table manners, and you must decide what works for you and your family. Furthermore, these will change as your child matures: what you can expect of your five-year-old is very different to what you can expect of your 13-year-old.

If you're reading this and it's resonating, don't worry. It's never too late to change things. If you'd like to, explain to your children what you have learnt so far. Tell them about your early experiences of family meals and start to do things differently. Begin by taking the focus off food and eating and instead view the meal itself as the least important part of the mealtime. I know this sounds counter-intuitive but if you view mealtimes as a protected time each day, to be together as family, you remove the focus from food and eating becomes easier. If you have young children, engage them in a game or let them tell jokes or ask questions. As your children get older, you can hear about their day, tell them about yours, have conversations about how you're going to spend the weekend, about the world, and their hopes and aspirations. My children loved quizzes at the table – going round the table, with questions being made up by one parent, calibrated to the age and knowledge of each family member.

If mealtime conversation is unfamiliar to you from your own childhood, you may feel anxious and worry that it will cause anger or tension. If so, remind yourself that you are now an adult, that these are your automatic responses influenced by your own history, and that you're choosing to create a different environment for your family. Your partner and children will support you if you're open with them about what you're feeling and that you are trying to do something different and better. It may feel artificial at first, but persevere and you'll be surprised how easily the meal is eaten and how quickly and, most importantly, how enjoyably the time passes.

Everything we've discussed in this chapter links to how you have previously felt in relation to food and eating – your food legacy – and how you currently feel. Feelings lie at the heart of our relationship with food; sometimes they are easy and comfortable, often they are not. Whatever we feel will emerge in how we talk to our kids about food and the food legacy they inherit.

> **CHAPTER TAKEAWAYS**
>
> - Everyone has a food legacy and it consists of multiple factors from our infancy right through to the present, with childhood experiences forming the bulk of it.
> - Everyone has a relationship with food and with their body.
> - Your relationship with food is multifactorial and includes your food legacy, your genetics, health issues, any history of eating difficulties, your relationship with your body and your psychological make-up.
> - Understanding these different factors is important as it helps you to understand the foundation of your relationship with food.
> - We often recreate dynamics and patterns that are familiar to us from our childhood, especially if we are unaware of what these are.
> - The primal brain – the amygdala – is our threat-detection system, and when it senses danger it floods our bodies with adrenaline and cortisol take over.

- Traumatic experiences get stuck in the amygdala and remain unprocessed, causing us to feel and respond to anything that triggers memories of it as we did when the trauma happened. This is why it's important to process the difficult experiences you've had (with or without a therapist).
- If you grew up without enough to eat, it will impact your relationship with food and how you feel and behave around it with your kids – and this can be transmitted from generation to generation.
- If you and your partner came from opposite positions – for example, if one of you had abundant food and the other not enough – this can cause difficulties both between you and in how you interact with your kids around food. Take time to work through this together.
- Developing an association between eating and screens can be problematic. It teaches mindless eating and prevents kids from tuning in to their body, connecting with family and enjoying the flavours of food itself.
- If you bond with your family over films with popcorn, great; but if you use a screen to keep your child calm and quiet, there are better ways to improve mealtimes. For example, play games, tell them about your day and hear about theirs – take the focus off eating and place it on connecting.
- Make connection the focus of mealtimes (rather than food).

CHAPTER 3

Feelings

'You can't stop the waves but you can learn to surf.'

Jon Kabat-Zinn

Before we dive in, think back over your life and reflect on your own emotional world. How were feelings dealt with by your parents? Did they help you name what you were feeling, validate your emotions and encourage you to work through them? Did they give you cuddles, comfort you and have your back when you needed them to? Or maybe they gave you hugs but they were passive or detached whilst giving them? If so, you may have learnt to provoke a response by getting angry and shouting or becoming very distressed. Or you may have learnt to be somewhat cut off from yourself. Maybe your parents couldn't cope with feelings. Perhaps they dismissed them, leading you to feel rejected or unimportant. Or, possibly they wanted to take away your upset so tried to fix things all the time. This communicates that having feelings is a defect that needs correcting and can leave you feeling, broken or like a problem that needs solving.

If you were shamed for expressing emotions, you will likely have cut off or learnt to ignore them as a means of self-preservation. Now, when they inevitably surface, you feel embarrassed and inadequate and need to suppress or get rid of them. Did you have a sibling or parent who took up a lot of emotional space? In these circumstances, you may have developed as the quiet one, the peacemaker or the mediator and so became used to ignoring your own feelings or subjugating your needs to care for others. These are only a handful of examples, but whatever your emotional style now, it will have originated in your childhood and your kids will observe, receive and learn from it too.

For better or worse, whether they make you comfortable or uncomfortable, feelings are a universal, constant and ever-fluctuating part of life. We all regulate our emotions every day, each of us in our own way. Emotional regulation includes how we understand what we're feeling, how we interpret it, respond to the feeling and express it. Then, on a more meta level, how we feel about what we are experiencing and how we learn from it. In turn, these things affect our future emotional regulation and its development.

Some of us have more strategies for dealing with our feelings and a greater ability to regulate them, whilst others have fewer strategies and are less able to regulate themselves. People who struggle to self-regulate and have difficulty tolerating their emotions and are prone to overwhelm. They're also more likely to have unhelpful thinking styles that add to their distress, such as 'all or nothing' thinking. They may turn to unhelpful coping strategies, such as emotional suppression, withdrawal, using food or substances, workaholism, dependence on social media, reliance on external stimulation or soothing, and self-harm. These may work in the immediate moment, but they cause problems in the longer term. Emotions and distress are inevitable.

Learning to understand, name, articulate, permit and tolerate our feelings are some of the most important life skills. Feelings don't need to be fixed, they need to be heard and acknowledged with compassion and attention.

We've all heard of comfort eating, emotional eating and losing our appetites when feeling low or anxious. I'm sure you've experienced one or more of these and you know that eating and feelings can be strongly linked. Restriction, binge eating and using food to manage emotions are very effective strategies in the moment, as they distract you from your distress. However, they cause a multitude of problems and significant pain to yourself and others once the immediate relief has worn off. Emotional or comfort eating occurs when we use food to self-soothe or suppress distressing emotions, whereas the appetite loss that often comes with anxiety and depression is more of a biological process.

Feelings are just like clouds and the weather: some are light and fluffy, whilst some are dark and ominous, harbouring a storm; some days are filled with bright blue skies and sunshine, others with wind, rain or snow; some storms come and go in a flash and others last for days. But whatever the weather on any given day, we know that it will blow out at some point and change. We accept this with the weather, but we struggle to accept it with feelings and moods. Instead, many believe that their mood should always be upbeat and stable, without fluctuation. This causes anxiety when mood inevitably changes and makes you more prone to using unhelpful strategies to cope.

Anxiety is a natural emotion that we need to keep us safe and ensure survival. As we learned in Chapter 2, when our amygdala – our primal brain – senses danger, it alerts us with a flood of adrenaline (see pages 24–7). There are many physical and psychological effects of adrenaline, and one is the impact on our digestive system. When we're faced with danger, all of our energy and attention need to be focused on that danger to keep us safe. Our digestive system stops working because the energy used to run it is needed elsewhere, which leads to undigested food remaining in our stomach. At the same time, our body prepares to flee by emptying of waste products through vomiting, urinating and diarrhoea, which makes us as light on our feet as possible. It is these two things that cause the typical, familiar 'anxious tummy' and why we tend to lose our appetite when we're very stressed or anxious.

When the stress is less acute but persistent, it often leads to an increase in appetite due to lower cortisol levels and higher levels of insulin, ghrelin and other metabolic and reward-signalling pathways in the brain.[21] The same seems to be true with depression, where changes to appetite and weight are one of the biological symptoms. Whilst more people experience appetite and weight loss, there is a subgroup who have an increased appetite and weight gain with a depressive episode.

Emotional eating, on the other hand, is not the same as the biological appetite feature of depression. It occurs when you are feeling emotions that you find upsetting: a relationship breakup, in the run-up to exams, or just when your mood is low. To numb the feelings, and distract yourself, you eat. You think about what food you want and buy or prepare it. Whilst eating it, you engage your senses of taste, touch, smell and sight as well as focusing on the food and literally pushing and swallowing the distressing feelings down inside you. In the immediate term, this is an easy and effective strategy for managing emotions as it gives you something to do and attends to an emotional emptiness. However, thereafter it is unhelpful and leaves you feeling worse than you did when you were simply upset.

Bingeing is a very common form of emotional eating; whilst bingeing, you can't think about anything else and thus your initial distress disappears. Once the binge is over, you become flooded by feelings of despair, hopelessness, defeat and self-loathing, in addition to whatever initially upset you and led you to binge, causing a double whammy of distress. If you are someone who binges, know that you are not weak, defective or lacking in willpower. You have found the best coping strategy with which to manage your distress. Ultimately, it's not a good strategy but it works in the moment. Every behaviour has a function and we all choose the behaviour that best serves the function that we need in the moment.

Given the powerful relationship between food, eating, mood and emotions, it's important to equip your children with as many tools as possible to help them manage their emotions so that they don't have to use food. I use the phrase 'using food' because when you eat or restrict food to manage emotions, you are using food as part of a strategy rather than eating it for nourishment or enjoyment. In many ways, it is the same as using alcohol, cigarettes, drugs and other harmful substances. It does not engender the same response in most people because food isn't mind-altering, illicit or harmful. But actually when used to manage mood, its function is very similar. When you realise this, it is easier to think about how you might change, which in turn brings you hope and a sense of agency.

Our Emotions

Emotional Vocabulary Exercise

We start helping our children to label their emotions from the moment they're born. Newborn babies have one mode of communicating their needs: crying. It's our job as parents to interpret and respond to our baby's cries, and usually we talk aloud to our babies when doing this. 'What's wrong?' we ask, not expecting an answer. 'Are you hungry?', 'Do you need a clean nappy?', 'Does your tummy hurt?' And so on. Simultaneously, we offer food, check their nappy, rock or bounce them, and cuddle them to ascertain what is distressing them and decode what they're telling us. This is the genesis of emotional labelling and emotional regulation. Without this, babies can't learn what they're feeling, acquire the words to name the emotion or have an experience of being understood and having their needs met. These are the foundations upon which emotional regulation and the ability to self-soothe are built.

So, even though babies are pre-verbal and seem not to understand, they get a felt sense – a bodily awareness or knowledge which is bigger than just a feeling – of being understood. It's a vital stage for their emotional development.

How many words can you think of, without help from anywhere, for happy, sad and angry? Maybe five or ten for each? There are in fact many words to describe each feeling.

Before reading on, see how many different words you can come up with for anger. I'd imagine somewhere between 10 and 20 ...

In fact, there are more than 80, each giving a slightly different level of intensity and meaning. See Table 3.1 on the next page.

Angry	Crotchety	Grouchy	Irascible	Peeved	Splenic
Annoyed	Disagreeable	Huffy	Inflamed	Petulant	Snappy
Affronted	Displeased	Hacked off	Infuriated	Pissed	Storming
Agitated	Enraged	Hot	Ireful	Pissed off	Sullen
Antagonised	Exasperated	Heated	Irked	Piqued	Sulky
Apoplectic	Furious	Impatient	Livid	Provoked	Stewing
Bitter	Fuming	Incensed	Mad	Put out	Tetchy
Cantankerous	Fierce	Incandescent	Maddened	Raging	Testy
Cross	Ferocious	Indignant	Miffed	Ranting	Turbulent
Chafed	Fiery	Ill-humoured	Narked	Ratty	Terrifying
Convulsed	Fractious	Ill-tempered	Narky	Raving	Tumultuous
Choked	Fretful	Irritable	Nettled	Resentful	Upset
Choleric	Galled	Irate	Outraged	Riled	Vexed
Churlish	Grumpy	Irritated	Offended	Sore	Wrathful

Table 3.1. Different words for 'anger'.

If your child only knows one or two of these words, their ability to understand and articulate what they're feeling will be inhibited and they'll often be confused by what they're feeling. With confusion they'll be more likely to turn to an external strategy, such as lashing out, withdrawing from people or using food to manage the emotion.

It can be a fun exercise to go through different emotions with your child and see how many different words you can find to describe them. It doesn't have to be heavy or serious. You can do it playfully and make it into a game. If they enjoy art or music, they can draw a picture that describes the word or play the feeling on their instrument. They're never too young to start this and there is nothing harmful or negative that can come from growing your child's emotional vocabulary. Indeed, the same is true for you — you're never too old to increase your emotional vocabulary and most adults have a smaller emotional vocabulary than they realise.

The Emotion Wheels

Emotion wheels, originally designed by the psychologist Robert Plutchik,[22] are a great resource for helping yourself and your kids understand emotions and develop emotional literacy. Plutchik's wheel was based on the idea that there are eight primary emotions: joy, trust, fear, surprise, sadness, disgust, anger and anticipation. These eight emotions appear in a ring around a circle, with another outer ring encircling the primary emotions, as you can see in Figure 3.1 overleaf. The inner circle and outer ring also each contain eight emotions, which are linked to the primary emotions.

To use the wheel, identify the primary emotion that you're feeling on the middle ring, then look at the adjacent related emotions to see whether one of those more accurately describes what you're feeling. Each petal represents a continuum of one of the eight primary emotions, with the outer, palest part of the petal expressing the milder side of the emotion and the inner, darkest section showing the stronger side of that emotion. Often, we feel more than one emotion at a time; for example, joy and anticipation combine to be optimism. Optimism is a belief that something good will happen in the future, so it requires anticipation about the future but from a perspective of happiness (joy) rather than worry or sadness. It can be very helpful to realise that you are feeling more than one feeling and to take time to analyse your feelings and what they combine to become.

FEELINGS | 65

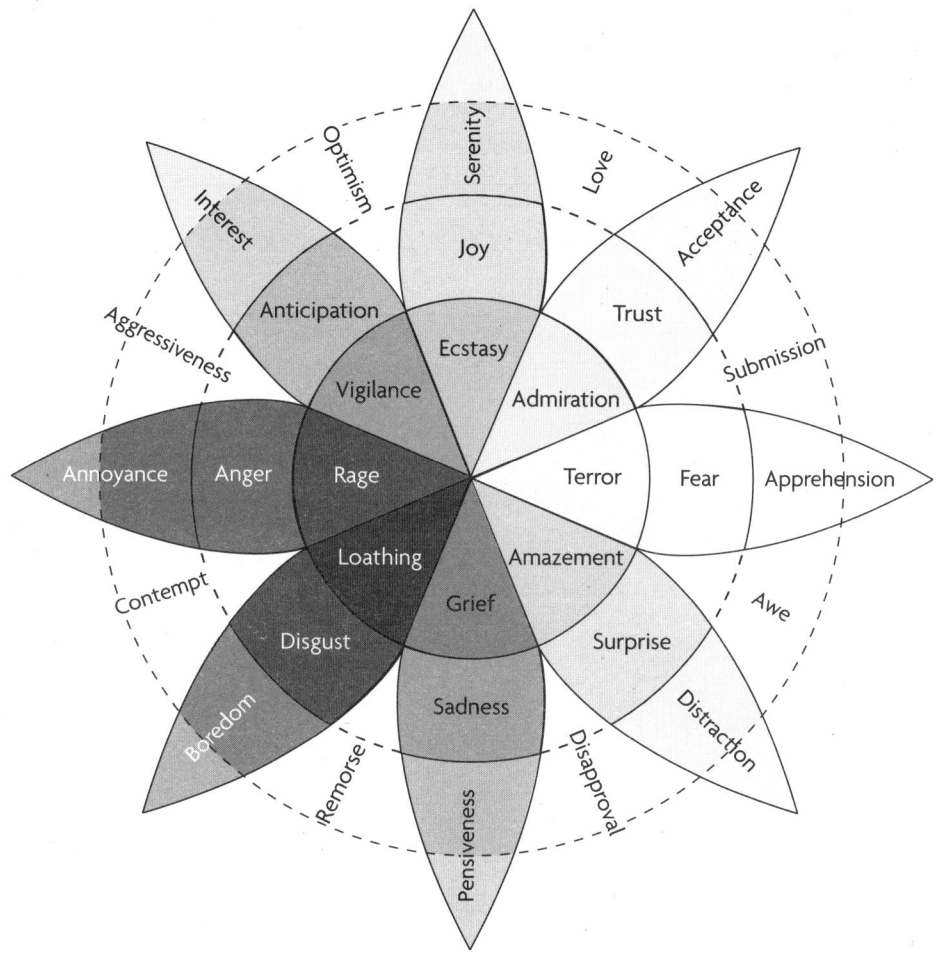

Figure 3.1. Plutchik's wheel of emotions based on the eight primary emotions.

Since Plutchik's initial wheel, emotion wheels have developed and been adapted for all ages in varying levels of detail (see Figures 3.1 to 3.6). The simplest being for young children, aged two plus, and the most detailed for adults. You can use an emotion wheel multiple times a day to help identify and name feelings. It's important to remember to identify positive emotions as well as negative ones; the broader your emotional vocabulary, the better. [23]

66 | HOW TO TALK TO CHILDREN ABOUT FOOD

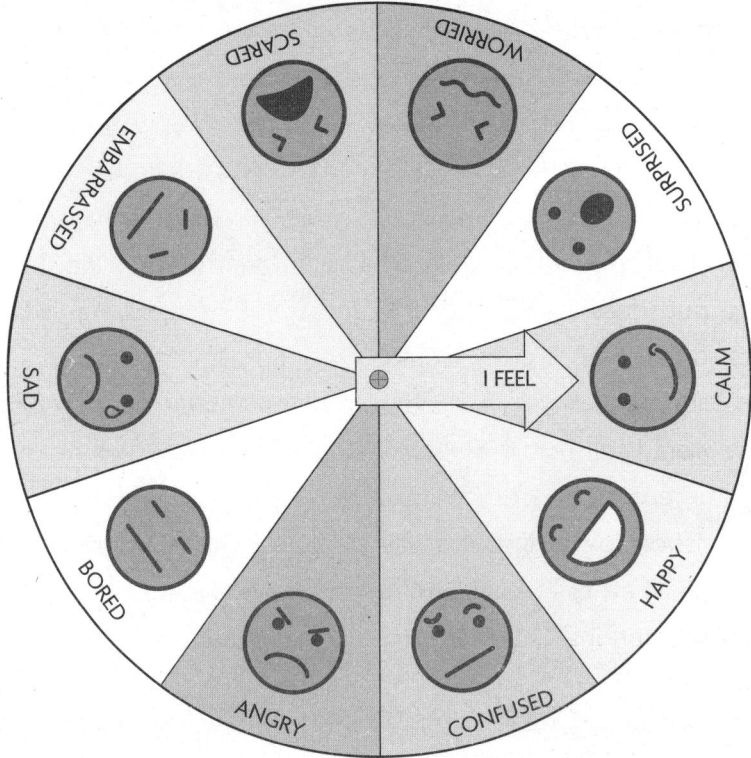

Figure 3.2. A simple emotion wheel for children aged 2.5 years and above.

'But won't I put ideas into their head?' I am often asked and the answer is: no. Children are very straightforward. If you suggest that they might be feeling something that they've not articulated, they'll feel relieved. If you suggest that they're feeling something they're not, they'll tell you – either by simply saying 'no', or by looking at you as though you are mad! This is exactly what happened with Jenna and her son, Xan.

Jenna brought her eight-year-old son, Xan, in to see me.

'I don't know what's wrong with him,' she said. 'He's so rude and naughty at the moment. He shouts at me and is being nasty to his little brother – they usually get on well. I've tried everything – telling him off, a star chart, hugs – but he pushes me away and I can't get through to him.'

I asked about school, the family and what else might be going on to contribute to Xan's change in mood and behaviour. Xan's dad, Sam, Jenna told me, travelled a great deal with work and always had done; indeed, throughout the boys' lives. I wondered whether Xan was missing Dad. 'No, I don't think so. He's used to it,' said Jenna.

When I asked whether she had asked Xan, she said, 'No, I don't want to put ideas into his head. I don't think he's missing Sam. He hasn't said that he is, so why would I suggest to him that he is?'

I explained that if she checked in with Xan and he was not missing Dad, he would tell her. If he was, he'd feel relief that his mum had named the emotion, helped him understand it and indirectly given him permission to feel it. Jenna was unconvinced and left our session considering whether to say anything.

The next morning, I received an email from Jenna.

> I was really worried about asking Xan if he was missing his dad, as you know. I was sure he wasn't, but he was really difficult again last night, and as I'd tried everything and run out of options, I tentatively asked him if he was missing Sam. Immediately, he nodded and then cried, saying that Sam was away too much. I asked him if he was also angry, which just popped out; I hadn't planned it, and he nodded again, saying that everyone else had daddies who were at home, had dinner with them, put them to bed. Why didn't he have the same? It was amazing! I had no idea he was feeling this way and as soon as we acknowledged it, he let me hold and cuddle him for the first time in weeks. We talked about it, then we called Sam and had a really lovely end to the evening, which had started so badly. Xan was so much happier and easier this morning, too. I can't believe that was what was going on and I was worried about asking.

It is not always the case that such a simple intervention resolves a problem so quickly and easily, but it is always the case that your child needs to know, understand and learn how to express their feelings so that they can avoid communicating behaviourally. Life becomes so much harder when children have to act out in order to be heard.

Emotion wheels aren't just the domain of children. As children grow through adolescence into adulthood, emotion wheels evolve too. They are one of my most commonly shared and appreciated resources in sessions. I've included a range of emotion wheels, from very simple to more detailed in Figures 3.3, 3.4, 3.5 and 3.6. All of the emotion wheels in this chapter can be used at any age. However, as a guide, the simplest wheel is for young children and as their emotional vocabulary grows, move on to a wheel with more emotions. The most complex wheels in Figures 3.5 and 3.6 have the largest range of emotions so those are helpful for teenagers and adults with a good emotional vocabulary. They can all be used to identify what you or your children are feeling, as well as a tool to expand emotional vocabulary and as conversation starters.

To use these emotion wheels, start in the centre and work outward.[24] For the wheels in Figures 3.3 and 3.4, begin by deciding whether your emotion is comfortable or uncomfortable. Next, move one ring out and choose one of the emotions that best matches how you feel. Once you've done this, become more specific in describing your feeling by identifying the emotion in the outer wheel that most accurately reflects how you feel. The wheels in Figures 3.5 and 3.6 are very detailed and divided into comfortable and uncomfortable emotions. The process of identifying what you're feeling is the same for every emotion.

FEELINGS | 69

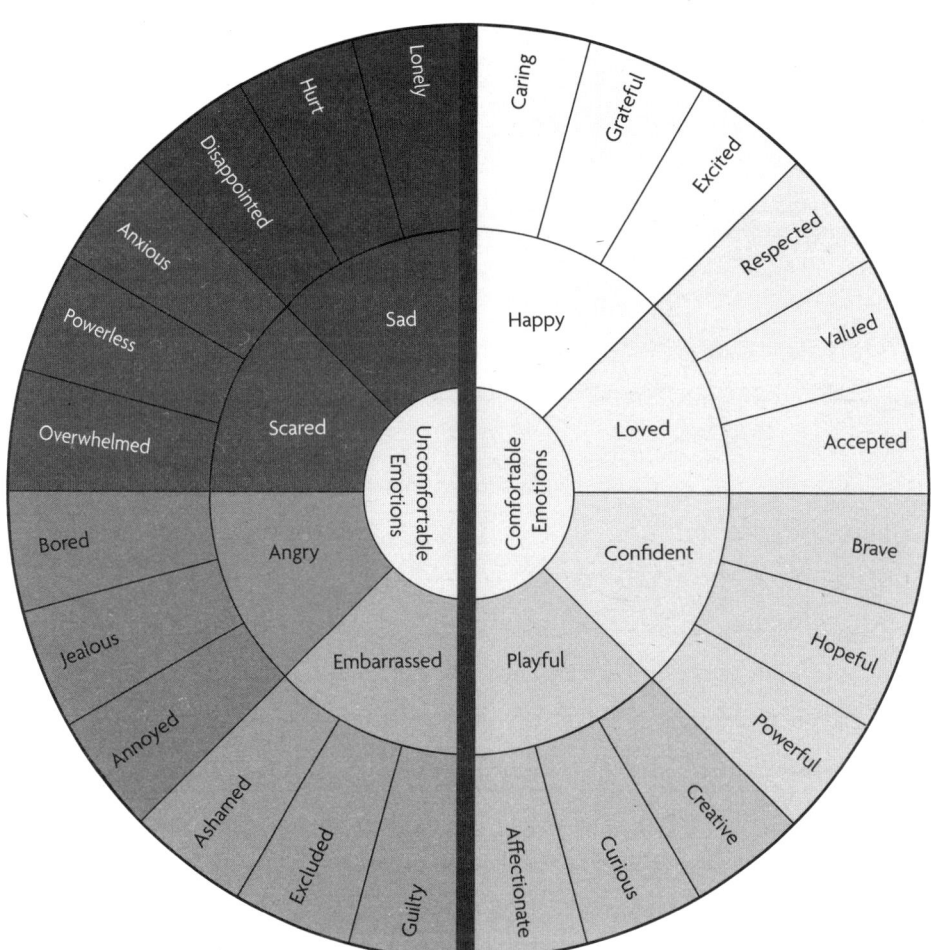

Figure 3.3. Emotion wheel showing 32 different emotions.

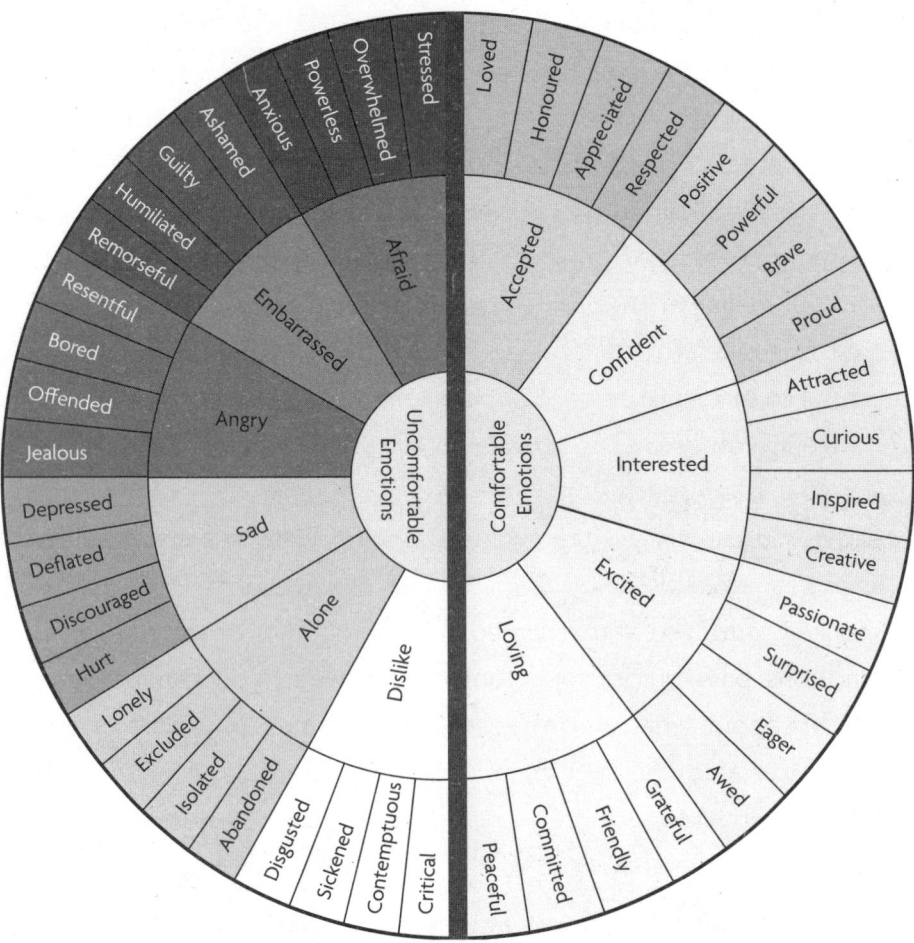

Figure 3.4. Emotion wheel showing 54 different emotions.

How many of the emotions do you name easily, as a matter of course? And how many can your child name? How does it make you feel to be more specific about what you're feeling? Does it help you to understand your feelings and reactions better? Does your behaviour make more sense? Are you able to tune into how your body is feeling more easily?

Imagine, for example, that your child is struggling socially at school. You feel tearful and sad. But sad is a very broad emotion so if you use the emotion wheel you might realise that you are feeling aggrieved and hurt on behalf of your child along with feeling inadequate that the situation is out of your control and dismayed by the school's apparent lack of help.

If you have had an argument with your partner about the washing up, your feeling of anger might really be that you feel furious that you are being taken for granted, indignant and belittled by your partner's refusal to see things from your point of view.

When you break the main emotion down like this your understanding is so much richer and there are a number of different paths you can pursue to resolve the issue. Knowing that you feel angry, for example, is different to knowing that you feel a mix of shocked, outraged and ashamed. You will also discover that tricky emotions pass quicker and more easily when you can be super specific about what you're feeling. The more you're able to name, the better able you'll be to recognise and understand what you're feeling, with more subtlety and nuance. With more nuance you are able to tolerate, regulate and process your emotions without becoming overwhelmed.

It's good to use these more detailed emotion wheels with your children as often as you can. They help to develop their emotional vocabulary, understanding and, most importantly, their emotional processing. If they've had a bad day at school, you can use a wheel to help them work out what they're feeling and why. Whilst developing these aspects won't directly prevent their eating becoming untroubled, it will make it easier for your child to articulate what they are feeling by using words. Therefore, they are less likely to communicate via other means and behaviours, such as through their food.

72 | **HOW TO TALK TO CHILDREN ABOUT FOOD**

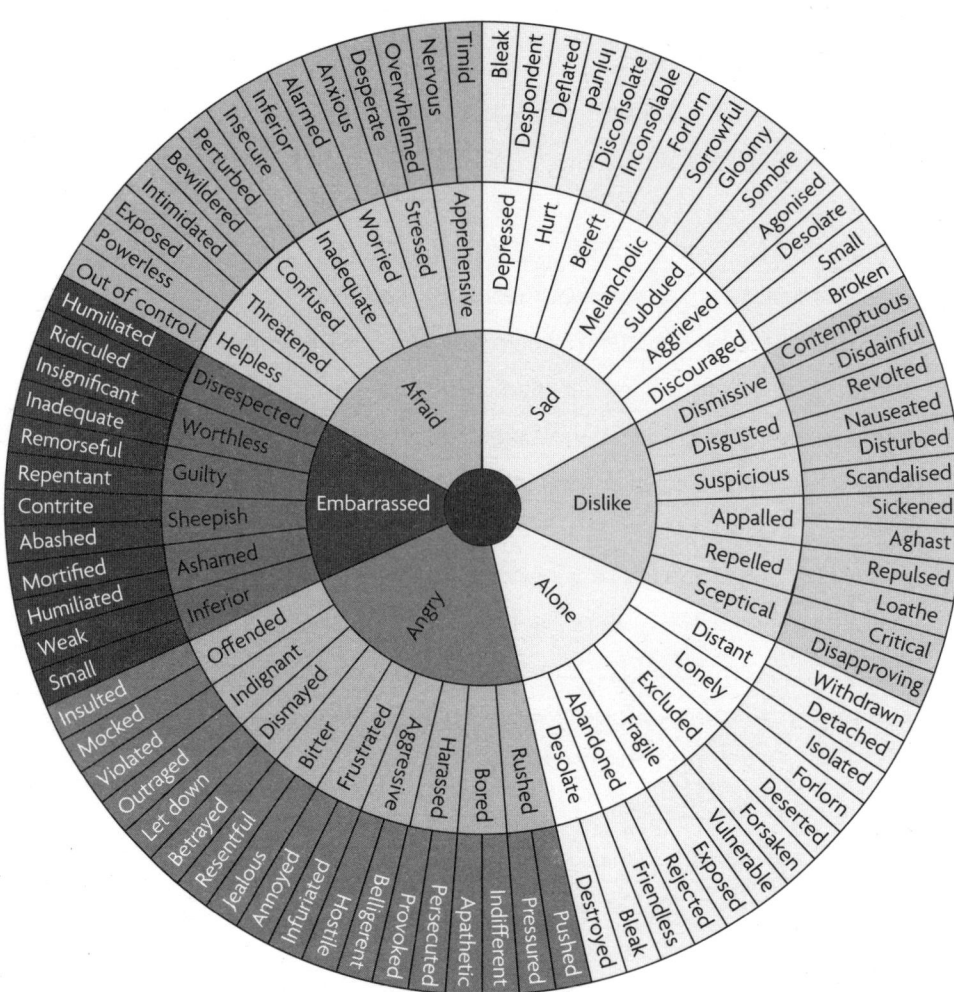

Figure 3.5. Emotion wheel showing a spectrum of uncomfortable emotions.

FEELINGS | 73

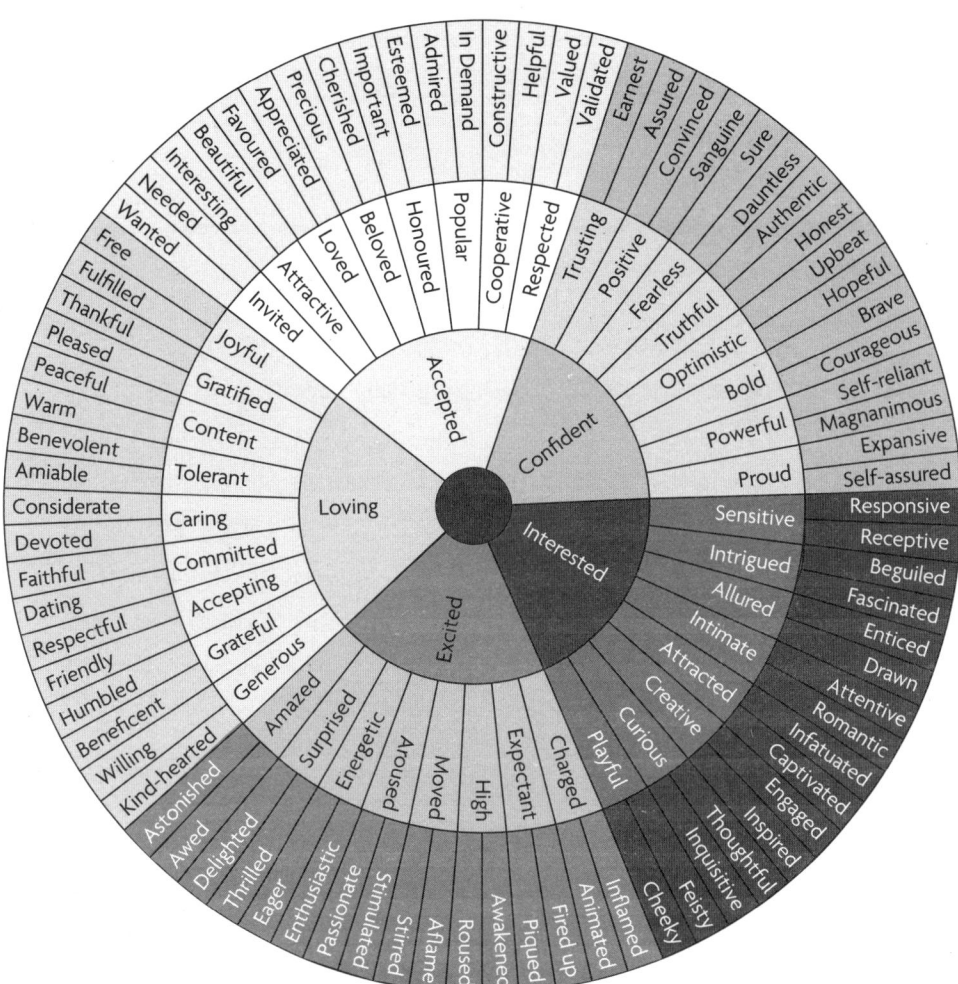

Figure 3.6. Emotion wheel showing a spectrum of comfortable emotions.

Distress Tolerance

It's all very well, I hear you say, being able to name loads of emotions – but then what? There are many ways to process emotions. These include: learning to understand them; talking and creating a narrative about them that makes sense to you; laughing; crying; exercising; and using cognitive strategies such as challenging thoughts, surfing emotions and distraction, or behavioural strategies such as meeting a friend, getting out in to nature or engaging in self-care, for example, having a massage. One of the most important things we can teach our children alongside developing their emotional vocabulary is 'distress tolerance', a concept developed by the behaviourist Marsha Linehan in the 1970s. It doesn't have a terribly glamorous or fun name, but it is exactly as it sounds. Life can be tough and we all experience difficulties at some point. It's inevitable. The question therefore is not 'how do we avoid distress?', but 'how do we best tolerate it?' We *must* learn to tolerate it, and the better our ability to do so, the less we have to employ unhelpful coping strategies, such as using food by comfort eating, bingeing or restricting, withdrawing from social engagement, supressing our feelings and pretending everything is fine, and using harmful or illegal substances to numb the emotional pain. Just like in the children's book *We're Going on a Bear Hunt*, 'We can't go over it. We can't go under it ... We've got to go through it!'

Imagine that you are paddling in the sea. The waves are building and you don't want to get knocked over by them. What do you do? You can't stop the waves building and breaking on the shore, and you can't block the waves with your body – indeed, if you try to, it is more likely that you will get knocked down by one. Waves build in size and intensity from very small to their peak, and then they reduce as they come into the shore. The only way to avoid being taken out by a wave is to ride it, as surfers do. They wait for a wave to build, then catch it with their board when it is big enough so that they can travel with it until it dies down (see Figure 3.7 below). This is what we need to do with emotions.

PEAK
The emotion reaches it's most intense point, often feeling overwhelming and like it will never end.

RISE
The emotion becomes more intense.

EMOTION
Triggered by a person, place, thought, memory or anything else.

FALL
The emotion starts to fade, losing its intensity until it passes.

Emotions come and go constantly. Just like the waves in the sea, the more we try to stop them, the harder they 'hit' us. Think about a time when you have tried not to feel a feeling because it was uncomfortable or inconvenient. It probably disappeared for a bit and then returned stronger. I see it like a child knocking at the door when you're busy. You tell them to wait. They wait a bit, then knock again – louder – until eventually they burst in and demand immediate attention. Feelings are the same. You can keep pushing them away, but at some point, they will come back demanding attention. And, in my experience, these moments usually come either as angry outbursts or tears when you least want them.

So, just like surfing waves in the sea, we must teach our kids to surf emotions. They come in waves, and we need to jump onto the wave of emotion as it swells and continue to ride it until it falls and passes. To be clear, emotion surfing is not a tool to help you instantly feel better. Instead, it is a tool to help you shift your perception of your emotions from being irritants to be pushed away and avoided to being messages bringing information about what we need to listen and attend to, safe in the knowledge that they will fall in intensity and pass when we allow ourselves to notice and sit with them. This will help you to feel better in the medium and long term, rather than having the instant but fleeting sense of relief that comes from suppressing your emotions in the moment.

Many people fear their emotions, particularly ones that are perceived as negative, such as sadness, anger and anxiety, and this often leads to a desire to get rid of them as quickly as possible. I like to think of feelings as messages containing important information that are sent to us by our mind. When describing this to kids, I say it's like receiving texts or snaps on our phone that we need to read. We can ignore texts from our friends and family, but if we do, we risk missing important information, such as a social arrangement, or upsetting people, which can cause problems that could have been avoided if we had dealt with the message when it first pinged onto our phone. Our feelings are exactly like these texts and snaps, and we need to notice and attend to them. If we don't read the message, the notification doesn't go away. If you notice that you feel angry, the message is that you feel hurt in some way (anger is a response to feeling hurt). If it's that you are happy, then something good has happened. If anxious, then there's a communication of threat, and so on. When you and your kids start to view feelings through this lens, they are much less frightening, instead becoming things about which to be curious.

Having this analogy, and that of surfing in your mind, helps you to emotion surf and tolerate distress. Often, the first sign of an emotion is a physical sensation rather than a thought or clear feeling. It may be a tight chest, that your heart is beating faster, a lump in your throat, butterflies in your stomach. When it lands, instead of pushing it away, be curious about it as if you were talking to your closest friend about themselves. Good questions to ask yourself are: what is the communication here? What am I feeling? What do I feel physically, in my body? What does it feel like to feel this way? What would I say to my child if they were feeling this? How would I help them go through it? What do I need now to get through it? Are there actions that I need to take? These questions help you lean into the emotion and jump on the wave, rather than run away and avoid it. It may feel counter-intuitive, but leaning into an emotion will help it to pass quicker and with less intrusion and distress.

Notice emotions that make you feel good as well as the trickier ones and notice, too, that the intensity falls after a while. The more you practise, the easier it becomes and the more comfortable it feels. In the longer term, you will negotiate the ups and downs of life more easily, navigate conflict and relationships, deepen your connection and intimacy with others, and make decisions about your life that are aligned with your values and needs. Don't judge yourself for your feelings because when judgement creeps in, it shuts the door on curiosity, slows the falling of the wave and inhibits processing.

You may be reading this thinking, 'This is meant to be a book on talking to my child about food. Why is she going on about this? It's not about food.' The answer is that learning to notice, name, tolerate, accept and release feelings is one of the most important protections for your child against using food and eating to manage their feelings. And you need to be able to do this first, so that you can teach and help your children to do it.

It is easiest to start to do this with your children when they have obvious feelings, such as excitement, joy, anger, upset or frustration. More complex emotions like jealousy will come, so the earlier you start on the basics, the better. As soon as you notice an obvious feeling in your child, pause and ask yourself what's going on for them. This will help you to help your child to notice and think about the feeling with you. Name the overriding feeling for them, for example: 'You have a big feeling and you seem cross. Is that right?' In this small sentence, you have shown them that you have noticed them, and that you are interested in what they are feeling. You have named what you are seeing and are not judging them. Instead, you are checking with them that you are on the right track and there is implicit permission for them to tell you that you're wrong and change the feeling, giving them ownership of it. This statement alone helps the wave of emotion reduce because your child feels seen, understood and contained. If they are able to, go on and explore their feelings in more detail. If they are very distressed, having a tantrum or pushing you away, once you have named their feeling, be with them quietly until the wave drops and the peak intensity of the feelings have passed. If your child is very angry, trying to talk about it will exacerbate things further, so the best you can do is tell them that you're there with them. If they're very upset, you might just need to hold them until they feel calmer. Whichever, wait until they are ready to think with you about what was happening for them.

Many parents say to me, 'I hate tantrums. They make me so

angry; my child won't listen and they kick off in front of others. It's embarrassing.' But remember, if your child is having a tantrum, they are communicating something to you: they are angry, frustrated or upset. Telling them off for throwing a tantrum or putting them in another room until they calm down won't help them: it may quieten them after a while because they're not being responded to, but it doesn't address the cause or teach them to understand and manage their feelings. They need your help. It's your job to help them work out what they're feeling, to name it and understand it. If your buttons are pressed by your child having a tantrum use an emotion wheel to work out exactly what you're feeling so that you can deal with your response and be freer to help them.

Using rewards or threats is a common method to stop unwanted behaviours: 'there'll be no TV later if you carry on screaming'. Or 'calm down and I'll give you some sweets'. But both miss the point and inadvertently prolong the tantrum. Likewise, putting children outside the room or in a different room alone leaves them feeling more angry, unseen and overwhelmed. It communicates that they are being naughty – a word and view that I don't like – and that they have to navigate their big feelings alone because they are either too powerful or unacceptable for you as their parent. More effective is: 'You're telling me really clearly that you're very angry and upset. I'm here with you.' This names the feeling(s) and lets them know you can cope, which enables them to feel seen and safe. The tantrum, like a storm, will blow out, just as it blew in. Using an emotion wheel mid-tantrum may inflame things further, so sit tight until your child is calmer and ready to talk about what was happening for them.

As children mature, they communicate emotions differently, but their need to feel understood remains as it does for us all. It feels awful to feel invisible, invalidated and ignored. You might adapt what you say to your teenagers but the basic communication of 'I can see you're distressed, I'm here for you when you are ready, and I'm not judging', stands. It can be hard because one of the primary developmental tasks of adolescence is separation and they do this through ruptures and arguments with parents that they love and to whom they are deeply connected. I'll come back to this later when talking about adolescence.

'It broke my heart,' said Naomi. 'Uma yelled "I hate you" and stormed off. I was devastated. I mean, I have poured so much love into her since the day she was born and she repays me with this. I didn't know what to say. I was so shocked and hurt. I haven't been able to look at her the same way since. How can she hate me?'

Whilst I am sure Uma hated Naomi in the moment that she yelled it, she did not hate her. It was the expression of strong anger because Naomi had laid down a boundary and said that Uma couldn't go to a party on a school night. She was communicating loud and clear how furious she was with her mum for this. Things became more complicated because of Naomi's profound distress in response to it, which Uma could not fail to see. Then Uma became conflicted because she was furious but had caused her mum distress that was intolerable. Uma felt that she had wounded her mum, potentially preventing her from showing this level of anger again. And when young people are not permitted to show their feelings, the risk of them using food or other strategies increases.

It's very common for our teenagers to feel and say they hate their parents. In the heat of the moment, it's exactly what they're feeling; but know that, as with all feelings, it passes. They don't and won't hate you for the rest of your lives, and it does not mean that you don't love them or that you have parented them badly. Indeed, it's not even about you. Don't take it to heart as Naomi did. Yelling 'I hate you' is an extremely effective way of communicating rage. And feeling this allows your teenager to move away from you as parents and towards their friends, which is part of the developmental task of separation.

You can discuss the rupture later, the next day, or even in a few days. Do as described above. Be curious about what happened to cause it. Name your part in it – 'When I said you couldn't go to the party, you were really angry with me' – and allow them to tell you about why they were so angry, how unfair it was, what they were missing, how they felt their friends would feel or judge them. Don't assume you know, and even if you do know, give them the space and time to tell you, and, again, don't judge them or dismiss their feelings. Acknowledge them and take responsibility for your part in it. Tell them that saying they hate you, even in the heat of an argument, is hurtful so that they have the opportunity to hear your feelings, apologise or make amends, should they choose. The only thing I really caution against is communicating to them that you are deeply wounded by them or cannot cope with their anger and feelings, because this hinders their ability to express themselves and pushes them towards other methods of emotion management.

Thinking 'Errors'

We all think in different ways, with a number of styles of thinking, known in the clinical world as cognitive (thinking) distortions. These are specific styles of thinking that tend to get us in trouble by increasing anxiety and distress and, as you've seen, many children, teens and adults manage tricky feelings by using food. Noticing these cognitive styles helps mitigate this. I've outlined below the ones that most often accompany difficulties in eating. You may notice you have some — they are common — and if your children are old enough, you'll notice these in them too. It's good to be aware of these to teach your kids to challenge them when they appear.

Black-and-White Thinking

Also known as 'all or nothing' thinking, this type of thinking is extremely common. It takes the form of believing that something is one thing or another: it is black *or* white, right *or* wrong, true *or* false. It lacks nuance, shade of grey, and leads to polarised thinking. You catch it by noticing 'either / or' in what someone says. For example, your child is good or bad. You are either fully committed to eating 'healthily' and stick to every rule of your meal plan or you have fallen off the wagon. You are either a perfect parent or an abject failure. With reflection, you can see the inflexibility of this way of thinking, and how it increases anxiety and perfectionism — if your child thinks they *either* have to be perfect *or* they have failed: the cost of making a mistake, no matter how small, is extremely high.

This is a super common cognitive style in those with both eating disorders and anxiety. With anxiety, this thinking style initially helps people feel in control: if they are, for example, scared of getting food poisoning from shellfish and they avoid shellfish, the anxiety will drop. If a teenager fears getting bad grades, they might try and mitigate this risk by working extremely hard — often too hard. However, despite best efforts, there is still no certainty and so the fixed thinking style provides only temporary relief. Indeed, the worry only increases because you will delay the inevitable (we all get food poisoning or a bad grade occasionally) and so you won't learn that you can survive it.

In the context of eating disorders, people usually have food rules by which they try to live and a common thought pattern is 'if I break my rule, I will fail'. For those able to continue restricting, this contributes to the development of anorexia. For others whose hunger overwhelms them, leading to a binge, the thinking flips from all – restriction – to nothing – binge with an 'I've blown it now, so f*** it' mentality.

With older children, naming this tendency, and discussing the possibility of 'grey' between the black and white, helps them. Younger children's brains are not developed enough to manage nuance and they need more concrete descriptions than teenagers and adults. A good way of doing this is to introduce the notion of 'both and' rather than 'either/or'. For instance, 'Mummy can be annoyed with you and love you at the same time', or 'you can eat healthily and have pudding'. Indeed, to me, having pudding sometimes is the epitome of healthy eating.

If this is resonating with you and I am describing the way you think, challenge yourself as I have outlined and work towards a more flexible thinking style. It's a game-changer when you embrace 'both/and', because life is nuanced, we're all flawed, we don't always act in accordance with our values, and most situations are a shade of grey. Thinking in all or nothing terms feels easier as it gives a feeling of clarity and certainty, but these are illusions, and the real world will always intervene.

Emotional Reasoning

'I feel it, therefore it must be true' is the crux of emotional reasoning – we believe what we feel as though it were fact. 'I feel anxious, therefore I am in danger.' 'I have read that sugar causes diabetes [I'm not saying here that it does, but this is a common fear] and I feel anxious when my child has it. My anxiety is evidence that it's bad for them to have sugar and so I must prevent them eating it.' Or, 'I'm worried about obesity, therefore my child gaining weight is dangerous.' These are food-specific examples of emotional reasoning, which may or may not resonate with you, but I'm sure that you have slipped into emotional reasoning at some point because everyone has.

It makes sense that when we have strong emotions, we believe that they're telling us something real, but this isn't necessarily the case. Our emotions trick and lie to us all the time and the more deeply we feel our feelings, the more easily they hoodwink us into believing that they're facts. But just because we feel something does not mean that it's true. For example, you may feel inadequate and think that your partner is a better parent than you, but that doesn't make it true. If you worry that your child might struggle with friendships, it doesn't mean that they are or will. Often, people tell me that they're worried about their relationship, and it's a sign that they ought to break up. It isn't. It's a sign to be curious about what's going on. It may be a sign that they are taking a risk, or it may be nothing at all. This is a really important distortion to notice and challenge because it is rife and it can negatively impact mood, anxiety and self-esteem.

Anxiety is like a smoke alarm. We install smoke alarms to protect us by warning us when there's a fire so that we get out of the house in time and remain safe. Only sometimes smoke alarms go off when we burn the toast, when there is steam in the kitchen, when the room is hot or because there's a glitch. Just because the smoke alarm goes off doesn't mean that the house is on fire – we have to check and ascertain why it's going off, and the same is true with anxiety. With kids and food there are so many messages in society about the dangers of eating certain foods and of gaining weight that your alarm system might be highly responsive and easily activated. But again, just because you're anxious about your child's eating or weight does not actually mean they're in danger.

If this rings true, then the task is to become less emotionally reactive, rather than responding to your anxiety by controlling your child's eating. The steps below will help you to do this:

1. **Slow down your reaction.** Insert a pause between the emotion and your response. You could take a breath, count to ten, do ten star jumps, consciously close your mouth to stop yourself speaking for ten seconds, and so on. Whatever helps you to interrupt your automatic response so that you can build in a moment to think before reacting, giving you time to choose how you respond rather than reacting rashly on your emotions.
2. **Analyse what you're feeling and your emotional triggers.** Be interrogative of your feelings. What are they? What's the threat? What evidence is there for it? What evidence is there against it? Take the time to do this because the more aware you are of your triggers, the more you'll understand them and the more easily you'll be able to predict them, spot them when they happen and intervene rather than operating on autopilot.
3. **Do the opposite.** Whatever your instant negative response is, do the opposite. If you want to shout, talk quietly; if you want to leave and avoid the situation, stay put. With food, if you want to restrict, eat; if you want to deny your child pudding because you're feeling angry or emotionally activated by them, allow it. Doing the opposite action is one of the best ways to change your thoughts and feelings as it challenges your beliefs and gives you real-moment

practice in changing how you respond, along with immediate feedback.
4. **Notice your emotional reasoning.** Over time, you will learn to notice when you are reasoning emotionally and you will have the ability to know how to challenge it.
5. **Adopt this mantra: just because I feel it, doesn't mean it's true.**

Catastrophising

You've probably heard of this. It's like looking through a magnifying glass for its skewing of your perspective. When you catastrophise, you exaggerate the likelihood of something bad (catastrophic) happening. For example, you might make an error at work and instead of viewing it as a mistake and no more than that, you spiral into a belief that you'll lose your job because of it, won't have an income and won't be able to support your family.

When it comes to talking about food, much of the narrative around today is based around fear: 'you need five portions of fruit and veg a day to prevent cancer;' 'sugar is addictive so if your child eats sugar, they will get addicted;' 'if you allow your kids sweets, crisps, chocolate, etc., they'll want more and more and will never be able to stop eating them;' 'if you don't teach your child to take responsibility for their dietary choices when young, they'll be given bad food at parties or friends;' 'if your child gains weight, they risk obesity'. I imagine some, if not all of these, are familiar to you. When we catastrophise, we massively overestimate the likelihood of the bad thing you're concerned about happening. It's like looking at a tiny spider through a powerful magnifying glass and thinking it is a tarantula.

This is really common, particularly if you are a little anxious. As we've discussed, our primal brain seeks out threat to keep us safe, and therefore when you are worried about your child's eating, your mind sends you more examples of danger than if you are not worried. This hooks you into the danger so that you attend to it and stay safe. Only in the instance of your kids eating some sweets and chocolate, this is disproportionate. To combat this, take a step back and employ your rational mind to sense check the threat. Ask yourself: 'Is their life in danger now? Is it an emergency I need to attend to right now? Do I have any actual evidence that this feared thing is happening? Is worrying going to help me manage it?' The likely answer to all of these is no. If, of course, your child isn't eating and is in need of medical attention, you're not catastrophising, and will need to get medical help as soon as you can, either by going to your GP, or in the case of an emergency to A&E.

Comparisons

Comparison is the thief of joy and something with which I'm sure you'll be familiar. Most people have slipped into the comparison trap at some point. When you compare yourself or your kids with others it usually leads to negative beliefs about you, and makes you feel inadequate. The comparison trap makes you think you are a worse parent than your friends, or a particular mum at school who you believe has parenting nailed. You'll think your child is fussier, less well-behaved, not as talented as little Jonny. You believe that you are allowing them more 'bad food' than other parents and are therefore a worse parent. It's endless and it causes an uptick in anxiety and a drop in mood.

Your children will compare themselves to their peers at some point in their childhood and adolescence – it's normal, and you can help them see how rubbish it makes them feel. The educational and academic systems rely on comparisons to grade students and select them for schools and universities. Diet culture, which I'll discuss in Chapter eight, thrives off comparisons. If you weren't interested in being like the wellness gurus or fitness influencers, they wouldn't be able to lure you with their quick-fix miracle products. Your kids are growing up surrounded by these, so it's worth being aware. Comparisons are rife and deeply unhelpful across society; being able to call them out when talking to your kids – and teach them that, whilst natural, comparing themselves to others is a fast-track to misery – reduces the distress they cause.

I hope that this whistle-stop tour through some of the main areas involved in emotions leaves you feeling more knowledgeable and better equipped when managing your own and your child's feelings. My main takeaways for you are below, but if in doubt, remember that life brings distress and you have go through it as you do the obstacles in the bear hunt. Teach your kids this, and at the same time give them as rich an emotional vocabulary as you can, help them surf tricky feelings, validate them and remember: most of the time when they are upset, it's not about you, but you can really help them understand, name and move through their big feelings.

CHAPTER TAKEAWAYS

- Distress is an inevitable part of life, so the question is not how to avoid it, but rather, how to tolerate it and move through it.

- Thoughts and feelings are like clouds and the weather – they float in and float out. Some are light and fluffy, others are dark and stormy, but whichever form they take, they never stay for ever.
- Teach your kids to name their emotions and tolerate distress. These are life skills.
- Emotion wheels are your friend: help your kids (and yourself) develop as broad an emotional vocabulary as possible.
- There is a strong link between distress and eating difficulties because using food to manage difficult feelings is effective – but only in the immediate moment and never long term.
- If you suggest to your child that they might be feeling a particular way and they're not, they will tell you – you won't put ideas in their head.
- Learn to emotion surf and take your kids with you.
- Thoughts and feelings are like texts. They are messages to which you need attend. If you ignore them, they stay on your radar rather than going away, becoming increasingly a source of stress. Notice them and attend to them, then they will pass.
- Don't take your child's anger personally – if they are able to yell at you, it is a sign that they feel safe and are developing independence (I know it's no fun).
- Beware the thinking errors that are 'all or nothing' thinking, emotional reasoning, catastrophising and comparisons. Challenge them in yourself as well as in and for your kids.

CHAPTER 4

Communication Through Food

'Laughter is brightest where food is best.'

Irish proverb

Communication

Noun: The imparting or exchanging of information by speaking, writing, or using some other medium. (*Oxford Languages Dictionary* definition of communication.)

Like it or not, you almost certainly communicate through food: making a special meal for your partner; sharing platters with your friends; a birthday cake for your children; a ready meal for the family when you are too tired to cook; a withdrawal of pudding when you're angry. These are all ways of telling others how you feel about them or about yourself. In addition, there are foods that are specific to your culture and identity, and sharing these inside or outside the family is a powerful form of communication. Food is used to connect with others, express your culture, create and share your identity, bring pleasure, and to communicate gratitude and love. At the same time, the deprivation of certain foods, and the providing of others, is used to convey displeasure or anger, to punish or control, and even as a form of abuse.

Food tells stories. About how and by whom it is prepared, where it comes from, the dish upon which it sits, and the bonds created when it's shared that are strengthened, weakened or broken across the table. It transports us to other countries and cultures. It is deeply rooted in our histories, cultures, religions and traditions, and through it, we impart these and pass them on, down generations and across to friends and others. We connect through the sharing of recipes as well as meals. Food is so much more than mere nutrients. Emotional connection, memory, storytelling, sharing, a feeling of belonging, community, heritage and cultural pride. It is love, memory and rage on your plate.

I have separated this chapter into sections, all closely related and intertwined, and not the clear, mutually exclusive topics to which the subsections profess. In sum, communication through food is the building of connections, the expression of love, modelling for the next generation, and a way of rewarding and punishing – and sometimes, it is all of these at once.

Connection, Eating and Mental Health

One of the most important protective factors for mental health is meaningful social connection. I'm not talking about making small talk or saying hello to people in passing, because such fleeting and superficial interactions can leave you feeling more alone than had you not had them. The connections that are protective are reciprocal relationships: with family, friends, work colleagues, or through hobbies or groups in which you are involved. They need to be enduring and caring: connections where you feel held in mind and important to others, and they to you.

We have seen consistent increases in the rates of depression, anxiety and mental health problems over the last two decades,[25] without discernible differences between those with wealth and those without. This is despite the increase in available medication and the rate of prescribing. If we take a biological view of mental illness, then this does not make sense. Surely, the numerous medications will treat and alleviate the suffering? Unfortunately not.

It is increasingly recognised that the epidemic of depression[26] is significantly associated with the loss of communities and consequent connection with them.[27] We're a social species. From a purely evolutionary perspective, we're hardwired to connect with others in order to thrive and evolve (we were safer hunting with our tribe than alone, and to reproduce and keep the species going, we had to connect with others). For our own wellbeing, we must continue to do so.

For most people, disconnection from their tribe(s) is a significant factor in their distress. Social relationships are fundamental to good mental health. With globalisation and the ease of working and living abroad, communities are both weaker and more scattered, bringing less opportunity to rely on the wider family for childcare, seek parental support and pass down intergenerational knowledge.

People vary in how much time they can happily spend with others before needing personal space to rest and recharge, but everyone needs some social interaction. Studies on social isolation show that the processes of ageing, cognitive decline and Alzheimer's all accelerate with isolation,[28] and that it decreases longevity of life.

Desiring little or no interaction is both a cause and a symptom of psychological difficulties. Given the importance of interpersonal relationships, whilst medication can help to ease depression and anxiety, it will not be enough on its own.

A great deal of our social interactions include consuming food and drink: a meal out; a celebratory drink; a party; having friends round for dinner; Christmas lunch; and – my favourite – brunch. All frequent ways in which we connect with others, share successes, celebrate special occasions and experience pleasure. Communal eating is universal amongst humans, and whilst large communal feasting is relatively infrequent, being the domain of events such as weddings or religious festivals, humble family meals are common to all cultures. Inviting people to your home and cooking for them is regarded as the height of hospitality. Even in a world where the acquisition of ready meals and fast food is easy, and sharing a meal with others takes longer, sitting around a table to eat with family and friends remains both desirable and essential. So, what it is it about the involvement of food in social interactions that is important?

When we sit and share a meal with others, our time with them is usually longer than if we speak on the phone, meet for a walk, have a drink after work and so on. Research conducted at Oxford University found that eating together led to social bonding. Furthermore, it found that eating evening meals together was the meal that resulted in the greatest feeling of closeness between people.[29] It is likely because people often have more time in the evening and so are more relaxed, and more likely to laugh, reminisce and share. The feeling of togetherness is powerful and protective.

This is when we get to bond, deepen our relationships and solidify our social networks. We get a good old hit of endorphins – the feel-good hormones – when we spend an evening nattering and putting the world to rights with others over a meal and a glass of wine, bringing a broader effect on mood and enhancing self-esteem. When eating with others, we are more likely to laugh, sing, dance and engage our playful side, all of which have positive health benefits. The stronger the bond we have, the more we engage, and it becomes a virtuous cycle. It's true that you can do these things without consuming any food or drink, but even a glorious walk with a friend often involves a coffee or a pause for tea and cake.

In addition to all of these great emotional and psychological benefits, those who eat regularly with others are more likely to be involved with communities and communal activities, which themselves have benefits on our mood, satisfaction and mental health. Finally, there is much evidence that the quality and size of our social circle has significant health benefits in terms of diminished susceptibility to illness, and increased longevity, improved cardiovascular health and better mental health. Anything that strengthens our bondedness with others is not just enjoyable but actively good for our health.[30]

I realise that having gone on about the benefits of eating with others, you might be thinking 'but I can't possibly do that'. Home cooking takes time and eating out can be prohibitively expensive. But the point is the social interaction; your culinary prowess is secondary. Equally, if you struggle with eating due to disordered eating, an eating disorder or social anxiety, eating with others may feel profoundly challenging or even impossible. But eating with others will ultimately help you. You don't need to eat in a big group. Start with one or two people you trust and with whom you feel safe, and build from there at your own pace. This creates connection and brings you support, distraction, a shift in your focus away from yourself and towards others: you will feel less isolated and alone.

One of the most damaging consequences of anxiety is withdrawal. The consequent retreat from aspects of your life – even if it gives relief in the immediate moment – causes increased anxiety and more withdrawal. It becomes a vicious cycle and has the opposite, detrimental effect to the benefits of social eating and connectedness. It is why recovery from an eating disorder has to include eating with others and socialising, and it's the reason treatment for social anxiety focuses on slowly increasing your exposure to the social situations you fear. My motto with my clients is to 'do the opposite' to that which the anxiety or eating difficulty demands.

Once you have children, the focus shifts, and eating with others involves your kids, especially when they're young. However, the importance of maintaining social interactions remains and potentially becomes more important with the stressors of parenting. Eating out with children can be stressful. Babies cry, toddlers and young children shout and create mess, and older children can be loud, silent, bolshy, shy ... The list is long. But it can also be enjoyable: a time for you to be with your kids in a different environment, where they behave differently and one in which you don't have to cook or wash up. If, on a particular day, your child is struggling with their behaviour or meal when you're eating out, you'll cope. You may choose to leave the restaurant or your friends early, you might step outside and have some time alone with your child, but remember, most of all, you and they will cope.

This is a common conversation that I have had hundreds of times in clinic. The feeling that your parenting isn't good enough, the fear of being on display in public, of being judged for your children's behaviour can be overwhelming. You may feel, as many do, that you can't cope with such anxiety, or that it's safer to stay home until your kids are old enough to behave perfectly with beautiful table manners.

Sure, this would make you feel more relaxed about eating out, but you'll be waiting a long time, during which you'll feel increasingly isolated, anxious and you won't discover whether your predictions come true. Plus, if your kids never eat out, they won't learn the changed expectations that come from eating in different environments. These were the conversations that I had with Michelle.

Michelle hated eating anywhere but home. She felt that her two older children, aged eight and five, had bad table manners, eating partially with their fingers and pushing their plates away when they'd had enough. Meanwhile, her 18-month-old made a mess of himself at the table and dropped food on the floor. She found mealtimes at home stressful enough when solo parenting, but more stressful when her partner, Beth, was there too; she felt that Beth was judging her and blaming her for their children's behaviour. When it was just Beth there, there was a calmer, happier environment. The kids were still messy, but the three of them had fun at the table, which eluded Michelle.

Michelle knew that children made mess. However, as the youngest child from a small family, she had not grown up with exposure to babies and young children and had no internal model of what to expect. She felt that her children's mealtime behaviour was a reflection on her parenting and felt ashamed and a failure. Her reluctance to see friends, even those with children of the same ages, was due to these feelings and a belief that her friends would negatively judge her parenting. She could not envisage otherwise, nor could she believe that her friends' children were less than 'perfect' at meals: eating with cutlery, staying at the table, being sociable and polite.

By understanding the meaning that Michelle took from mealtimes – the sense that she wasn't a good enough mum – it was easy to see how she felt the children's behaviour had to be 'perfect' and that anything less reflected her inadequacy. With this realisation, Michelle could explore the ways in which she was a good enough parent and build her confidence. Bit by bit, she took risks and shared her concerns and feelings with a friend. She discovered she was not alone. Her friend convinced her to join her family for a meal alone, leaving Beth and the children at home. Michelle saw that her friend's kids were similar in behaviour to hers: it wasn't something to feel ashamed of – it was pretty normal for their age and stage. This felt like a lightbulb moment because she was able to observe without simultaneously fretting about her own children. Over time, Michelle grew in confidence and understanding of her children's behaviour. She and the children began to join family and friends with whom she felt secure for meals and the atmosphere improved. In addition, her kids enjoyed eating with friends, their table manners improved due to modelling and they too were happier. For Michelle, although withdrawing had initially felt like the only option, it was the opposite of what she needed.

You may have similar concerns about eating anywhere other than at home with your children and often, when parents are finding mealtimes challenging, it can feel better to be alone even in your home. Since you've read this far, it won't surprise you that I suggest you do the opposite! Like Michelle, many parents have difficult times with their children at mealtimes or eating generally. It feels awful when you are engulfed in it, but you won't be the first, or the last.

Take the risk of eating with others with their children. It is as important for your children as it is for you. They too benefit from social connections, and they are more likely to eat well and try new foods when there are other children doing so, as they copy their peers. If you have withdrawn or not ventured to shared eating yet, don't worry – it's never too late to start and reap the benefits.

Begin by choosing whomever you feel most comfortable with and share any concerns you have in advance of the meal so that they know it might be tricky for you. The more you do it, the easier it will become, and I promise: you are not alone.

Parental Love

What happens when you cook for your kids and your food is rejected or tasted but left uneaten? How does that make you feel? It's often particularly difficult for parents, when their children refuse or reject the food they have made. Many parents take this in their stride and view it as a common part of parenting that's frustrating. Other parents, however, imbue significant meaning in their child's rejection of their home-cooked meal and the depth of the distress it causes can be directly linked to what they believe about their role as a parent, as well as the meaning of food in their life.

Mina told me that her mother had expressed her love through food. She never said 'I love you' but made delicious meals and snacks, often asking Mina what she would like to eat before making dinner. On birthdays, special occasions and celebrations, Mum's time, care, attention to detail and presentation of the food was raised to 'restaurant standard'. A simple Victoria sponge, no matter how delicious, was not enough because it was too plain for a celebration; if Mina requested a Victoria sandwich for her birthday, her mother would surround the cake with beautiful hand-crafted decorations made from fondant icing with a handmade centrepiece on top. The clear vehicle for communication about nurture and love was through food rather than words. Meanwhile, Mina learnt that a mother shows her love for a child through food and therefore a mother's role is to feed her child.

To be clear, there is absolutely nothing wrong with expressing love through food and gestures. However, it can become tricky when there is anger or hurt around, and then food, or its withdrawal, becomes a mode of communicating that too. When Mina's mum was angry, she didn't want to cook for her daughter, but nutritious food remains essential regardless of our feelings for our children in any given moment. This was difficult for Mina to receive and it must have caused internal conflict for her mum, who knew she needed to feed her child well but didn't want to. When her mum was tired, poorly or away, Mina felt that there was no way for Mum to show affection or communicate her love – Mum's only love language was food and she had no other mode of expressing it. Thus, the importance of Mum's food production was paramount and without it, especially pre-adulthood, Mina felt insecure about Mum's feelings for her.

As Mina grew up, she too struggled to demonstrate her feelings for her friends and boyfriends verbally or using touch because she had no internal model. She was a great cook and, like her mum, made delicious meals for friends and gave them wonderful baked goods in times of need. However, Mina didn't feel that her needs were met with her love language being food, and so she had to actively learn to articulate her feelings – to tell her husband that she loved him, and to accept being told he loved her – when it felt so alien. She also had to practise giving and receiving hugs and physical affection and although it felt strange initially, she really valued it too. Mina was able to do this because she recognised what her mum had been unable to give her and knew she wanted to be different. This awareness and desire to change are the essential ingredients to breaking family patterns and intentionally creating your own way of doing things.

Whilst many people express love and gratitude using food, you need more modes of communication. Words, touch and physical affection or even emojis – it really does not matter, you just need variety.

Modelling

Much of our communication is non-verbal and indirect. Children learn predominantly by watching and copying, not by following verbal instructions. This is known as modelling and is used to describe how, from infancy to adulthood, we watch others behave and learn from it. Have you noticed that sometimes your child will be playing with a friend and you'll suddenly hear your words and your tone of voice come from them? It might be something that you've said to them, a sibling, your partner or anyone else. It can be uncomfortable if it's a tone or comment that you dislike when hearing it back. Or, they'll imitate the way you praise or chastise them? In those moments, your child mirrors the way that you interact with them and with others. I certainly rarely liked it when it happened to me, which, with four children, was often, and I found it a humbling and somewhat salutary lesson every time – I still do. Young children do not have the intellectual or cognitive maturity to understand complex conversations about why they should behave as asked, or what has caused their parent, friend, or teacher to get cross. As children mature, they're increasingly able to do this, but nonetheless, much of what we learn and teach, particularly as adults and parents, is through modelling.

Have you heard of mirror neurones? They are pretty cool! Discovered by neuroscientist Giacomo Rizzolatti in the 1990s,[31] mirror neurones are one of the most important recent discoveries of neuroscience. They are responsible for two distinct processes of information that we get from observing an action done by another: the what is being done and the why. They are active with both behaviours and emotions and explain how we 'read' other peoples' minds, infer the intent underpinning behaviours and emotions and feel empathy for them, all without conscious cognition.

This neural network is automatic – we don't have to think about what other people are doing or feeling, we simply know. These neurones create a direct link between the sender and receiver of a message and explain how when you observe someone's actions you understand what they are doing and why. The why – the automatic understanding of intention – is really important, describing how we develop theory of mind: empathy and the ability to put ourselves in another's shoes. (There is a hypothesis that in conditions such as autism, where people struggle to understand others' emotions, there might be something amiss with the mirror neurone system.[32]) This is why emotions can be contagious: if you are with a friend who is very distressed, you will likely feel distress. When you're with others whose mood is great, your mood will lift and so on. It explains why humans learn by copying and imitating. Mirror neurones are reciprocal and fire off each other. So, when your child watches you, they will understand your emotions and be able to infer why you are feeling and behaving as you are without you telling them.

'Do as I say, not as I do' sounds ideal, but kids do as we do, much less as we say. So, if you tell your child that food is important and delicious but they see you picking at it, leaving it or skipping meals, this will be what they learn. Similarly, if you talk about the importance of sitting at the table to eat a meal but you eat standing up, don't be surprised when they want to eat on the hoof too. Sometimes you'll be rushed, and you might have your breakfast as you leave the house, and that is fine. An infrequent behaviour does not teach your child a habit, but if you always eat breakfast as you leave the house your child will think it is normal, and they will want to do it as well.

COMMUNICATION THROUGH FOOD | 103

'I need to lose some weight'; 'I want to get back to my pre-baby body'; 'You can see by my thighs that a piece of cake is not necessary'; 'I've larded out and don't fit my clothes anymore'; 'I've got to stop eating the kids leftovers, I'm getting so fat'. You'll certainly have heard comments like these standing at the school gate, or you might have said them yourself. It's not a problem for you to have such thoughts – they're very common – but the problem comes when your children overhear you saying them or see you acting on them. Depending on their age, having a parent who is dieting or concerned about their body image communicates that the aesthetic is important and that the way to improve the way you look is through restricting food. When children see this, they internalise any, some or all of the following:

- Food is something that you can control to make yourself look a certain way.
- Food is not just about fuel, and potentially not even predominantly so.
- They are the cause of their parent's unhappiness with their body.
- Their parent eating their food (leftovers) is causing upset or is bad.
- Weight loss is something to which they should aspire.
- Food/eating causes unhappiness or anxiety.

When your child internalises these messages, whatever you say will be trumped by your indirect communications – the way that they see you behave around food, the comments you make to others, the distress and angst it engenders. It is extremely hard to tell your child that they need to eat if you are not, unless there is a genuinely good reason for your abstinence, such as a medical one or a rare lack of hunger in a specific moment — but only when in the context of otherwise normal, balanced eating.

Seventeen-year-old Holly was recovering from anorexia when she came to me. She was doing well but still struggling in some areas. She found eating with her family challenging because whilst her medical team had emphasised the importance of this, her mum tended to 'hide behind cooking the meals' as she saw it. Mum ate, but tiny portions, frequently separate from the rest of the family, either standing by the hob or at a different time. Even though Dad and Holly's siblings ate together and with her, Mum was communicating very clearly that she was not comfortable with sitting and eating with the family. Holly was angry because family meals are a part of treatment for anorexia and she felt that Mum was being hypocritical; because Mum had such sparrow-like portions, Holly felt that she was being targeted as the one with the problem when Mum had food issues as well. Before Holly had become unwell, Mum's eating had not caused a problem in the family: they'd just accepted that Mum was 'funny' around food. However, for Holly's recovery, it was important that her mum addressed her own eating, which, it turned out, had always been a problem for her and with which she, too, needed support.

Imagine that you hurt your arm. You pop a plaster on and cover it up, but you constantly knock it in the hubbub of everyday life, so the scab keeps coming off and it doesn't heal properly. You need to uncover the wound and expose it, to allow it to get air and heal properly from the inside out. If the cut is deep, you'll need to go to the doctor for stitches or other treatment. This is a helpful analogy for emotional wounds. If you've had a difficult time with food, you might try to cover it up in front of your kids. However, they'll undoubtedly knock your wound frequently, and you'll have to work harder to protect it. With or without professional help, you need to heal your relationship with food properly so that you don't have to cover it up. Then, there'll be nothing there for your kids to accidentally touch and cause pain.

Of course, anorexia and its treatment are extreme, but they illustrate the importance of positive parental modelling of healthy eating behaviours.

Darcey contacted me because her eight-year-old son, Rory, was an extremely fussy eater and would only eat certain foods. Rory ate a variety of foods and a reasonably well-balanced diet. However, Darcey was exhausted trying to get him to eat the 'perfect' diet and the battles that went with this. Curious as to what this was about, I asked about her and her partner's beliefs about food.

'I just want my kids to eat,' she told me. 'I don't mind a bit of fussiness, as long as they're happy, healthy and eat OK, but Anthony, their dad, is insistent that they only eat healthy food. He eats a paleo diet and thinks that the children don't eat well enough. I hide veg in pasta sauce, but he's unhappy with that as he wants them to like vegetables and know that they are eating them. He gets really stressed when Rory leaves some of his meat or vegetables. He doesn't want them to have chocolate or sweets, and he thinks it's bad for them to snack in between meals. If we go out for a burger, he won't have the bun and talks constantly about how bread, wheat and sugar are bad for you. I let the children have it all, but Rory is still so fussy, and it causes so many arguments. He's just getting worse.'

You can see that Anthony and Darcey — both with the best of intentions — gave mixed and confusing messages about food. Dad had very clear views on healthy and unhealthy foods, and these were inconsistent with Mum's, which gave more flexibility to what the children ate. Rory may well have been a bit of a fussy eater regardless, but he was very confused by the contradicting communication from his parents and did not know who to follow or what to believe.

Are you a parent who believes that you are what you eat? Do you think that eating healthily is extremely important? Do you tell your children they can have all foods in moderation but then talk about how terrible sugar, fat, salt or other foods are? Are you desperate for them to have a healthy relationship with eating and their bodies but are unhappy with your body and never eat dessert yourself? These contradictions are common and frequently lead to difficulties for children who, as sponges, absorb lessons – intended and unintended – from the actions of their parents.

A child whose parent never eats pudding does not need to be told explicitly, with words, that pudding is troubling. They will understand from observing their parent that there is something bad about it. I'm not advising pudding at every meal, but it is essential that you model eating it sometimes; and if you don't eat it, you need a coherent explanation – one that's not about the evils of sugar, fat or weight gain. I oddly don't like ice cream and so very rarely eat it, even if we're abroad with fabulous gelaterias. My kids have always seen me refuse it, but I'm clear that I just don't like it, and never have. However, when I fancy it, I eat sorbet or frozen yoghurt in a cone. I also eat other desserts, so the narrative they have (correctly) developed is 'Mum's odd – she doesn't like ice cream' and not something with a meaning wrapped up in weight or 'unhealthy eating' which could damage their relationship with food. Of course, it is essential to get variety and balance into your children's diets, but not at the expense of relaxed mealtimes and flexibility with food.

Modelling and beliefs are closely intertwined because most of our behaviours are guided by our beliefs. If you believe that family meals are important, you'll probably ensure your family eats together. If you believe children shouldn't feel distress, you'll be unlikely to get angry with them or deny them things that they'd like, for fear of upsetting

COMMUNICATION THROUGH FOOD | 107

them. If you feel strongly that eating fruit and veg is essential, you're likely to eat them yourself, so your kids will watch you and learn to do so themselves.

Cast your mind back and reflect on the eating behaviours of your parents. They, too, will have modelled behaviours to you, and much of what you learnt and the beliefs you acquired will have come from them. When thinking about this in relation to your childhood, think about the beliefs your parents held and relate these to their actions. There is a lot of overlap with your food legacy as that comprises a mix of verbal communication, modelling, and both direct and indirect communications. Once you start to notice and understand your parents' behaviours, you have more choices about your own.

A word of warning for parents on linking your dissatisfaction with your body to your children, whether through having been pregnant or given birth if a mum, or parenting generally. Many parents (both mothers and fathers) bemoan the lack of time they have to exercise and keep in shape once children arrive, especially in the early months and years. It's really tough, especially if you're working, tired and juggling multiple people's needs as most parents are. Be kind to yourself and your body – having children is a huge transition and the adjustment takes time. As we've discussed, just as you settle in and feel comfortable things change. It's OK to feel and say you're frustrated about not getting to the gym, but don't let your kids hear that it has anything to do with them as it can make them feel that your unhappiness is their fault. They can also pick up messages about the importance of how their body looks at a very young age, laying the foundation for a tricky relationship with food.

Most women's bodies sustain some permanent change post-pregnancy and it can take time to adjust to your 'new normal' body. It's important that you allow yourself time to adapt and come to terms with that. If you're struggling, focus on how extraordinary it is that we can grow another human inside us and tune into the wonders of your body. If gratitude is a practice that you find helpful, use it here and tap into those feelings for having been able to carry and have your beautiful child. If, however, when your child hears you say that having a baby 'ruined' your body, or that you want your pre-baby body back, they can take this to heart and feel responsible, sometimes extrapolating that if they hadn't been born, you would be happier or your body would be better. They don't know that you didn't mean it and in the worst case scenario, children internalise this and believe that you wish they had not been born, which in turn can lead to low mood, anxiety, low self-worth, guilt and shame. They may try to compensate or make up somehow for their existence, or withdraw and be as small as possible. They aren't to know that you are not necessarily associating them with distress about your body, or blaming them personally, but rather you are probably commenting more generally on the changes and challenges that pregnancy or birth brought for you.

If you or your partner have said this in front of your child, don't worry. Just change what you say going forward and make clear to your child that when you have made comments in the past it is not directed at them, that you love them and wouldn't change having them for the world. How you repair this will depend on their age: if they're a little older, you can be explicit about what you said, why and how you mistakenly led them to believe they were to blame for something that they absolutely are not. Repair is always possible and it is better to address an issue than hope it doesn't exist and avoid confronting it head-on, allowing it to fester. The worst, or best, case scenario is that you raise it with your child and they laugh or tell you that they never took what you said to be about them personally – that's the ultimate win-win; you realised you might have caused distress to them, you addressed it, discovered it was not a problem and modelled beautifully to your child how to do all of these things.

Methods of Communication

A Note on Children's Behaviour

Most of this chapter focuses on our communication as adults, through food, but it is also the case that kids communicate through their behaviour. Indeed, their behaviour is their primary mode of communication for much of their childhood and your job as their parent, or the adult, is to decipher the meaning behind their behaviour and help them to name and understand it.

Tantrums are frequently deemed 'bad behaviour'; however, they're not. They're a communication of distress and the distress is expressed in the form of a tantrum. It feels terrible for children to feel the level of upset that leads to its expression through a tantrum. That upset can be disappointment, anger, rage, sadness, jealousy, grief or anxiety, none of which feel comfortable. Even as adults, most of us don't enjoy feeling any of these, but hopefully, we have the cognisance and language to understand and articulate what we are feeling in a way that elicits support rather than discipline.

Your child may also communicate through their eating or behaviour at mealtimes. When they push their plate away it can mean numerous things. They may simply not like the taste. They might be feeling anxious and therefore unable to eat, or it could be that they are sad or tired. Possibly they were hoping for a different meal and they're disappointed or annoyed. Or maybe they had a difficult day at school and are feeling full of emotions that they need help to express.

The key as the adult is to go for the communication – that something's wrong – and explore that.

So take the pressure off eating in that moment and be interested in what's going on for them. Be curious and compassionate. Avoid judging them or their feelings as this will potentially lead to trickier behaviour in the moment but more importantly, your child will feel invalidated and less willing to confide in you next time. View the behaviour as communication and see your role as helping problem solve with your child – this might simply take the form of a cuddle – rather than telling them off or disciplining them for the behaviour itself. It is hard to do because you too will have feelings, especially if you are exhausted, hurt or have made their favourite meal, which they've rejected. Remember, however, that your child's refusal to eat the food that you have prepared for them is probably not about you. It's most likely to be about something going on for them internally and once their emotional discomfort or distress resolves, they'll be able to return to their food.

If you find yourself getting repeatedly frustrated about your child's mealtime (or other) behaviour and you know it's not about their inner emotional state, then a great strategy is to comment on the behaviours – however small – that you like. This will feel strange and potentially tricky if you are used to correcting them by saying 'don't eat with your fingers'; 'don't lick your plate'; 'stop shouting over your brother' and so on. You might also believe that they need to be told that they're behaving badly, but I urge you to give this method a go. When you start with a 'don't' all that the brain hears is the command: 'eat with your fingers', 'lick your plate' and 'shout'. The tone will convey displeasure and your child will know you are telling them not to do something but it's much better to tell them what you'd like them to do: 'please use your cutlery', 'put your plate down', 'please talk quietly'. In addition to this, comment on everything your child does that you like. You don't need to make the praise gushy or disingenuous, simply let them know you noticed what they did and that you like it. Some examples are: 'I liked the way you just used your fork to eat your pasta'; 'lovely calm speaking, thank you'; 'great job sitting at the table today'. You can say any of these within a few seconds of them happening. Don't wait to be sure because by the time you've waited, they may have done something you don't like and you'll have missed the moment.

Most kids really like to be noticed and appreciated so doing this might feel artificial to you but it will feel less so to them. And if they're a bit older, they'll probably notice the change and may even comment on it. That's fine, just say you want to let them know all the great things they do and keep doing it. When I first did this with my kids, one of my ten-year-olds looked at me like I was mad and said, 'why are you ... being weird, Mummy!' We had a laugh together and I replied it might feel weird but I didn't like telling him off so was stopping doing it. It took about 36 hours but he got into it and all of my kids' behaviour improved as did family life in general.

Contrary to expectations, when you take the additional time to unpick the meaning of their behaviour, or focus on the small behaviours that you appreciate and would like more of, rather than engage with the behaviour itself the situation resolves itself much quicker than when you start with the discipline. And if your child has pushed away their meal, more often than not they return to it and eat it once they feel understood and comforted.

Treats and Rewards

Over the last couple of decades, reward charts have become prominent, motivating children to behave in ways which adults desire.

These charts are based on a concept called 'operant conditioning',[33] a method of learning that involves rewarding behaviours that you want repeated, and punishing unwanted behaviours. Such a chart is based on the premise that children want to please the adults and seek rewards via desirable behaviours, by which I mean behaviours adults like and want repeated. When the child has collected a certain number of stars – one per demonstration of the required behaviour – they receive a reward. The success of such a behaviour change technique lies in: 1) making stars attainable quickly and easily enough for a child to feel that they are succeeding; and 2) ensuring that the reward, once received, is wanted by the child. Frequently food, which is deemed a treat, is given as the prize.

Eight-year-old Isaiah, for example, loved tidying up but got angry and upset when he came home from school and the house was tidy. When he was younger, he and his two brothers would play with their toys but resist putting them away. To encourage them, their parents rewarded a tidy playroom with chocolate buttons, which the boys loved. This did the job in the moment – the playroom was left tidy whenever their parents asked – but, over time, Isaiah developed an association between tidying and chocolate as treats. He learnt that if he wanted these sweet treats, he needed to tidy but it also meant that when there was nothing to clear up, he had no access to chocolate. The strength of this link also prevented him from receiving specific praise from his parents and from realising that there were other benefits to putting toys away.

You may not have created such a strong link between one of your child's behaviours and a reward, but it is common to reward them for doing things they don't enjoy – homework, good table manners, putting away their toys – with a treat. Children are pleased to be given sweets, chocolate or ice cream, but this sets these foods up as being special and better than other foods, which they are not. These foods have attained treat status because adults tend not to want their children eating the high volume of sugar and ultra-processed foodstuffs found in such foods. There is a confusion in the language of 'treats' that we use here. On the one hand, a 'treat' is something which is particularly desirable, and the reward for good behaviour; on the other, and contradictorily, it is something had only rarely, because it is not really ideal or appropriate in any great quantity. This may make sense for a parent, but it can be confusing for a child: it links good behaviour with something which should happen only rarely. In Isaiah's case, his parents wanted him to tidy up, but they didn't realise they built a neural pathway that linked tidying up with chocolate rather than with having a clear space or happy parents.

When food is used repeatedly as treats, throughout childhood and adolescence, it creates an association with food and reward – and food as a form of validation, both emotionally and neurologically. Reward pathways in the brain are built through laying down and reinforcing neural networks (brain pathways). So, when sugary food is linked with reward, acceptance, praise and validation it creates wiring that connects the two. Once this wiring develops, it continues into adulthood and you may reward yourself with food even when you don't want to eat it. It is not a problem if you are happy to have the food and the association, but often it leads to distress.

I saw this in Val. She had excelled at school, received a first-class degree and became a solicitor in a top law firm, where she was excelling too. However, this success was overshadowed by her eating. She could not understand why she was so health-conscious yet ate sweets, chocolate and cake when she did not want to and without thought. She had tried to control her eating through cutting out sugar but had never managed it. Her parents had been strict and very focused on good behaviour. They did not show physical affection, and, instead of praise, gave sweets and sugary treats on special occasions, such as when Val achieved good exam results. Once she realised the link that had been created by her parents in childhood, she could pause before validating herself with treats and question whether she actually wanted the food. If she did, she had it, but if not, she was able to nurture herself in other ways.

Focusing on the contradictions from the treat status of food, however, misses the main issue with giving food as a reward. What children really want is praise, appreciation, connection and time with their parents, teachers and peers. Food does not provide these. A much better reward is one that notices and appreciates your child's behaviour for itself. In schools, this is often achieved by giving a 'star of the week' celebration or an acknowledgement in front of the class. At home, it is often enough to actively notice and acknowledge whatever it is that your child has done that you like. Saying 'you've been so patient whilst I've been on my work call, thank you' will make your child feel seen and valued. They will feel proud of themselves and want to feel this again. Another really great way of rewarding your kids is with your time, especially in today's world, where many parents work and are time-poor. This can be playing a game together, watching a TV programme with your child, going to a café or having an outing. These are more time-consuming than giving a food treat, but much more valuable for both you and your child: these activities will communicate that you want to be with them, that you appreciate the effort they have made to behave as you'd like, and, in turn, build their self-esteem, which is a vital part of healthy child development. Rewarding with your time and attention also assists with bonding and making memories.

Giving kids an edible treat that you know they love after a tricky day to cheer them up or soothe them can be tempting but I advise you not to. When we try to comfort a child with food rather than attend to their physical and emotional needs, we leave them feeling uncontained and not understood. Instead of learning that they'll receive appropriate comfort and attention, they receive the message that their needs can't or won't be met appropriately. Consequently, they understand one of the following: that their needs are not valid; that they are too much for their parent; that they are being silly; that next time they should keep quiet; or that they need to shout louder to be heard. If, after tending to your child's emotional and physical wounds you want to offer some chocolate, ice cream or a trip to McDonald's, that is, of course completely fine – but it must not replace the nurture.

I'm not criticising giving your children treats. I believe that we should offer children all foods, including treats, but we need to think carefully about when, and our motivation for giving them. If it's to shut them up, stop them crying, coerce them into doing something or as a replacement for spending quality time with them, then it is unwise. If it's because you're sharing some cake, having a hot chocolate with them in a café, enjoying dessert, or just because you or they fancy it in that moment, then go for it.

Anger and Punishment

'No pudding for you tonight'; 'If you don't do your homework, there'll be no sweets for a month'; 'You didn't eat your broccoli so you can't have ice cream'. Unfortunately, statements and threats such as these are common. There are many problems when we express our anger through food or use it punitively. We don't want children to develop an association with food that makes them scared, angry or resentful.

We must not increase the potential for them using food as a form of communication or expression of emotion: it confuses issues and once they start to use food to communicate, express or suppress feelings, it becomes entrenched quickly and is difficult to shift.

Leilani came to me with severe anorexia. She had been unwell for many years after suffering domestic abuse. She had always been very slim but her father had called her 'greedy' and told her she was fat when she ate. He would deprive her of food frequently and if she asked for it, he wouldn't give it. When she wasn't eating, he force-fed her and then ridiculed her. He was extremely cruel and it continued until she left home. Why this awful story in the middle of a book on talking to your kids about all things food? Because Leilani internalised these taunts, began to believe them and inflict them upon herself. Her internal monologue about her body and eating was punitive and very difficult to change this even once out of the relationship. She had been unwell for many years after suffering abuse by her father, after her mother had left her father and the family.

We internalise voices and messages from important people in our lives. You'll have heard of the phrase 'inner critic', referring to the negative, disparaging voice you hear in your mind. It's often the voice of a parent who, in trying to do their best for you, was critical or corrective. In cases like Lelani, where there is abuse, her father wasn't trying to do his best – he was abusive – and the critical inner voice is frequently as abusive as the parent. More commonly, it comes from harsh comments made by teachers at school, through bullying or difficult relationships where you received unkind messages about who you were or your performance in certain areas. There can be a cultural component too via scripts like 'big boys don't cry' and 'a woman's place is in the kitchen'. Once internalised, they become your own voice and you continue inflicting harmful, denigratory messages on yourself. We have huge impact on our kids and we need to help them internalise benevolent, positive messages about themselves, their body and their eating.

Consequences for behaviours need to be thoughtful and most importantly, logical – they must make sense to your child. For example, it makes no sense for rudeness to receive a consequence of no ice cream. There's no relationship between the two. It makes much more sense to say to your child, 'Because you were rude to me, I feel cross and hurt so I don't want to play a game with you right now.' If you were about to go out for an ice cream, for instance, it would make sense to say, 'When you were rude just now, it hurt my feelings and I feel cross, so I don't want to go out for ice cream now as we'd planned.' The consequence is logical because we don't want to spend time with someone who makes us feel upset. With homework, you might say, 'If you don't do your homework you will have to tell your teacher, explain why, and they might be cross with you.' If you tell your child off, make sure it makes sense. This is challenging in the heat of the moment, when you're angry. Consequences can always be postponed until you are calmer. You can also give them logical consequences in advance to help them make decisions and you will be amazed at the choices they often make.

Catherine, a working mum, described how when her partner was abroad, she messaged her children, aged nine, 11 and 14, to say that she was leaving work and heading home. They replied asking what was for dinner, to which she responded with her planned meal but added 'I can cook when I get in, but it will mean dinner is late and we won't have time to play a game after, before bed. But if you guys make supper whilst I'm travelling home and we eat when I get in, then we will have time for the game. Whichever is fine, it's your choice.' Catherine was amazed to come home and find dinner made and the table laid. She told me that one of her daughters who thoroughly disliked cooking had helped her other daughter and son with dinner too. She had expected them to choose to continue with whatever they were doing before she got home and to leave the cooking for her.

Without realising it, Catherine had laid out a logical consequence for her kids: I don't have time to both cook dinner and play a game, so I can only do one or the other. There was no threat in her words – a threat would have sounded like: 'If you don't make dinner, I won't play a game with you.' She could have set up an 'if then' that sounds like it is from a place of tit-for-tat, or anger, which would not make sense. Catherine communicated the same issue as a statement of her circumstances with two responses that would lead to different outcomes. She genuinely didn't mind which option her kids chose – she just wanted them to be clear that they had a choice. There was no threat, no anger, no punishment and she came home to a communication from her children that they wanted to spend time playing with her before bed.

Using food to punish also reinforces the good food/bad food split. You never hear a parent say 'because you were rude to me, there'll be no broccoli for a month', or, 'no chicken for you tonight'. Why? Because we have unwittingly set up a culture where sugary foods are seen as treats and other foods, such as fruit, veg, grains, are seen as undesirable staples. So, when adults punish using food, it tends to be using foods that support this assumption. When children learn that sweet, sugary food is desirable, they understandably want it. Then, if they are deprived of it through punishment, it feels punitive; they're likely to seek it out secretly, and unlikely to tell you about it.

Finally, when we muddle food and discipline, teach them that food can be withheld, made to taste unpleasant, used to communicate anger, dislike, and to punish and hurt potentially teaches them to use it in this way. This can manifest in the way they treat a pet – for example, if the cat knocks over a vase they may say 'naughty cat, no supper for you' or they might internalise it further and deprive themselves of food if they have received a negative comment or assessment. It can emerge at any time throughout childhood into adult life. It may be something they do with their own children as it is what they learnt in childhood – though I know that feels a long way off. It could also lead to an association where any deprivation of food is associated with these negative feelings and so they eat much more of the 'treat' foods later in life to comfort or reassure themselves and those close to them. This becomes an unhappy strategy, which, because of its roots, is difficult to relinquish.

If you're reading this and noticing that you have expressed anger or punishment to your children through food, don't worry. You are human, food is a complex area and parenting is the hardest job we do. We all do things as parents that we wish we hadn't, and I have made and continue to make many mistakes with my kids and food, despite my background and my job. When I screw up, all I can do is notice and repair by acknowledging it, apologising and explaining my error to them. You, too, can do this by thinking about consequences being logical going forward. I have put some questions below to help you think more logically and that promote logical consequences. These are interchangeable across areas, and once you get the hang of them, they come quite naturally.

Questions to ask yourself:

- Is the consequence I have in mind linked to the 'behaviour'?
- Is the issue mine (you're tired, stressed, impatient) or my

child's? If it's yours, the best thing to do is say, 'I'm very tired and not as patient as usual, so please could you do X to help me out?'
- Does the consequence make sense logically (not emotionally)?
- Am I reacting from a place of emotion or responding with thought?
- Am I lashing out?
- Is this a thoughtful (and compassionate) consequence?
- Do I want to impose this consequence because I am hurt / angry / upset?
- If so, is it proportionate?
- If so, is it logical? For example, not wanting to read with you because you just hit me, which is logical; or saying no pudding for a week because you just hit me, which is illogical?
- Is this a punishment or a consequence (they are different)?
- What's my motivation for imposing this consequence?
- If I asked my best friend, would they think this consequence made logical sense?
- What alternative consequences can I come up with? Then go ahead and pick the one that is the most logical.
- Will it make sense to them? Will my child get it?
- Will it confuse them?
- Will this consequence set up an association that I don't want? E.g. sugar being special.

Table 4.1 that follows gives examples of logical consequences in different domains: eating, homework, rudeness, helping around the house and conflict with siblings. These are all interchangeable, so if there's a consequence in the homework section that you feel is applicable to a mealtime situation in your home, then great, use it there.

Topic	Questions & Examples
Eating	Consequences based on hunger / mood / you not making more food until the next meal (you can think of this as the kitchen being closed): • Are you sure you don't want to have something to eat? I won't be making more food until lunchtime. • You often feel cross and sad when you're hungry. Are you sure your tummy isn't hungry enough for a snack? • You seem a bit grumpy. Might it be because you're hungry? • You don't have to eat if you're not hungry, but I want to check that you're sure because you know being hungry can make you feel sad and angry.
Homework	The consequences need to be from school, because school set the homework. • You will need to explain to your teacher why you haven't done your homework. • Your teacher might be unhappy if your work is that messy (then leave it to them to decide what to do). • You can watch TV once you've done your homework but not before. As they get older you may want to nudge them regarding their self-esteem or exam results.

Topic	Questions & Examples
	- I get that this is hard, but you will feel good about yourself if you do it. I can help if you'd like?
- How will you feel if you go into school tomorrow without having done your homework?
- How will your teacher react when you tell him you didn't do your homework?
- How would you feel if you pushed yourself to do the work and did well?
Rudeness	This will be about an emotional wound and so the consequence will be based on that. - Because you were rude to me, I feel hurt and don't want to hang out right now. I need to calm down.
- You hurt your brother's feelings, so he doesn't want to play.
- That was an unkind thing to say/do, so you will need to apologise or your friend might not want to stay.
Help around the house	You can tap into time or mood consequences here as if you have to do everything, you'll have less time to spend with your kids. - I can do the tidying up but then we won't have time for a story. If you help me, we will. You choose.
- When I do the clearing up, I feel taken for granted and then I'm grumpier and less fun.

COMMUNICATION THROUGH FOOD | 123

Topic	Questions & Examples
Lashing out at siblings	It's important to help your child to name and understand their emotions as well as coming up with a logical consequence. • You broke up your sister's puzzle. What were you feeling? What made you do that? • You broke your sister's puzzle. When you have calmed down, you will need to put it back together for her. • You hit your brother. That's not OK. What was going on for you? • You hit your brother. That's not OK and now I need to be with him for a bit because he's hurt. • What were you feeling? We need to spend some time understanding that and thinking about how not to do that if you feel that way again.

Table 4.1. Examples of logical responses in areas of conflict.

If your child is older and you have responded with a consequence that is, on reflection, punitive rather than logical, you're not alone. Don't beat yourself up – we've all done it. Take the opportunity to understand what happened and repair with your child: talk to them about what you've done and why, apologise for it, explain you hadn't realised. So, for example, 'I didn't let you watch TV last night because you didn't eat your supper and that doesn't make sense. You said you weren't hungry and I didn't respect that because I was irritated. I'd gone to the effort of cooking dinner and then you didn't want it and I lashed out in the moment. That was my problem, and I know you weren't hungry. I'm sorry.' It is never too late, and modelling how to repair is a gift to them.

The Dessert Conundrum

This brings me to the dessert conundrum. I'm often aften asked how to tread the balance between not setting dessert up as something special even though the sugar usually makes it more highly palatable and more desirable.

It's better to say nothing about dessert until you get to dessert. If you have chosen to make dessert, then it is available and when you get to it, you will offer your child some. I will talk about this in more detail later, but in brief, they can decide whether they are hungry enough or fancy it. If they have not eaten their main course, you have the choice to give them either a small portion or to say, 'I don't think you seem hungry enough for dessert because you weren't hungry for your main course.' This is a logical conclusion rather than a punitive one because it makes sense. If your child, or indeed an adult, is not hungry, they are not hungry irrespective of the food. Your child might have room for a small spoonful of dessert but if it has been set up as just different food, rather than better food, it's much more likely that they will be indifferent towards it and able to say no when they don't want it. When it's set up to be conditional or a treat, the feeling of deprivation arises which causes distress. One of my kids used to differentiate his 'stomachs', saying that he had a separate pudding stomach that could manage much more than his main course stomach. This has been a standing joke ever since, but it also really helped us to manage how much dessert he ate, and we used his description of his dessert stomach, which he had come up with and understood.

Another option, if you want them to know that there is dessert on a particular evening, is to let them know earlier in the day that pudding will be on offer later. So, for example, you could say, 'I'm making stir fry for supper tonight and there'll also be apple crumble if you have room for it.' Or, 'We have a main course and some fruit and ice cream tonight.' Then, if your child follows up with how much they love ice cream, for instance, you can say, 'I know you like it. Hopefully you'll be hungry enough, but if you're not, there'll be other times you can have it.' Both options emphasise eating when hungry and not when full, respecting the body, rather than imposing behavioural conditions or illogical trades made for sugary food. The latter example also makes clear that ice cream is not a one-off, tonight-only food and that there's no drama – if your child doesn't want it this time there will be a next time, thereby helping them to lessen the urgency attached to having it today.

Before we continue, I want to ask you why you worry about your child having pudding or treats? It might seem obvious, but it's always wise to consider whether your concerns about anything related to your kids' eating are because there's something to be worried about or because of your own feelings about food?

Whilst none of the above guarantees that your child will always turn down pudding when they are full or remain sanguine about not having it when they've not eaten a main course, it will help them to understand that they need to respect their body's signals and have the filling, nutritious food as well as the sweet, less nourishing food. Notice the *as well as*. Much better for them to know that they can have main *and* pudding, savoury *and* sweet rather than their being an either/or, black and white choice. The binary makes it harder for them as they feel they have to eat everything or have no pudding. 'All or nothing' thinking which we discussed earlier in Chapter three, leads a higher risk of tantrums, overriding their body's signals and disordered eating.

Katya was a free-thinking seven-year-old who knew her own mind. Her parents found her tricky to handle, believing that she was 'wilful' and disobedient. Their 'go-to' consequence for bad behaviour was to deny Katya pudding or 'treaty foods'. The messages were clear: do things differently to how we'd like and you will not be allowed sweet treats. Do as we say, and you might be allowed them.

There are many problems with this strategy: removing something (pudding) as a punishment is only meaningful if a child already has it. If they don't definitely have pudding, taking it away because they don't comply with parental expectations doesn't matter to them. It's also not a logical consequence and it sets up unhelpful communications around food.

It's tough when we struggle with our children, when they're angry, tired, rude, or behave in ways we don't want. The key words are 'when we struggle' because it's us as parents who are having a hard time with the feelings our child's behaviour is provoking in us. It's often not about them. Our task, rather than disciplining, is to pause before reacting and engage with what our child is feeling when they tantrum (disappointment, exhaustion, overwhelm, etc). Next, name this and help them manage their emotions. Remember, your kids need your help to understand and name their feelings. Until they can do this, they have no option but to express themselves in the best way available. If this way of thinking is challenging for you, because, for example, you think it's pandering to bad behaviour, take a moment and recall a time that you were angry. Did it help when you were told to calm down or stop shouting? Were you comforted by that or did you feel dismissed and even more upset? I expect the latter, and this is what your kids will feel too –

it's why the traditional methods of dealing with 'bad behaviour' are so often ineffective.

Kids develop their relationship with food based on our communications as parents, about food and eating. You'll have seen that communication is not as straightforward as direct, verbal imparting of information. Modelling, family meals, rewards and punishment all contribute. The traditional attitude of 'children should be seen and not heard' is, thankfully, now much less common, but anything that prevents children from experiencing the joy of communal eating is detrimental to their relationship with food. Navigating the multitude of communications your kids receive around all things food is challenging. To keep it simple, hold on to these four main points: they learn primarily by watching and modelling, so be vigilant about what you show them; reward with your attention and time; make consequences logical and enjoy sharing food and meals with them.

CHAPTER TAKEAWAYS

- Eating with others is a fundamental part of human connection. It is in our evolutionary wiring and improves mental health and our wellbeing.
- It leads to bonding, deeper relationships, increased support, sharing, reciprocity and endorphins – what's not to love?!
- The evening meal has been shown to be the best for social connection.

- Whether you can cook is secondary. Hospitality is about relationships ... you can make toast, or buy in. It's the connection you're after.
- Anxiety and eating disorders both lead to social withdrawal, especially around mealtimes, and this perpetuates the feeling of being alone and increases anxiety about eating with others.
- Eating out with young kids may feel stressful or worrying but it's important to do it, nonetheless. Take the risk.
- Food can be a way of showing love, but if it is the only way a parent expresses love, it can cause problems when angry or away from home. If food is your main love language, you need an additional method of communicating it.
- Modelling is the main way children learn – they watch and copy so be aware when there are little ears and eyes listening and observing.
- Avoid rewarding with food because it muddles the issues and sets up reward pathways in the brain that link behaviour and food, and these last into adulthood.
- Avoid punishing with food. It removes neutrality from food and causes disordered eating and eating disorders from an early age.
- Practise finding logical consequences – it feels so much better when you do and is easier for you and your children.
- Food is a method of communication and the communications from it are easily internalised.

CHAPTER 5

Developmental Stages with Eating

'It's all just a phase.'

My mother-in-law

Becoming a parent is a momentous moment. Despite the preparation, it can feel overwhelming as your life changes forever and you have a tiny new human to feed and nurture. The cascade of feelings that come with having a baby are overpowering, particularly if some are uncomfortable or if you are feeling low.

The nutritional needs of children change continually from birth to adulthood, as does the progression from 100% reliance on being fed to complete self-feeding. What does not change, *as long as your child is taught and allowed to respect it*, is that they know how much they need and want to eat.

Ellyn Satter was a registered dietician, feeding expert and family therapist who devised the division of responsibility model:[34] a method of implementing what's commonly known as responsive feeding, to which I and many feeding experts subscribe. In summary, the model says that the parent is responsible for the *what* (foods to offer) and the child is responsible for the *how much* (to eat). You, as the parent, respond to your child's needs and communications, of hunger and satiety, teaching them to tune in to their body and observe how it feels when hungry, full and after eating certain foods. This helps them to notice and respond to themselves so that they can internalise this and learn to respect and trust their body's cues.

In infancy, parents choose whether to breastfeed, bottle-feed or use mixed feeding, and the baby decides when and how they feed and how much they take. As babies grow, their stomachs can take more food and this is when it is possible to get into a routine and move towards more structured feeding times. When solids are introduced and throughout childhood, parents choose what food the child is offered and when, and the child chooses whether to eat the food offered and how much. I'll discuss this in more detail, and for each age and stage, in the sections that follow, but the strength of this model is that children learn from birth to observe and respect their body's hunger and full signals, to eat as much as they need, and then to stop. This takes the pressure away from parents and children about how much a child eats and creates a calm, minimal conflict environment around food, which reduces the likelihood of feeding and eating difficulties during childhood.

Pregnancy and Birth

Our bodies change enormously when pregnant and whilst it is an amazing natural process, and an extraordinary piece of biology that allows us to grow another life inside us, many women struggle during pregnancy.

There are a wide range of experiences of pregnancy and diverse physical and psychological symptoms that accompany it. I had hyperemesis (severe vomiting) with all of mine, though thankfully only for the first 14 weeks. Having had friends who experienced only a bit of queasiness in the morning, I was shocked initially by how sick I was, but the doctors said that strong pregnancy symptoms were indicative of hormones helping the placenta form and the foetus grow. Thankfully, this helped me view the sickness as an unpleasant but positive symptom from which I took comfort when heaving over the toilet or pulling open yet another sick bag. Consequently, I didn't resent or blame the babies inside me for it, but that is not the case for everyone.

If you have previously had an eating disorder or difficulties with body image, pregnancy is a time when the risk of recurrence is high.[35] This is no surprise as it is natural to revert to old coping strategies in times of distress, but also because 1) there are many recommendations on foods that are safe or unsafe to eat during pregnancy; and 2) the multitude of changes to your body can cause body image distress.

I am aware, writing this that reading these words may cause you to feel stressed either in advance of having your baby or after. My intention is not for that to happen. Rather, to acknowledge how challenging pregnancy can be to raise awareness of the importance of looking after yourself. Likewise, the challenges that occur when considering how you develop a relationship with your children in relation to food and bodies. If you are struggling or would like a space to explore your feelings about your pregnancy, becoming a parent or the changes to your body, seek support. There is nothing to be concerned about or ashamed of: pregnancy is a time of change and anticipation in all aspects of your life. Don't underestimate its enormous significance and treat yourself and your partner with kindness and compassion.

Having your baby brings profound joy, but due to your fluctuating hormones, sleep deprivation and the adjustments that becoming a parent bring, changes in mood are common. The 'baby blues' leave many mums feeling emotional, anxious and irritable in the first few weeks after having a baby,[36] and tend to pass within a few days. If low mood continues, it can be a sign of postnatal depression (PND). PND is not a condition solely experienced by women; men suffer with it too[37] and it can start at any point in the first year after the arrival of your baby. You may experience a loss of pleasure in previously enjoyed activities, feel down, anxious, exhausted, unwell, tearful, hopeless and that you cannot cope. Other biological symptoms include insomnia or changes in your sleep, and a loss of appetite. See your GP and seek help as the symptoms can last for months and have a significant impact on you, your baby and your family. It is thought to affect one in ten parents and treatment is usually effective. Having a new life for which you are responsible is a seismic event, emotionally and physically. It's one that literally changes your life forever, so it would be extraordinary if you did not have feelings about it, some of which may feel negative and tricky.

If you have struggled with an eating disorder or have a troubled relationship with food, this can re-emerge when there is a baby in the mix. If you want to breastfeed, you will need to eat and drink more than you are used to, to make enough milk, which might feel difficult. Bottle feeding may bring challenges for either parent, male or female, though I appreciate much of this section is mum-specific. Having spent your pregnancy with a constantly changing body, it will be changing again. You might want to breastfeed your baby but struggle with the physical sensations that come with your breasts filling with milk and your baby sucking it from you. You may experience pain when feeding or find that the idea of it turns your stomach, deciding that it's not right for you. You might feel frightened about whether you'll be able to adequately feed your child or want to return to an old but effective emotional management strategy of using food or restriction yourself.

Any of these can generate feelings of inadequacy, not being a good enough mum, feeling selfish, ashamed, humiliated, disgusted, angry, sad or a mix of all and more. Know that you have nothing to feel shame about. Nothing in your life stays the same when you have a baby and however you feel is how you feel and that's OK. Take the time to notice how you're feeling in yourself and your responses to feeding your baby. These emotions are important messages alerting you that there is something happening in you that needs attention. You can only make choices about how you respond by first noticing what you are feeling: otherwise, you are destined to react without conscious thought or choice.

If at any stage in your pregnancy or parenting you find yourself struggling, seek help. It is never too early, nor is it ever too late. Anything that you do to improve your emotional wellbeing will have a positive impact on your children and family, as will anything you do to aid your relationship with your body, food, eating and feeding.

Infancy and Early Childhood

Every child develops at a slightly different pace. For this reason, there is some overlap in the ages heading sections and in phases of development I describe in this chapter.

From Birth to Three Months

Your baby comes from the safety, solitude and comfort of your womb into a loud, bright, stimulating world. This can be overwhelming and many need quiet and calm to feed and stay awake. Babies are born with the sucking and swallowing reflexes already developed and open their mouth to suck, especially if hungry.

All babies are born liking sweet tastes and disliking bitter tastes. They show this in their response to the different tastes in their mother's breast milk depending on what she has eaten. By two months old infants show a preference for familiar tastes.[38] By this point they play with the nipple or teat when no longer hungry and are able to regulate their milk intake to meet their growth and energy needs. By three months they enjoy exploring different shapes and textures using their hands and mouth. Allow this exploration as it leads to better acceptance of foods with varying textures during the weaning process and beyond.

When it comes to 'demand' feeding – I prefer to talk about responsive feeding (using the division of responsibility) as demand implies that your baby is demanding, which they're not – versus routine feeding, my preference is to follow the needs of your baby. Their stomach is tiny, and they know when they are hungry and how much to eat. They may need to eat little and often – there's not much space for a large meal – or they may want more. How and how much they eat during any feed will change, just as it does with you. If they're not hungry, they won't feed and that's OK. The speed at which your baby feeds is also determined by them and there is nothing that you can do to alter or control that – things get difficult if you try. They may complete their feed in one go or stop and start. If their previous feed was short or they ate little, they'll probably eat more at the next feed. This is the division of responsibility with newborns – you decide what you feed them and they decide the rest. Once they've finished eating, they'll show you by relaxing, slowing down and stopping. At this point you respond by ending the feed and playing with them before putting them down to sleep.

Angie was distraught. Her second child, Felix, was six weeks old and was not doing anything in the same way as Freddie, her two-year-old. Freddie, she told me, had 'been a dream'. He'd hardly cried, ate well, was easy to get into a routine and was sleeping through the night at three months. The first of her friends to have children, Angie had no one with whom to compare Freddie and she thought this was normal. For some babies, it is, but it's not the norm. So, when Felix cried frequently, wanted to feed little and often, and seemed to struggle with colic, Angie thought that she had done something wrong. 'It's my fault,' she sobbed. 'I got it right with Freddie but now I'm doing it all wrong. Felix just cries so much and is rarely happy unless I'm carrying him. There must be something wrong with him; he's not like Freddie – he's not normal.' Angie wasn't doing anything wrong. She had a baby who had colic, was uncomfortable and had different needs to her first child. Felix was just as normal as Freddie – they were just different babies and she was responding accordingly.

Every baby is different and what's 'normal' encompasses a broad span. A baby can only communicate by crying and their cry demands that we pay attention, which is why it is called a coercive cry. It's incredibly difficult as a parent to ignore it, which is also normal and necessary. Your baby has no other way to get their needs met and thus their coercive cry is a survival mechanism. The tricky part comes when you have to work out what they need. Sometimes, they'll be hungry, at other times, tired. They may need a clean nappy, a cuddle, need to suck (the primary reflex at this age), want to be jiggled around, have trapped wind or colic. Not all crying means they want to be fed. Over time, you'll get to know and differentiate their cries. However, there will be times when they just cry and whatever you do, they won't be pacified and will continue to cry. All you can do is be with them and comfort them until they feel better. Sometimes, babies just cry.

If you feed responsively, you may well need to feed your baby frequently and at inconvenient times, especially during the night. This is natural and if you can tolerate it, do. It will pass as they grow, as their stomach holds more food and they become more autonomous. The first few months with your gorgeous baby can be exhausting and are full of change. Be kind to yourself as you are to your baby and if you're struggling, speak to friends, family, your health visitor or GP.

To address a concern I often hear, you cannot indulge or spoil a baby. Babies aren't demanding, they're just communicating their needs. They won't become entitled or spoilt because you meet their needs and feed them when their body requires nourishment. Indeed, the opposite is the case. Babies whose needs are met become children who know that their parent will respond appropriately. They feel safer and more secure and therefore will be less anxious and demanding.

Finally, your emotional health is paramount so if you need to put your baby, or babies, into a routine so that you can cope, look after yourself and do that. A baby will thrive with parents who are loving, responsive and emotionally stable whether or not they are responsively fed or in a routine. And the converse is also the case: they will pick up that you are unhappy, exhausted, at the end of your tether and fare less well. So, look after yourself and make sure your own needs are met so that you're in the best possible place to meet your baby's.

DEVELOPMENTAL STAGES WITH EATING | 137

A word on multiples. I started with non-identical twins, and it was a great lesson in the difference between two babies born at the same time, to the same parents, living in the same environment. They had different appetites, eating habits, growth rates, needs and internal rhythms. They hit their developmental milestones at similar, but not the same, times and they evolved differently.

We humans are not biologically made to carry multiple babies as animals are, so we are not programmed or set up for it. The most invaluable nugget that I took from a talk we went to when I was pregnant with our twins was this: we are not wired for multiples and we might not recognise both of our babies as ours if they look quite different (as mine did). We are not programmed to bond with multiple babies and therefore you may not bond with both or all three equally or at the same speed. This is OK and, more importantly, it is normal. Feeling differently towards your babies is distressing but knowing this really helped me in those first few weeks. Multiple pregnancies, births and parenting is different. Your expectations need to be specific to having more than one baby at once and different to those of your friends and family with a singleton. It is not better or worse, just different. If you need additional support, ask for it. It is not a sign of weakness or failure. Having one baby is life-changing and difficult enough. Having more than one can be more so, and it is certainly logistically more challenging – it's also fabulous, joyful and great fun.

Many more multiples are bottle fed, at least part of the time, because it is much harder to breastfeed twins or triplets. Feeding two babies simultaneously is doable, but challenging. Feeding three simultaneously isn't unless you have a second person to help. If you breastfeed your twins simultaneously, you need space and cushions to support them – it's not possible to do so on the move. If you feed them one after the other, even on routine, you will be feeding for double the amount of time to those with a singleton. If you feed 'on demand', you will be feeding for most of the day and night for a number of weeks or months and it can quickly become unsustainable. I highlight this because I want you to do whatever you can and accept that. It is enough and it is good enough. You are, and will be, a good enough parent.

Two to Six Months

The moment that your baby starts to smile meaningfully and responsively is wonderful. It's the beginning of their social development, when they seek connection and reciprocity. Those first smiles are a joyful developmental milestone and usually happen between six and 12 weeks. They are engaging with you and seeking connection and response, and the more you interact with them and respond to their cues, the more they will reciprocate. If you've had a tough first few months this can feel like the beginning of a new phase, bringing rewards for the nurture you have given so far.

Continue feeding responsively as you have been, following the cues and meeting the needs of your baby when they want to eat. Ensure that they feed when they are awake and calm. Trying to feed a baby who is sleepy or not hungry is going to be unsuccessful. They will refuse the bottle or breast, dribble or spit out the milk or, if they do take the feed, they may well then be sick as it is too much for their stomach. The least ideal scenario is that they learn to eat when they don't want to because you become distressed if they don't. This begins a pattern of overriding their body and eating to please at a pre-verbal stage. To avoid this, be attentive to their cues and feed them only when they want to eat. If, reading this, you realise that you've fed your baby when they weren't hungry, don't worry, simply change the way you feed them. All you need to do is feed them when they're hungry and not when they're not. If you feed to a routine this is OK, but you might just need to increase the gap between feeds. Remember, feeding your baby and your child is a continually evolving process. I found that with all of mine, every time I felt we were in a great rhythm, things changed again. Just keep evolving with them.

By about four months, your baby will open their mouth in response to a spoon, move food to the back of their mouth with their tongue, and be able to cope with some puréed and mashed foods. They'll move towards the spoon for preferred foods and turn their head away or keep their mouth shut when they don't want to eat. They're interested in the foods that others are eating and show a preference for some foods and a dislike for others. UK guidelines recommend beginning to introduce solids at around six months, but remember, initially solids are offered to introduce different textures and tastes rather than as a source of nutrition.

Usually, at around six months you'll notice that your baby becomes hungry more often and is not sustained for as long by feeds. This is an indication that they may need more than just milk and the time for solids is approaching. Discuss this with your health visitor or GP, but as a general guide, wait until your baby can sit up, see food coming and open their mouth in anticipation.

Five to Nine Months

This is the time when your baby starts eating solid foods in addition to their milk, though milk remains their primary source of nutrition and energy. The introduction of solids is not to magically get your baby to eat a full, nutritional meal, but to start the transition to food: to introduce them to the taste, smell and texture of foods. You have a head-start here as you know how food looks, feels, smells and tastes, but your child does not. This is their first experience of these things and so every time they taste a new vegetable or a different flavour it's novel, and they have no idea what's coming. This is vital to remember because it can take children a long time to become accustomed to new flavours and textures, so don't give up if initially your baby rejects a food.

Your baby will watch you eat, copy you and show an interest in their surroundings. Start slowly by offering food and notice what they do with it. Remember, you choose what food you offer and when, slowly transitioning to more of a meal and snack time structure. Your baby chooses the rest: the speed at which they eat, the way they interact with the food and the quantity they have. Allow them to explore the food at their pace and in their way. This can be a lovely stage and an opportunity for playful interaction and fun between you and your baby. There is usually a lot of mess: smeared and dropped food, clothes with encrusted solids and much cleaning up and laundry. Bear with this: it is an extremely important phase in your child's feeding and eating development and contributes to shaping their relationship with food.

Aged between six and eight months, babies begin to imitate the behaviour of others. They can cope with the introduction of lumpier foods and can chew soft lumps and soft foods, keeping most of the food in their mouth. They can close their lips to clear the spoon and, because more solid food is given, they learn to move it around their mouth with their tongue. They will try foods and put foods that they like in their mouth. As your baby gets used to textures and tastes their gag reflex becomes less frequent.

Some babies accept solids quickly and easily and others slowly and with caution, but all get there. By following their lead, you'll help your baby feel safe and secure, knowing that food and mealtimes are times of calm and discovery. Not all babies enjoy solids initially and that is OK. They don't have to; what's most important is that they feel no imposed stress or anxiety from you, because whilst this may prompt them to eat (or not) it will link stress, food and eating from a very young, pre-verbal age and when associations are made this early, they are much harder to break.

Seven to 15 Months

During this stage, your baby changes hugely as they move towards toddlerdom. They will play, give and take turns, and show an interest in self-feeding. They will progress from happily being fed by you to wanting to feed themselves and this can happen quickly and without warning: one day they are content with you feeding them the next day they refuse the spoon, push it away and will not eat unless they are feeding themselves. They seek increasing independence and autonomy and want to touch, feel and eat whatever they can, exploring with all senses: the taste, smell, texture, sound and look of food. This is at the root of baby-led weaning, which has gained popularity over the last 15 years. There are many excellent weaning books, so I'll only clarify that baby-led weaning has self-feeding as a core principle.[39] Continue with the division of responsibility – your responsibility is to choose what food to offer and when, and your child's is to decide how much and whether to eat.

At this stage, your baby will accept lumpy foods and soft foods that they can chew. They'll start to drink from a closed cup and will want to hold it themselves. They'll begin to feed from a spoon without spilling the food and once their teeth start to come through, bite into hard foods. They'll clearly communicate likes and dislikes by closing their mouth, turning their head and pointing to foods they want. As their language develops, they will also say 'no' to foods that they don't like or want. Some babies are very sensitive to the feel and texture of certain foods or objects and whilst this is OK, it is good to encourage touching those foods, nonetheless.

Mess increases during these months, with your child frequently wearing their food as well as eating it. I remember thinking that mine could not possibly have had enough to eat as so much food was on them, the highchair, table, floor and occasionally walls. Allow the mess as much as possible. Not doing so increases anxiety around eating and removes some of the exploring and play that's vital for their development and their relationship with food. If you're stressed by the mess, you're more likely to be impatient, snappy and upset and your child will pick this up instantly, potentially feeling that it's their job to make you happy, or that mess is bad and eating stressful because the mess must be avoided. I realise that babies cannot express these feelings verbally in the way that I have here, but anxiety and distress is clear to see in situations where feeding is fraught.

Samara arrived in clinic with her 18-month-old, Zack, who she described as 'eating like a sparrow, very picky and tentative around food'. He had dropped off his centile line (a measurement of a child's expected growth over childhood) on his growth chart, and although he was not losing weight, he was not gaining as he should have been. Zack didn't want to feed himself as his friends did and as he did when he first moved to solids. He was happier eating very small amounts of finger food such as cucumber sticks, carrots and breadsticks than he was eating yoghurt, soups and purées.

Zack was breast fed for six months, feeding easily and growing well. He was keen to feed himself but, when he did, he got food over himself and Samara, thinking this would be uncomfortable, wiped him up each time and said, 'oh dear', or, 'what a mess', or, 'you're all messy'. Zack initially turned his head to avoid having his face wiped or pushed the flannel and wipes away, but Samara made sure that she kept him cleaned up. Over the weeks and months that followed, Zack's enjoyment of food reduced and he became reluctant to feed himself.

This kind of story is common. You need to wipe your baby's face and hands every meal, but only once the meal has ended. Doing it at the end as you get your baby out of the highchair or down from the table is part of the communication that the meal is over. When babies and toddlers are not allowed to make mess with food, it communicates that mess is bad, eating must be a careful activity, it's not OK to get any food on their face, hands, clothes, that food is not to be explored and that mealtimes are not fun (they can't be fun if the focus is on tidy eating). This then extends and prevents children from discovering textures, not only with foods but also more broadly, for example with sand and paints when they are in nursery and throughout life. I am sure you can think of a child who gets upset at the arrival of a speck of dirt, and, likewise, an adult who is pernickety about cleanliness.

So, with this in mind, allow mealtimes to be relaxed and engaging. Wherever possible have meals at the same time as your child. They'll want to mimic you and so will learn by modelling as well as feeling part of the family. Offer small amounts of food for them to try, without overloading their spoon or highchair tray. Give variety, mixing finger foods and foods to eat with a spoon or fork, and let them eat in their own way and their own time. Give opportunities to try new foods over and again. It takes time for babies to acquire new tastes and textures so don't feel defeated if they reject foods many times –

they may well still like them in a few weeks or months. Tastes also change and evolve throughout life, so your baby might reject a food at eight months but then love it at 18 or later, and vice versa. Don't read into this – it's completely normal.

Similarly, their appetite will vary like yours: some meals they'll be hungry and eat well, and others much less so. Don't be alarmed. Babies' appetites change constantly and if they are not hungry for a meal or two, it doesn't matter. By trying to get them to eat when they don't want to, you communicate that they should override their body, and that you're upset, and this leads to more eating difficulties rather than fewer. Just go with them, allowing them to lead on how much they eat, and the rest will fall into place.

As your baby gets older, moving towards toddlerhood, avoid too many snacks in between meals as you want them to arrive at the meal hungry and ready to eat: it's no fun for anyone to sit down to a meal when not hungry. It's never too early to start talking to your child about how they feel when they're hungry, full, wanting to eat, and the younger they can understand and develop trust in their body's signals, the better. For more guidance on the details of what foods to introduce at which stage, there are numerous weaning books available. In terms of how to feed and help your child and you avoid stress around food, I've popped some that I recommend in the Resources and Further Reading section under Weaning on page 289.

One to Three Years

Another period of significant growth, development and change in your child, these years see your baby develop from babyhood, through toddlerdom and into early childhood. They move from being fed to feeding themselves, from using a bottle to sippy cup, then onto an open cup or glass. At around 20 months, toddlers start to seem anxious about new foods, rejecting them at sight without trying them. By three years old, they can name foods, tell you what they do and don't like and are able to chew most foods served in a family meal (though their chewing will not be fully developed). Between two and three, they start to imitate the behaviour of other toddlers and similar-aged children and show a preference for restricted or withheld foods. Their food preferences by age three predict their food preferences throughout childhood.

Only yesterday, your toddler was eating everything easily and happily. Today, they are picky and whingy, cautiously eyeing up food that they usually love, having a nibble or a couple of bites and leaving the rest. Tomorrow, they may eat more than you ever thought was possible. This is the pattern over these years and it has the potential to leave you feeling confused and anxious. Rather than trying to control what your child eats, stay calm, offer foods that you are happy with at meals and snacks, sit down and eat as a family and let them decide how much they eat. Children self-regulate as long as they are allowed to, so some days you have a sparrow at the table, taking tiny bites of food, and other days you will feel that your child is making up for it and eating loads. Keep the structure of sitting down for meals and snacks and avoid increasing snacks between meals because your child has eaten less – they need to be hungry for the meal. Roll with it all, it's developmental and will change again as they grow.

Gabe arrived deeply concerned about Ivy, his two-and-half-year-old daughter. She had been an easy baby, fed well and transitioned smoothly to solids. However, over the last six months she had become erratic in her eating: fussy, picking at or refusing foods she had previously enjoyed, whining and sometimes misbehaving. Ivy was continuing along her growth centile, was healthy and outside of meals and snacks was her usual happy self. The primary carer and an excellent cook, Gabe could not understand what had happened. He had cooked and plated delicious meals, eaten the same as Ivy and now the enjoyment of eating together was fast disappearing. He was insisting Ivy stay at the table until he and his partner, Tony, had finished, and he was trying to coax Ivy to eat more, often resulting in her eating less. Tony was not worried, saying that this was 'just a phase' – it would pass.

After I explained that this was developmental, Gabe was less anxious, but he felt a sense of sadness that his beautiful meals were no longer 'worth it'. I encouraged Gabe and Tony to follow the division of responsibility. I also encouraged Gabe to allow Ivy to choose how much she ate without coaxing or cajoling, and to shift the focus onto her feelings and behaviour rather than the food. Once she had had enough, it was better to let her get down from the table, leaving Gabe and Tony to enjoy the rest of the meal together. It was also important that Gabe understood that he and his thoughtfully created meals were not being rejected. It wasn't personal; it was purely Ivy's developmental stage – at some point, she would embrace his cooking again. Quickly, once Gabe relaxed, Ivy relaxed and although her eating was less consistent than before this change, it improved, along with the atmosphere during meals.

Our primal instinct is to keep our children safe and well, and when we feel that they're not eating enough it can be hard to remain sanguine, particularly if you, another child, or family member have had eating difficulties. As discussed earlier in Chapter 2: Your Family Food Legacy, your relationship with, and identity around food, has a bearing on how you feel about situations like this. There is nothing wrong with you if it causes you distress when your child's eating changes and becomes less straightforward.

Most importantly, take the focus *off* the food. Instead, notice how your child is feeling and behaving at meals. Let them use utensils or their fingers – table manners are not so important at this stage and it's key you pick your battles. Even if your child has previously liked a food, in this stage they may well be wary of it.

Ensure that there are a couple of 'safe foods' you know they'll eat at every meal and along with other foods that the family are eating. Make eating fun and keep serving foods even if your child doesn't like them. If you avoid these, and serve only safe foods, your child will never eat them and their diet will become more restricted. Allow your child to eat in the order that they choose, perhaps even serving dessert alongside main food, so they can choose to eat dessert first. I know that this sounds counter-intuitive, but the focus is on being food neutral and making all foods equal, with no treats or special foods. When all foods are viewed equally, children will often eat the healthier foods as well as, or instead of, the biscuits or cake. When certain foods are set up to be desirable and scarce, such as chocolate and ice cream, they will be much less likely to leave them or choose broccoli instead.

The trickier your child's eating becomes, the more important it is to have family meals as often as possible. These help in a number of ways: they lessen the attention on that particular child, diffuse the tension through family chat, and provide modelling for your child. When it's solely you and one child at a meal, the intensity increases and emotions often run high.

Toddlers are emotional beings. They are active and inquisitive. They learn what they can and can't have, where the boundaries are and how they can be pushed, and they are prone to getting upset and throwing tantrums. They know exactly how to press your buttons, and they can be relentless. This leaves them at risk of learning to use food emotionally because it can be extremely tempting, when they are distraught in the supermarket, to give them something to eat to quell their upset. Avoid this and instead pull from your armoury the techniques of focusing on what they're feeling so that you can name it, understand it, help them to understand it and comfort them. For example, you might say, 'You're feeling angry because you want to be at home playing. I understand that and we'll be home as soon as we can. Then you can play.' They may not calm down immediately but this is much more helpful to them and their immediate and long-term emotional development than giving them food. It might also be that they are hangry, and it's helpful to know how to spot it as it often manifests as whining or a tantrum. As with other emotions, name it for them so that they learn to understand what's going on in their body. If you need to give them something to eat because they are too hungry, do so – this is responding to their cues and needs.

Starting School: Ages Three to Six

At this stage, things get easier again. Your child has grown and emerged from being a toddler into a more sentient being who is eager to please. Their horizons broaden as they go to nursery and school and become increasingly social. They might be playful and quirky, beginning to develop a sense of humour, and they'll love to make you laugh. Feeding becomes more straightforward and you can ask them to use cutlery, teach them table manners and encourage them to eat a wider array of foods once more. Phew!

However, beware. Because your child will want to please you, they'll often be compliant and eat foods you want with utensils even when they'd rather eat something else with their fingers. If you start to insist on cutlery before they're ready, they'll feel bad about letting you down or stressed about eating. Similarly, if there are too many foods that you want them to eat that are new and varied. So, continue to offer meals consisting of some foods you know they like and others that might be new and that the whole family are eating. Eat together as a family and allow your child to manage what and how much they eat. At this stage, let them serve themselves from dishes on the table, or help you to dish up their food, increasing their sense of agency and reducing the risk of food becoming a battleground if they aren't compliant, or if food and eating is becoming a source of angst and negative emotions.

The preference for withheld or restricted food begins around ages three to four, and if certain foods are controlled, your child will want them more. It can feel anxiety provoking to give your child foods you believe are unhealthy or that other parents are forbidding but try to surf those feelings, allowing your child to have cake, chocolate, sweets and crisps: foods you'd rather they didn't. The discomfort you feel in the short term will be well worth it. In the not-too-distant future, they won't crave those foods unless they actually feel like them, and because they know that they are available, they'll refuse them when they'd prefer something else and leave them when they've had enough.

If your child became fussier between the ages of one and three, they may still be so, and you may feel a more urgent desire to increase their repertoire of food as time ticks on.

Barbara phoned me in despair over her six-year-old son's, James, eating. 'He won't eat any fruit, the only vegetable he'll eat is cucumber and he loves chocolate and treats. I manage to hide vegetables in spaghetti Bolognaise and tomato sauce and then he eats it, but not if I put the same vegetables on his plate. It's the same with his packed lunches. Every time I put an apple or other fruit in his lunch box for school, he throws a tantrum and refuses to eat it. I get so worried about him not having enough that I end up giving him biscuits or chocolate in the car on the way home from school. He's quite skinny, so I'm worried that if he doesn't eat the chocolate, he won't have enough food.'

Barbara was so worried about James's eating and weight that she was giving him control of the 'what' (food) as well as the 'how much'. When we unpicked this, it became apparent that as a child, Barbara's parents had shown her much love through food and treats and she felt that not to give her children these was depriving them of love, rather than simply not offering them food she would rather they did not eat regularly. Indeed, caring about their health to this degree was one of the many ways in which she was loving.

I explained the division of responsibility to Barbara and although it made her anxious, fearing that James wouldn't eat, she tried it. The first few days were bumpy, with more tantrums than usual, but thereafter James became used to having a different snack in the car on the way home, and he began to have some of his fruit for lunch on some days. However, Barbara wasn't convinced and came back to another appointment saying, 'It's better, but he still chooses the Coco Pops when I put Coco Pops and Weetabix on the table for breakfast.' I asked her why she offered Coco Pops at breakfast and Barbara replied because the kids liked them. I reminded her that she chooses not only what she cooks for meals but also what food she buys in the supermarket. If she doesn't want them to eat Coco Pops, she doesn't have to buy them, and if they're not in the house then children won't have the option to have them for breakfast.

Later that day, I got an email from Barbara saying that she had gone home and cleared her kitchen of all foods that she didn't want the children to eat. She felt liberated: until that day she hadn't realised that there was an option not to have sugary cereals, chocolate, crisps and biscuits in the house. When we met again, she described a transformation in James's eating. He was still fussy and would always have a sugary option when available, but not having it available at home had helped Barbara to remain calm and show James that she was not pretending not to have Coco Pops, for example. This had helped James to accept other cereals with which Barbara was happy. He was eating a little more fruit although she was still putting 'hidden veg' in tomato sauces. She said, 'Sometimes I take him out for a hot chocolate or ice cream and we enjoy it together. It's so much better: we have a lovely time together and James still gets the sweet food he loves, just not all the time.'

You may yourself have added vegetables to sauces and soups, blending them so that your child eats more than they would usually. Doing this sometimes is fine, particularly if you are making a mixed vegetable soup or other dish. Other than these dishes, though, don't hide veg, especially if your child is fussy or a picky eater, because when they discover this, they'll lose trust in you and the problem will grow. You want your child to know what they're eating so that they have a sense of agency over what they eat, learn what different foods taste and feel like and broaden their repertoire. If they're anxious about food and discover that you have been 'hiding' food in sauces, they will become even more restrictive.

Your aim is a food-neutral approach where no food is better than any other. You might be worried that this is permissive, that your child can eat biscuits all day long. It isn't. You wouldn't be happy if they ate cabbage all day long and you'd help them eat more variety.

This is the case with any food. Remember, you choose what food comes into the house and they choose whether and how much of it to eat. Sure, you can offer a plate of biscuits and cake before a main course, or a snack of chocolate. If you do, your child may eat more of it for the first few times, but once they realise that it's available and they're not deprived of it, they will stop having so much and choose more savoury, sustaining food much of the time. It's the deprivation or perceived deprivation that causes rumination about and cravings for a food.

If a food is 'not allowed' there will be an instant attachment to that food. It immediately moves from something neutral to something emotive, value-laden and of which we are deprived. If this is due to an allergy, or religious or ethical principle, the explanation is easier and your child will need to understand it. Without such a reason, they feel that the food is special, is being withheld, that they are being deprived and so the yearning begins. This is why it's so important not to label foods in this way or make having them conditional on anything.

Middle Childhood: Six to 12 Years

Your child's development continues apace during these years as they grow physically, emotionally, intellectually, in independence and begin the transition into adolescence. Girls tend to be about two years ahead of boys developmentally until late adolescence (around 20). They enter puberty roughly two years earlier, too, which is why parents of daughters often describe them as being 'seven going on 17' – something one rarely hears from parents of sons.

The act of feeding your children becomes less arduous in these years as, by now, they'll be eating independently, at school, at friends' houses and with the family. You have an idea of your child's likes and dislikes, any idiosyncrasies that they have around tastes and textures and whether they have any anxieties about mealtimes or eating. They gain independence every day and want more autonomy, but they still need you to have responsibility for, and control over meals, as well as providing a consistent structure to eating.

Through these years, it remains important that you do your job with feeding and have responsibility for what food comes into your home, and the meals that you put on the table. Your child should do their job, taking responsibility for whether, what, how much and how they eat. Continue to let them to eat at their own pace, choosing the order in which they eat their food and how much they have. Allow them to have more of a food if they wish to, even if they've not finished their plate – plate clearing is not a helpful rule. If your child needs to eat after school and before dinner, give them a snack but ensure it's small enough that they are hungry at suppertime.

Make the boundaries around meals and snacks clear and allow your child to be free within these boundaries. These rules are about the structure rather than the content of eating occasions. For example, if your rule is that snacks and meals are had sitting at the table then this is what you expect. Within that, what they eat follows the usual division of responsibility. Likewise, with family meals where everyone sits down for a meal together. Don't give your child a meal alone unless there is an exceptional circumstance. Again, within that they're free with regards to eating. If your child can choose their own snack, then really allow them to choose whatever they wish, including traditionally 'treaty' (high-fat, high-sugar) food, remembering that you have responsibility for the shopping and therefore what's available to them.

Iris was eight when her mum, Siobhan, called me. She was beside herself because Iris had been found 'stealing' chocolate from other children's lunches and from bags of other parents at school and on playdates. Siobhan was mortified and deeply ashamed of Iris. She could not understand it because she'd never given Iris chocolate. It wasn't allowed in their home because Siobhan, a very diligent and thoughtful mum, had read many books on nutrition and feeding toddlers and children and knew that sugar was, as she put it, 'more addictive than drugs'.

Chocolate and sweets had become 'forbidden fruit' to Iris. Despite Siobhan's firm line and intentions, Iris had had chocolate at school and at parties and found it delicious. She knew that it wasn't allowed at home and, aware of Siobhan's animosity towards it, felt that she couldn't even talk about liking it or ask for some, and so when she'd craved it, she'd obtained it wherever possible: she took it surreptitiously from others without seeking permission, as she believed permission wouldn't be given.

It's going to sound counter-intuitive, or possibly worse, but the only way to really resolve this kind of issue is to take away restrictions around your undesired food. Don't simply remove the prohibition, but clearly let them know that they can have it at home. Buy the chocolate and store it in a place that they can easily access and help themselves. Show them that you have done this and however hard, actively give them permission to help themselves. Indeed, this is the advice I gave Siobhan.

I imagine that this might be causing a rising wave of anger or panic in you, especially when you have worked so hard to follow nutritional guidelines and give your child wholesome, nutritious food, avoiding all things ultra-processed and highly palatable. Stay with me... The primary cause of children stealing food is prohibition. As we've discussed,

DEVELOPMENTAL STAGES WITH EATING | 155

the stronger the ban, the more special that food becomes in their mind and the more they want it. Because they see their friends eating it, have it at parties and see other parents allowing it, they know it's not dangerous, but also that it'll never be allowed at home. They can't ask for it or buy it without you or money: their only option, if they really want to eat some chocolate, is to obtain it secretly.

When you first bring the forbidden food into your home and give your child access to it, they may start by eating a lot of it. They need to discover that it being allowed is not a one-off and this will take time. They might test you by finishing it all or taking some and hiding it. It's important you don't tell them off or they'll know that you aren't really OK with their eating it. Help them notice how they feel emotionally and physically when they eat the chocolate and after. It's part of the learning that they need to do, which doesn't develop naturally with forbidden foods and cravings. Ask them how their tummy feels, whether they actually enjoy the first and last mouthful in equal measure. Most of us enjoy the first biscuit, for example, but by the time we get to the third it's not as tasty. This is responsive eating – noticing all the ways a food makes you feel and responding. You can say, for example, 'I see you finished all the chocolate really quickly. How did it taste?' Then, if they seem happy to chat about eating the chocolate with you, you can follow up with any of these questions: 'was the last bit as good as the first? How's your body feeling now? Are you full? Are you wanting more and, if so, is that because it's still new to be allowed it?' They don't have to be in this order, nor do you have to ask any or all of these questions – they are just ideas to help you think with your child about how the chocolate made them feel; to help them to notice all the effects. If they have a lot, get excitable and then 'crash', point it out to them and help them make the link. This will assist them in tuning in to their bodies and learning to listen and respect them in a way that deprivation and bingeing won't.

If you find they're hiding chocolate it may be that they don't yet trust that they will be allowed it again. You can say something like: 'I noticed you have hidden some of the chocolate in your bedside table. Maybe you think I've only bought it as a one-off and I'll stop? I won't stop, so you don't need to hide some just in case. I'll get some more.'

I know this is a massive mental shift and may well go against everything you believe, but try it. You might feel angry and anxious in the short term, but over time your child will learn to trust that they don't need to steal or hoard it, and they'll start to have a more balanced approach to the chocolate (or whatever it is). If you can't bring yourself to do this, you risk them continuing with this behaviour into adolescence and beyond. A poor relationship with food is much more damaging than some chocolate, crisps or sweets.

Allergies and Illnesses

Thirty-five-year-old Katie was referred to me for treatment for long-standing anorexia. She described how as a child she was anxious but ate reasonably well. In middle childhood, she started suffering from migraines, resulting in her missing a day or two of school. Her parents took her to a neurologist and there started the voyage of hopeful discovery of food triggers for her migraines.

However, without realising, she was not developing a comprehensive understanding of her migraines and how to reduce them but a fear of food. Every time she removed something from her diet to see if its absence improved her migraines, Katie became frightened of the food and struggled to put it back into her diet, even when it clearly wasn't a trigger. Her diet became less diverse as her food repertoire shrank. By the time I met her, aged 35, she was stuck in a severe and entrenched anorexia, terrified of all but a small range of foods. In addition, food colourings were found to be a trigger at one stage, so anything containing them, including prescription medications, was off-limits. Given that many medications have a small amount of white or other food colouring, she was unable to take most, causing major difficulties when it came to treatment options both for anorexia and other conditions.

Increasing the diversity of Katie's diet was profoundly challenging as her fear of food was so ingrained that she didn't remember life without it. Every time we tried to add anything with sugar, she believed that it would harm her. Likewise for chocolate, peanut butter (there was no nut allergy), hot drinks, drinks other than water or any new food that she ate. She was desperate to recover from anorexia, which she intellectually knew was much more damaging to her health than the migraines, but the pervasive food constraints had become so familiar they felt safe. Although she knew rationally that many of the foods she avoided didn't cause migraines, she wasn't prepared to integrate them back into her diet due to anxiety: the restrictions had started with medical guidance from the neurologists looking after her, so to her they were prescribed and wise. Inadvertently, whilst treating one illness, her medical team had contributed to another, more serious and life-threatening.

Of course, if you have a child or family member with an allergy you must attend to it and be cautious about exposure. Allergies have become commonplace over recent years, and the London allergy clinic reports that 50% of children have some form of allergy, with food allergies accounting for 8% of these.[40] In the UK, 2–3% of babies are affected by an allergy to cows' milk.[41] Most do the milk ladder and most outgrow their allergy during childhood. Allergies to eggs are also common and like cows' milk, it tends to start during infancy and rarely progresses into adulthood.

With the increased awareness of the risk of allergies and food intolerances, especially those causing anaphylaxis (a severe, life-threatening allergic reaction), comes increased anxiety. There are also certain foods we're advised by the UK government to avoid during pregnancy and weaning, which is meant to be helpful and protective but also increases fear around food and the potential harm that certain foods could cause your baby.

The difference between an allergy and an intolerance is significant. A food intolerance only affects the digestive system and whilst many of the symptoms are similar to those of an allergy, they are less severe and not life-threatening. A food allergy affects the entire immune system and even small amounts of the food can trigger a severe and sometimes life-threatening reaction[42] (see Table 5.1).[43] There are different types of allergies, too, ranging from mild irritation to hives, asthma, eczema, headaches and anaphylaxis. Coeliac disease (an allergy to gluten) is unusual because it affects the immune system and causes severe symptoms, but it does not cause anaphylaxis.

	Food Tolerance	Allergy
Symptoms	Bloating, gas, cramp, headaches, irritability	Hives, lip swelling, tongue swelling, cough, wheeze, vomiting, diarrhoea, chest pain, difficulty swallowing
Timing	Hours	Usually shortly after eating the offending food

	Food Tolerance	Allergy
Frequency	Inconsistently, not every time the food is eaten	Every time the food is eaten
Severity	Not life-threatening	Can be life-threatening

Table 5.1. The differences between food intolerances and food allergies.

In 2020, there were 36,000 children under the age of 19 with diabetes in the UK.[44] Like allergies, being vigilant about the food your child eats is an essential part of the treatment. With diabetes it's particularly important because calculations must be made every time a child eats to determine how much insulin they need. This teaches them to track macronutrients, particularly carbs, from a very early age. Whilst it's easier in the context of diabetes because there is a crystal-clear rationale and a medical necessity, teaching kids to track food or calories is not recommended.

With allergies or illnesses in the family it's both tricky and important to get the balance right between worry and vigilance and the communication to your child that food is safe. The type of allergy that your child has will determine how vigilant you and they need to be. When the allergy is severe or there are multiple food allergies, this is a complex task. Teach your child what they can eat and what they need to avoid. You will also need to teach them to recognise the symptoms of their allergy and how to respond to them. Learning to live in the world means learning to manage this risk and have the tools – medical and psychological – to do so.

Complete avoidance is not an option because you can't completely control your child's environment. Your job as a parent is to teach them how to respond when, not if, an allergic reaction occurs: to give them the tools to manage their own health and look after themselves. It's also your job to manage your own anxiety and find an outlet for this that is not your child. Anxiety is contagious and you don't want your child to be any more anxious than is necessary as this can cause increased restriction, avoidance of social situations and a pervasive increase in fear that impairs life. Conversely, during adolescence, young people can become fed up with a disproportionate amount of anxiety or restriction in their lives due to allergies and can flick the 'f*** it' switch, leading them to disregard their safety and take unnecessary risks. Appropriate caution and education, while avoiding excessive fear, is the key to minimising the chance of both scenarios.

So, how to do this without creating a situation like Katie's? Start teaching your kids about their allergies and how to look after themselves from a young age — ideally from so young that they won't remember being told, because they grow up with it being just another fact about themselves. If they learn that they are allergic later in childhood and it's a shock, they'll always remember discovering the information. And, depending on how it is delivered, the distress might always be with them and associated with their allergy and food. If they develop an allergy later in their childhood, you can't do anything about this other than be calm and teach them how to manage it.

Do what you can to educate your child about their condition in a matter-of-fact way, where they understand the seriousness but are not frightened. What and how much you tell them will increase as they grow. You might tell your two-year-old that they will feel very unwell if they eat the food to which they're allergic, but to a six-year-old you would add more information, and to a 12-year-old, more still. Remember mirror neurones and modelling: you are teaching them with your words, emotions and behaviour. So, if you are matter-of-fact and calm, they will be too. If they see you panicked and distressed, they'll learn to be upset and frightened about their allergy. Avoid words such as death, poison, toxic, dangerous and deadly unless the severity of the allergy makes them absolutely necessary. These words instil significant fear and a communication that food is dangerous, poisonous and can kill them, making food scary rather than enjoyable. In theory it's possible that children with allergies know which foods to avoid without all food becoming scary, but this can be hard to achieve, which is why it is so important to get the balance between teaching them how serious their condition is without excessive fear.

Allergic children and families can enjoy and share food just as much as non-allergic ones: it's all about the how. Show this by going out for meals, to friends, relatives and restaurants. Teach your kids what questions to ask, what to look for on menus or food packaging, teach them to refuse food if they cannot safely eat it, or are even just unsure about it. Let them practise asking the questions and taking charge from as early an age as possible, so that they can learn under your supervision. It might feel daunting, and you may feel out of control, but it's necessary for you both. The sooner you start to give your child the opportunity to manage their allergy, the quicker and more easily they will take opportunity.

Baked goods can be a big issue for allergic children, especially for those with an allergy to nuts, seeds, dairy or eggs. Many biscuits, cakes, chocolates and breads contain these, so children feel they are missing out at parties and friends' houses. Be transparent and keep a supply of their favourite foods readily available to take out with them or have at home any time they have to refuse the food on offer when out.

There are also social ramifications of allergies. If your child suffers from visible allergies, such as hives, bloodshot eyes or eczema, it provokes a response from others in a way that a less visible allergy such as a migraine won't. If your child is teased because of their allergy symptoms, help them explain what's happening to their friends and liaise with their school so that teachers can intervene in the teasing and prevent an escalation into bullying. Teasing around this is unacceptable and contributes to increased anxiety and avoidance around food for fear of a reaction from peers rather than the allergy itself. Exploring the interaction between fear around a physical reaction and the social consequences can be confusing, but don't worry about unpicking it: the bottom line is that when trying to create as healthy a relationship as possible between food and your child, anything that gets in the way is an issue that needs resolving.

There are some excellent websites and organisations that help you navigate an allergic or diabetic child – the links can be found under the Allergies and Diabetes sections in the Resources and Further Reading on pages 289–90.

If you're very allergic yourself, much of the advice remains the same, though you will be teaching your child not to be too worried about you. Be careful about your verbal and non-verbal communication about your own health. How did your parents react to your allergy when you were young? Was it something that you were brought up thinking was dangerous or serious? Was it a mild irritation or inconvenience? The answers to these questions will play into how you cope with your own allergies and those of your child, so it is important to reflect upon it.

How to Teach Your Kids to Recognise When They're Hungry

I realise that I have, and will continue, to bang on about helping your kids to recognise their hunger and full signals, but I've not given you any pointers so far on how to do this. Hunger is multifactorial with a number of physiological and psychological elements, as well as memory, taste, sensory and practical components also involved. At the most basic level, hunger is a survival mechanism.

We all feel hunger differently. In part this is because we are unique with different bodies and brains, and so have different physical sensations. But also it's because there's more than one type of hunger and so we have to know what type of hunger we're feeling before we can tune in and understand it. I'm sure you will have experienced most, if not all of these at some point.

The Different Types of Hunger

Biological (Physical) Hunger

This is the hunger that we tend to refer to when we talk about being hungry. We feel it when we're ready to eat after a gap since our last meal or snack, and most of us feel it a few times throughout the day. One of the signs that we're biologically hungry is that thoughts of food and eating come into our mind. We think about what we'd like to eat and we start to plan when, what and where we'll eat. It's not an uncomfortable feeling initially, but if we ignore it or leave it for too long it can become unpleasant as our body sends us increasingly insistent signals that we need to eat.

Although everyone feels it differently, there are a number of common 'symptoms', all of which tell us it's time to eat. For some of us, it's the empty stomach feeling, for others, it's a change in mood or feeling shaky. I've put the most common signs for adults and children in the tables overleaf.

Kids

Stomach	Body	Energy	Mood
Rumbling	Headache	Lethargy	Whiney
Gurgling	Floppy	Fatigue	Tearful
Physical hunger	Poor concentration	Tired	Grumpy
Feeling empty	Shaky	Listless	Tantrums
Stomach pains	Dizziness	Low energy	Bored
Nausea	Light-headed	Loss of focus	Miserable
Refusing to eat (past hunger)	Nausea	Withdrawn	Hangry

Table 5.2. Signs that children are hungry.

Adults

Stomach	Body	Energy	Mood
Rumbling	Headache	Lethargy	Low
Gurgling	Shakiness	Fatigue	Blue
Hunger pangs	Low energy	Meh	Grumpy / Moody
Feeling empty	Tiredness	Tired	Hangry
Stomach pains	Dizziness	Loss of focus	Irritable / Snappy
Nausea	Light-headed	Listless	Disinterested
Gnawing	Poor concentration	Withdrawal/ Withdrawn	Can't be bothered
Extreme hunger	Poor coordination	Depleted	Humourless

Table 5.3. Signs that adults are hungry.

It's as important to help your kids notice how they feel in these domains when hungry as it is to point out to them the changes in how they feel once they have eaten and are sated. These will be things like feeling satisfied, the hunger signs having remitted, having energy, being bubbly, finding their sense of fun, playfulness and humour, and being interested in things again. It's often very helpful to tell your kids how you feel so that they can learn to recognise it in you and know that it's normal to feel hunger in many different ways. They may then tell you they think you're hungry whenever you're irritable, but that's OK, it's all useful conversation.

Extreme Hunger

Extreme hunger occurs when you have gone past biological hunger. For whatever reason you miss the cues, you have to work through lunch, you've been dashing from pillar to post or you're on a diet. You may feel that you have 'gone past hunger' and that you're no longer hungry and this is common initially. What comes next, however, is extreme, unmissable hunger. It's uncomfortable and primal, causing you to feel 'I must eat now'. Often it becomes preoccupying, leaving you unable to think of little else other than what you want to eat and how soon you can eat it. All of the signs in the tables on the previous page can accompany extreme hunger too.

Sometimes, when we finally eat after experiencing extreme hunger, we eat too much. In part this is because we're less likely to eat slowly and assess how sated we are whilst eating. It's also partly because the brain thinks that it's been in a period of famine and so now that food is available, it needs to stock up to protect from the next famine. Eating more regularly prevents this from happening and allows us to eat in a more mindful, calmer fashion – it's hard to be mindful when you are feeling extreme emotions, urges or physical sensations.

Emotional Hunger

I'm sure you've experienced this: you feel low, stressed, have had a tough day and you eat to self-soothe, 'treat yourself' or numb out. Emotional hunger tends to occur in response to intense emotion. Stress often leads to emotional hunger due to the release of the stress hormone, cortisol, which increases appetite, especially for highly palatable foods.[45] However, it's not just stress that leads to emotional hunger; it can be wanting to reward yourself, to stimulate pleasure, due to low mood, or a desire to numb the pain that you are feeling. There's interplay between the emotional, physiological and cognitive (thinking) components and emotional hunger is a powerful driver to eat. A clear sign that hunger is emotional is when eating doesn't leave you feeling sated, or it doesn't change your feeling of hunger.

Given that your kids will experience emotional hunger at points in their lives, it's important to help them identify it. The strategy is exactly the same as with the other types of hunger – start by being interested in how they are feeling in their body (their hunger symptoms) and then how they are feeling emotionally. Be curious rather than directive, and ask how their day was, what they did at school – all the usual questions. If you suspect that they're feeling emotional hunger, you can raise it but don't prevent them from eating. You can give them a small portion and see how they feel afterwards. Remember, take it slowly and steady – you're wanting to give your kids knowledge that will help them throughout their lives and aid their developing a good relationship with food. Getting too prescriptive about what kind of hunger they're feeling and allowing them food or not, depending on it, is deleterious to their relationship with food.

Practical Hunger

This describes hunger that is based on habit and routine. You might know that you're working through lunch and therefore plan to eat at 11.30 to prevent yourself from getting too hungry in the afternoon. It may be that you like routine and so eat at the same times each day irrespective of whether you're biologically hungry. There's nothing wrong with planning, and sometimes it's extremely helpful, for example when travelling across time zones. It can be beneficial in preventing you or your kids from getting too hungry, but ideally it wouldn't be your norm. This is because if it's your usual way of eating then you're not tuning into your body and responding to it, which means that sometimes you'll eat more than you want and sometimes you may undereat.

This is a risk in trying to prevent your kids getting too hungry, because they need to learn to notice what their body is telling them. Hunger, as you know, is a fluctuating rather than a static state and responsive parenting or feeding depends on you and your child being able to respond to their physical cues.

Taste Hunger

'I love lemon cake'; 'toast and butter is my favourite'; 'crisps are delicious'. These are all statements about taste and with taste hunger, we often eat a food when we're not hungry simply because we like the taste of it. Memory plays a significant part in taste hunger, because it's our memory of the taste of a food that activates our desire to eat.

The converse is also true: if you have negative associations with certain tastes then you probably won't eat that food even if you are hungry.

Simply thinking about food can stimulate hunger and get your digestive juices flowing. Imagine that you have a fresh lemon. You cut it in half and then into quarters and pop a quarter into your mouth and start sucking out the juice (as you would with an orange). It's sharp and tangy, making you pull in your cheeks. Whether or not you like the strong, citrusy flavour of lemons, you'll notice that imagining this activates your salivary glands and your mouth starts to water in anticipation.

Memory and Hunger

Research has shown that memory plays a significant part in hunger cues.[46] When we have good memories of eating certain foods, we'll have some excitement at the prospect of eating them again, finding them enticing. However, those with few rewarding memories of certain foods – for example, fruit and veg – won't find these foods enticing and won't have a memory cue that stimulates a desire to eat them. Finally, people with negative associations of eating certain foods will have memories that cause them to reject those foods.

This adds even more weight to the importance of keeping mealtimes stress-free and happy, and to removing conflict from eating in general, and especially around the foods you really want your children to eat and enjoy. It further advocates for a food-neutral approach with no food hierarchy because when highly palatable sweets, chocolate, crisps, fast foods are set up to be treats your child will form positive memories of having those foods as a reward or on a special occasion and therefore have memories of them that generate a powerful hunger for that food.

In summary, knowing all of these different types of hunger will equip you to help your child really tune into their body and understand its signals. It'll also assist you if your quest is to educate your child on eating healthily. You'll have explicit (relaxed) conversations around eating for comfort and the foods that typically go with this. You'll chat about their favourite foods leading to taste hunger; the consequences of extreme hunger and so on. And now you appreciate the role that memory plays in hunger, you'll be able to focus on making positive memories for your child with foods you'd like them to eat.

So How Do You Educate Your Children About Nutrition?

How is it consistent for me to say teach your kids that 'all food is food, all food is equal' on the one hand and simultaneously say that it's necessary to teach children about nutrition, where not all food is equal? I realise the message can be confusing, but it's a nuanced conversation, and nuance is inherently tricky to understand. The younger your child, the more clarity and the less subtlety they need. Subtlety requires more complicated cognitive processing and the brains of younger children are not developed enough for this level of comprehension. So, your conversation with them will evolve and become more complex and less black and white as they grow up.

Be their role model. Eat well yourself and they'll learn by watching you. Eat a balanced, varied diet and they'll learn to do the same. Don't underestimate the influence that your eating has on them. They want to eat the same food as you, from the same crockery, with the same cutlery, and they feel grown up when they do. They'll copy you, it's modelling. They learn to eat as you do even if you say nothing at all. If you rarely cook, eat ready meals and ultra-processed foods, your child will too. Even if you make homemade meals just for them, they'll think that they're getting second best because it's different to your food. If they never see you eat fruit, they won't naturally eat it. If you don't like vegetables, rarely eat them, or only eat one or two types of veg, your child will do the same. They won't jump up magically and beg you for salad if they don't see you eating it.

When your child is very young and you're in control of what they eat, it's easy: you feed them, they eat it (hopefully), job done. However, once they go to nursery, school and friends' houses, they're exposed to different foods and family styles of eating. It's around this time that they may ask questions about why their friend Alice eats different food to them. How you answer shapes the conversations that continue from here. You can talk about every family having their own preferred flavours and foods, their own way of having meals together, or not, and you can refer to some people liking and having time to cook and others not, so that it does not seem that there is a right and a wrong way. Talking about right and wrong, good and bad is value-laden and places judgement on others. There is little more mortifying than your child going in to school and saying, 'My mummy says that your mummy gives you bad food.' Instead, try sticking with facts where possible: 'We love veg and eat more than them'; 'They eat meat every day'; or, go for a neutral guess: 'Maybe their daddy doesn't like cooking as much as I do'; or, 'Maybe it was a very busy day so no one had time to cook'.

When it comes to discussing which foods are healthy or desirable, I prefer to talk about nutrition and foods being nourishing for your body, good fuel, or sustaining, rather than 'healthy' and 'unhealthy', which are value laden. Tell your child that we need to eat a whole range of foods to make sure that our bodies get all the nutrients they need to keep us growing, energetic and healthy. Talk to them about different food groups and needing to have a balanced diet because too much or too little of any food is not good for them. Too much fruit, veg, protein, carbohydrates, fats all have consequences, as do too little of them.

Be specific. It may seem pedantic but 'unhealthy', 'not good' and 'bad' don't describe anything that food gives the body or the soul and they're loaded, pejorative terms. Instead, be accurate about what certain foods contain, what we need nutritionally, that the food tastes good and that we need lots of variety in our diets. How you talk to your kids will evolve. They need age-appropriate information – a single fact or two when they're young with increasing detail as they get older. I've popped some bullet points below to make it easy.

- Start by teaching them that food is fuel for our bodies like petrol is fuel for the car. You don't expect a car to drive with no fuel and you can't expect a body to work without food.
- Avoid using words like good, bad, clean, dirty, healthy, unhealthy, junk or rubbish.
- Be specific in telling them what foods do in the body. For example, these foods: give us energy / help you grow / make your bones strong / help our eyes to see / help our hair to grow / and so on.
- Name foods and food groups, for example: vegetables and fruits, or fats, carbohydrates and proteins.
- Describe how the different colours of fruit and veg contain different vitamins and minerals – that's why they are different colours.
- Get practical! Show them how foods change when you cook, wash or add something to them. For example:

- ◇ When you wash red cabbage, the water turns blue. They'll find that pretty cool. Then, add a squeeze of lemon and the water will turn pink.
- ◇ Watch egg whites de-nature when you whisk them and they change from a yellowish liquid into stiff, white peaks.
- ◇ Soups are completely different colours, depending on the veg that's in them.
- It doesn't have to be all talk – these things are fun and will capture their attention and interest.
- Explain we need to eat everything as part of a balanced diet, but we need more of some foods than others.
- Teach them to notice how their body feels after certain foods: which keep them full up for the longest? Which taste better to them? Be curious and help them to internalise what makes them feel good.
- Tell them we need as much variety of foods as possible – especially fruit and veg – to give us as many vitamins and minerals as possible.
- Make it age-appropriate, so for young children, one or two headline facts only, and as they get older, more detail and nuance.
- Make it interesting! 'I like apple cake because it reminds me of going to tea with my grandma' will engage even young children in their own family history, and how food is more than just what we eat.

I like to talk about foods that keep us fuller for longer, which is important because we don't want them to get hungry an hour after eating. So, we stay feeling sated by having a combination of enough food and sustaining foods. For less 'healthy' foods, explain that foods with a lot of sugar in them give a fast burst of energy but it gets used up in one go and then it's gone, leaving you feeling tired and hungry quickly.

Refined sugar is often a source of worry, with some parents even saying 'sugar is cocaine' or 'sugar is poison'. I know there have been headlines stating it's as addictive as drugs and research continues. To date, the research has been done on rodents and extrapolated to humans. Experts currently disagree on whether it's addictive and, if so, how addictive it is. Likewise, the links between sugar and poor health outcomes. There are indications that eating it gives a dopamine (reward) boost and that the deprivation binge pattern occurs.[47] You might think that I am advocating giving your kids sugar: I am and I'm not. I'm keen on balance and come from a psychological perspective, where I see the many problems an extreme position causes.

I implore you not to tell your kids that sugar is poison – it creates several problems. It's factually incorrect. Sugar is neither cocaine nor poison. If your child were offered a teaspoon of sugar and a teaspoon of cocaine or poison which would you rather they chose? Such messages create confusion and anxiety for your child when offered sugary foods at school, friends' houses or parties. They become confused as to why they are being offered 'poison'; it may cause them not to trust food that has been prepared by other adults. Later, as they grow older, they may stop trusting your nutritional knowledge and information, leading to them craving sugary food and hiding their consumption from you as they would an illicit substance, exactly like Siobhan and Iris described later. None of these are good outcomes, so avoid a stance as extreme as this.

With the growing research on ultra-processed foods and the negative impact on health, many parents feel they must be avoided completely and that their children need to know that they are 'bad' and 'not even food'. Whilst I agree that too much ultra-processed food is unwise, be clear about why. Refer to them as ultra-processed foods and then explain that this means that they are foods that contain many ingredients, some of which you would not have in your kitchen cupboard and foods that you could not recreate at home. 'Bad' food is not specific or accurate and talking about it as such can leave your child unclear as to what you actually mean. Sometimes you may be exhausted and unable to cook from scratch, with a processed meal being the best option: that's OK, your wellbeing is extremely important. There is also a socioeconomic component here. It is a position of privilege to be able to choose what food you want freely. Many can't afford this luxury and might have to choose between something highly processed or go without food altogether.

The concept of a rainbow on your plate is super helpful, if you have the freedom and funds to provide it. Again, it's a privilege. The rainbow on a plate describes having a whole range of different-coloured foods on your plate at a meal. The colours in fresh foods come from different nutrients so eating a rainbow means that you and your children ingest a wide range of nutrients beneficial for health. You can turn this into a fun activity with your child when you shop, prepare food and sit down to eat. Ask them to find different coloured fresh foods, get them to learn the names and count them. Use this as a dual-purpose activity: to teach about nutrition in a fun way, and to develop their vocabulary, spelling and counting. Use the different foods as an enjoyable way to discover new flavours, with you and your child tasting different foods together to see if they are sweet, bitter, sour, salty, mild or strong. Discuss how different foods grow and their purposes in nature. Play games to see who can come up with the biggest number of a certain colour or group of foods. Be as creative as possible so that your child becomes interested in food and enjoys learning about nutrition rather than feeling that it's a chore, or that the foods they like are somehow linked to their worth as a person.

When your child's older, introduce more nuance around different foods and styles of eating across different families and friends. Ensure that they know they can eat nutritious *and* less nutritious foods as part of a balanced diet. Your teenager may well want to eat foods that you regard as unhealthy. This might be due to their hormones, because they want to eat with their friends, or it may be part of their process of separation and individuation. The stricter the food rules at home, the more likely your teen is to go against them through their adolescent years because this is part of the adolescent process. Avoid going into battle over food, particularly if your teen is eating, is healthy and is generally doing their adolescence in an adolescent way. Just keep having family meals that are well-balanced and continue to have pudding sometimes, so that nothing is banned and your teen continues to have all foods at home. If you want to gently nudge them from time to time, to remind them that they may want to recalibrate the balance of their diet, it *might* be OK to do that, but it will depend on your relationship with your child and whether it turns into an argument. If so, it's a topic prudent to avoid. If your child is struggling with food, or with their body image, I will discuss this later in the book as these are different conversations with different needs and interventions.

If you've read this and feel upset or angry thinking that you have got this wrong, don't worry. It's a minefield and can be very difficult to navigate with the abundance of messages in the media, on social media, at school, from your family background, your partner's and your children's friends. There are many fear-laden articles readily available and whilst the content is often (but not always!) accurate, remember: attention-grabbing headlines are necessary to hook you in, and none are better at this than anxiety-provoking ones. In addition, anyone can be an expert so check that there is science supporting the claims you read rather than just opinion.

If you feel that this is poor advice because you want your children to know the difference between 'healthy' and 'unhealthy' foods in a binary way, then you can teach them this. Just know that it's not best practice as it becomes tricky for them if they like the taste of 'bad' foods. They may feel that they can't tell you because it's not acceptable at home, or because it makes them bad or anxious around food. Ultimately, work out what you want your children to learn from you – that is all you can control. The essence I want you to hang on to, irrespective of your child's size, is that the odd bit of chocolate, cake, pudding, crisps etc. isn't going to cause harm. An anxious, guilty or poor relationship with food will.

And finally, there's the issue of body size. Some children have bigger bodies. You might roll your eyes at this, thinking it's ridiculous to avoid saying that they are overweight, but living in a bigger body is much more accurate. We don't want children who are in bigger bodies because we live in a culture that doesn't accept it (more in Chapter 8, on diet culture). If we are scared of our child being heavy then we risk parenting around food based on fear about their size and in doing so, we neglect their physical and emotional needs. It doesn't work and it's ineffective.

When we try to control our child's body size it makes them feel shame and communicates that small is better. It causes significant anxiety and instantly marries food, weight and size. It tells them that they can't be trusted with food and prevents them from trusting their body. It hinders their self-worth and creates a very troubled relationship with food. Instead of being helpful or protective, trying to control our child's weight leads to increased weight gain, through restriction, extreme hunger, bingeing, dieting and comfort eating.

We need to detach the way we feed our children from their body size. We must feed all kids the same irrespective of their size (taking into account allergies and dietary requirements) so that we set up a positive relationship with food. We need to build self-trust and confidence with eating and with their body. Indeed, this is all the more important with children who are larger as they will get messages from school, society and the world at large that their body is too big and they are inadequate. We need to do everything we can to minimise the impact of this and trying to shrink them into a body that is too small for them isn't the way. We must do so through ensuring they know how to understand their needs and through building their self-worth and resilience.

> **CHAPTER TAKEAWAYS**
>
> - Responsive feeding using the division of responsibility is key: you are responsible for what your child eats and when, and they are responsible for whether and how much they eat.
> - When feeding your baby, think of responsive feeding with the emphasis on responding to your child's needs and cues, rather than to their 'demands' as implied by demand feeding.
> - Allergies and illnesses can lead to significant anxiety. Be factual with your kids about their condition and liaise with school and other parents so that the adults looking after them know what to do if they have a reaction.

- Help your child to tune into their body and notice their hunger and full cues.
  Help them to notice how different foods make them feel.
- Help them to understand the different types of hunger – in an age-appropriate way.
- Don't restrict or ban any foods other than for medical or religious reasons. Restriction leads to cravings, taking banned food surreptitiously and bingeing.
- At every age and stage, your child's needs will change, as will their independence – adapt accordingly. It's an ever-evolving process.
- Get creative and curious when talking about 'healthy eating'.
- Avoid 'good', 'bad', 'healthy' and 'unhealthy', etc., labels. Instead, be specific about different foods.
- Avoid trying to control your child's weight or size. It's ineffective and more damaging than them being larger.
- Having some chocolate, cake, pudding, crisps etc. isn't going to cause harm. An anxious, guilty or poor relationship with food will.

CHAPTER 6

Childhood

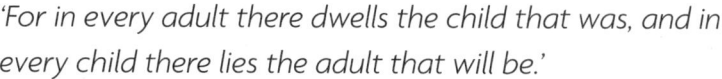

'For in every adult there dwells the child that was, and in every child there lies the adult that will be.'

John Connolly

Imagine that you go to a restaurant for dinner and order your favourite meal. When it arrives it smells off, looks a dodgy colour, the green vegetables are brown and putrid, and it's topped with what looks like spots of whitey yellow pus. Would you eat this? No. You'd feel a powerful aversion to something so disgusting and no amount of coaxing, cajoling, bribing or anger would make you eat it. When your child is presented with a scary or new food, or when they are a picky eater, they may feel and react similarly.

Six-year-old David was referred to the feeding clinic. His mum and dad nervously described how David had fed well as a baby and taken to solids initially but became anxious about eating different foods at about three years old. They had tried everything: cajoling, bribing, praising, getting angry and insisting he ate, but his list of accepted foods was short. They didn't understand what had happened, felt they'd failed as parents, and were ashamed. David was comfortable eating peas, grapes, melon, chicken, spaghetti Bolognaise, bread, butter, strawberry jam, cream cheese, chocolate, pasta, pesto, mashed potato, tomato sauce, rice crispies, Frosties and Petits Filous. Anything else led to tears and sometimes tantrums.

David was his parents' first child and they were worried about his physical health. His weight and height remained on the same growth curve as they had always been, and whilst his diet was a bit limited, he ate food from all food groups and enough of a range of foods for me not to be worried. It was much more important that he felt less anxious around food, so I suggested that his parents keep serving his safe foods and continue putting new foods on the table at meals – but not on his plate – so that he continued to be exposed to them without feeling frightened about eating them. This is a very common issue and one that usually resolves with this approach.

There is so much advice, much of it contradictory, about what kids *should* be eating and how parents *should* be feeding. The pressure to get your child to eat fruit, vegetables and a wide range of foods is immense and as a parent it feels like you are doing something wrong if your child refuses certain foods or food groups. However, it takes time for children to develop diverse tastes and try new foods, and if your child does this slower than other children you haven't done anything wrong or failed. A wide range of factors influence children and some strategies both help and hinder.

All children are picky to a greater or lesser extent. You've had decades to hone your taste buds, expand your repertoire, and discover a whole host of foods and flavours that you like. Your children haven't. Sometimes it's the taste, other times the texture or smell of the food that is off-putting. If you go into battle with them over a food, they won't want to eat it and probably won't

– pressure is a sure-fire way to turn them off a food or eating. As you become more insistent, your child more adamantly refuses, you both dig your heels in and entrench your positions. You usually lose because you can't make your child eat. Remember, any reaction – even a negative one – is better than no reaction to a child. So, if you react to their fussiness, even negatively, it increases the likelihood that they will be fussy again. And again.

You will have much more success if you offer them opportunities to try new foods along with 'safe' foods during a relaxed, family meal, where they see you eating those foods. If conflict over food happens more than a few times, your child learns that it's an effective way to provoke you, get your attention and really bother you. It becomes a mode of communication, a power play or a way of upsetting you and none of these are good.

Psychologically, the aim from day one is to help your child develop a positive relationship with food. The relationship we have with food from childhood is life-long and whilst it may evolve over our life, having a solid foundation is highly protective. By a solid foundation, I mean feeling comfortable with food and eating; having positive associations with it; trusting your appetite and your body; feeling free to eat what you fancy when you're hungry; nourishing yourself; not having emotional, pejorative or value-laden language attached to certain foods; and being free of anxiety and distress around food and eating in all areas.

Before you jump in and say that your child needs to know what is healthy and unhealthy and that they cannot be allowed to eat chocolate, crisps and biscuits all day long, I agree. I am not advocating a lack of nutritional knowledge nor a diet consisting entirely of ultra-processed foods. As discussed earlier, this all comes later, and can be taught throughout childhood in an age-appropriate way. You don't need to teach infants or toddlers about this. You don't need to offer them chocolate, sweets and crisps, but you do need to be setting up the good relationship with food from day one, and this comes from the attitudes to food and eating that you and your partner have, and model to your children.

Picky Eating

There are two main hypotheses about why so many toddlers and children become picky. The first is evolutionary,[48] suggesting that it's a survival mechanism (see Chapter 1, pages 10-11, for more detail). If children stick to foods that are familiar (safe), they reduce their chances of ingesting something poisonous. In addition, children's taste buds are different to adults. They taste things more intensely and they prefer sweet, salty and sometimes sour foods, with an aversion to bitterness.

Hypothesis two relates to the developmental stage of toddlers and young children. Physical, neurological, emotional and social development move on apace during this time, as dependent infants transition into increasingly independent children. Strong emotions, tantrums, a desire to do everything themselves and a dislike of adult direction are common, and with this comes an awareness of restrictions, often imposed by adults, in what your toddler can, or is allowed to do. With all of this, choosing what and whether they eat is something over which children have agency. Many also communicate their independence, autonomy, defiance or compliance through food. Others manage anxiety by managing their food. For some, boredom is the reason they reject food because a toddler's attention span is short. All children go through this – periods of being fussy and not wanting to try new foods. Usually it's not an issue, and they emerge out the other side by the ages of six to eight. It becomes an issue, however, when they get stuck being picky. Signs of stuckness are:

- Eating a small and shrinking list of foods, sometimes as few as five to ten.
- Getting upset or anxious at the sight of a new or unfamiliar food.
- Neophobia (a phobia of new foods).
- Gagging or retching at the sight of a new food.
- Normal, everyday life becoming disrupted due to food.
- Worrying about eating away from home.
- Parents making special meals that are different to those the rest of the family are eating to get your child to eat.
- Parents feeling upset about their child's eating.

Sticky picky eating is most often associated with four areas: anxiety, sensory issues, temperament and autistic spectrum disorder (ASD).[49] There are links between these areas as children who struggle with sensory sensitivity are often also anxious, and those with ASD likewise. If your child falls into these categories, it might be helpful to seek specialist advice to support both of you. You are your child's greatest advocate and champion, and you need the knowledge, tools and support to feel confident and empowered in helping your child. Even children who get stuck with picky eating usually grow and thrive physically, with most continuing along the same weight and height centiles as they have been on throughout most of their childhood.[50] If you are concerned about your child's growth, take them to the GP for a check-up.

If you're distressed, anxious or angry about their eating, seek support for yourself. There's no shame. Feeding and nourishing our children is primal and when it becomes difficult, it evokes strong emotions (so that we keep them safe and fed). However, there's more wrapped up for you in your child being fussy than a purely primitive, instinctive reaction. Were you a picky eater yourself and, if so, what was the response of your parents, peers and teachers? Were you taunted or berated for it? Were you frightened into eating everything or defiant in response to pressure? Did you grow up with exposure to anorexia or food poverty? I put these together because both frequently lead to profound fear about them recurring in one's own family. Was love and acceptance expressed through food in your family, so having a child who does not accept foods communicates that you are not loved? Did you have an eating disorder and remember the pain? Do you believe that part of your role as a parent is feeding your child a varied and balanced diet and therefore their refusal signifies failure? Whatever is cropping up for you is worth exploring. It helps you, your children and their relationship with food.

Below are strategies that help in broadening your child's accepted foods but be patient. It takes time and is best done calmly and slowly.

- Stick to a clear meal and snack structure, ensuring a good two hours between a snack and a meal, so that your child is hungry, but not too hungry for the meal. Children who are too hungry or have 'gone past it' will often not eat, despite it being what they need to regulate their emotions, gain energy and feel good.
- Maintain the division of responsibility so that you provide the 'what' and 'when' of food – what food and the time to eat it – and they have responsibility for the 'whether' and 'how much' they eat.

- Respond to your child's hunger, their fulness and any issues that arise around food. Help them to recognise their body's signals and trust them to do so.
- Eat together as a family. This reduces the risk of boredom, because there is stimulation from conversations, interactions and watching you and any siblings. It also enables them to watch you eat, a very important part of modelling.
- Always have at least one or two accepted foods that you know your child will eat. You can add others that they don't and that you'd like them to learn to eat, but they must be able to eat enough, meaning their safe foods need to be available.
- Don't offer alternative foods to those that you have prepared. Your child can leave food – this is their role in the division of responsibility – but for this to be feasible they must have safe foods available.
- Offer new foods alongside safe foods. You can mentally 'grade' the new foods so that you offer some similar to their safe foods and some that are different and more ambitious.
- It can be very helpful to have a self-service model of meals whereby all food is put in the centre of the table and you and your children serve yourselves. Of course, you may need to help your child, depending on their age.
- If you are plating their food, don't overfill their plate. A full plate can be overwhelming and put them off eating altogether. Allow them to have 'seconds' if they are still hungry. More small servings are better than loading their plate for a single serving.
- Tweak and rotate safe foods to ensure that your child continues to eat them and to create maximum variety in their diet.

- Try to make mealtimes relaxed and enjoyable. Take the focus *off* the food and place it on family connection and bonding. Talk about everyone's day, share yours, chat about things you enjoy and share humour. This environment is the most likely to enhance both your child's relationship with food and their willingness to try new foods.

A food feels unsafe because it's new and unfamiliar. You and your child have different views on risk, reward, change and newness. For example, if your child only eats beige foods but you want them to eat broccoli, the broccoli is a monumental jump for them and one they are unlikely to make. You need to offer them foods that have some of the characteristics of their safe foods. White beans or banana, for example, will be more likely to be accepted than broccoli, in the first instance at least.

If your child is struggling to move beyond their safe foods despite doing all of the above, try these extra strategies:

- Rather than having a goal of eating a new, feared food, make the goal familiarity with that food. It's more realistic and much less stressful. Start by just being interested in the new food with your child: try smelling it, touching it, mushing it, licking it, or picking it up and moving it towards the mouth or to the lips and then returning it to their plate. These steps move your child further towards taking the risk of trying a new food, in a slow and graded way. Much better to maintain patience and do this than force them to taste it, dislike it, feel an aversion or gag, confirming that it's dangerous or disgusting.
- Have a small plate or bowl next to your child's plate so that

they can keep the unfamiliar food separate from their safe foods. This is less frightening for children than having a new or unsafe food placed on the same plate as foods with which they are comfortable. It also safeguards the likelihood that they will eat because they will not become anxious about a scary food touching or contaminating a safe food.
- Create a 'food ladder' with a child by putting a safe food at the bottom – rung 1 – and a desired, unsafe food at the top – rung 10. Then add a series of steps, each building on the previous one, that creates steps towards the desired new food. The key is building on what your child will already accept.
- Try 'food chaining': start by making small changes to foods that they already eat. If they are happy with little chunks of cheese, give them grated cheese; instead of cucumber sticks, give slices. These are the same foods prepared differently and the first step in helping them accept difference. Try a different pasta shape. Once they have accepted the small changes, increase the challenge slightly: offer the pasta shape with which they are comfortable in a different colour – for example, green penne instead of white.
- As you work up the ladder or along your chain, build on the previous step, maintaining the features of accepted foods as you work towards the desired food.

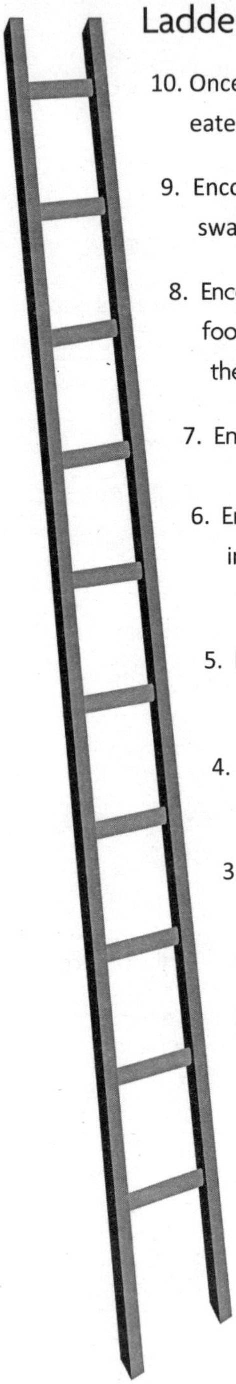

Ladder to Food Acceptance

10. Once they are doing this, increase the amount of that food eaten and start again with another new food.

9. Encourage your child to bite and chew the food and then swallow it.

8. Encourage your child to bring the food to their face. To 'kiss' the food and touch it with their tongue – again it helps to involve the whole family and make it fun and playful.

7. Encourage your child to pick up the food with their hands.

6. Encourage your child to touch the new food with cutlery initially, and then with their fingers. It can help if they cook with you and have fun with the new food.

5. Encourage your child to smell the food. Involve the whole family so you all do this together.

4. Start to put the new food on their main plate, but not touching any other foods.

3. After a few days, serve your child the new food on a small side plate or bowl that's separate from their main plate.

2. Add the new food to family mealtimes by putting it in the middle of the table for everyone to help themselves (don't pressure your child to do so).

1. Choose a new food. It can be anything but start with something similar to a food your child already eats easily. Take them shopping with you and encourage them to pick up the food and put it in the trolley.

Figure 6.1. Example of food ladder – work from bottom, rung 1, to top, rung 10.

CHILDHOOD | 189

Food Chaining

Food chaining is a technique where you link foods that your child already likes and accepts to new foods similar in texture, size colour and shape.

1. Identify the foods that your child likes, including texture, colour and shape.

2. Identify the foods that your child does not like, including texture, colour and shape.

3. Pair the foods that have similar texture, colour and shape, changing one thing at a time.

Cheesy Cracker to Broccoli

FAVOURITE CRACKER
- Disc Shape
- Cheese Flavour
- Yellow/Beige
- Crispy

CHEESE AND CRACKER
- ★ Disc and **Square** Shape
- Cheese Flavour
- Yellow/Beige
- ★ Crispy and **Soft**

CHEESE TOASTY SQUARES
- **Square** Shape
- Cheese Flavour
- Yellow/Beige
- Crispy and **Soft**

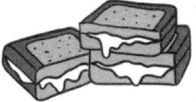

BAKED CHEESE POTATO
- ★ **Round Shape**
- Cheese Flavour
- Yellow/Beige
- Crispy and Soft

BAKED CHEEST POTATO AND BROCCOLI
- **Round Shape**
- Cheese Flavour
- ★ Yellow/Beige and **Green**
- Crispy and Soft

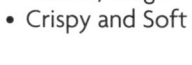

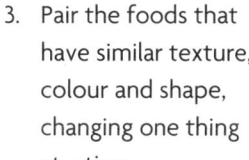

BROCCOLI AND CHEESE
- **Round** Shape
- Cheese Flavour
- Yellow/Beige and **Green**
- ★ **Soft**

Figure 6.2. Example of food chaining.[51]

Fussiness is normal. Maintain the fundamentals: the division of responsibility; not offering snacks too close to meals; mealtime boundaries; continuing with family meals; modelling; offering variety; and not reacting to your child's fussiness. Always remember that in asking them to eat something that they think they don't like, you are asking your child to do something that makes them anxious and for some children, scares them. This will help you to remain patient and compassionate. It's like the tortoise and the hare – slow and steady wins the race.

CHAPTER TAKEAWAYS

- Eat with your kids.
- Avoid going into battle over food or eating with your child.
- Most kids go through a fussy stage. You only need to intervene if the fussiness gets 'stuck'.
- Avoid food becoming a method of communication.
- It takes time for kids to try new foods and acquire new tastes. It's normal for them to be reluctant and for it to take time.
- If needed, try food chaining and / or a food ladder.
- Focus on nurturing a positive relationship with food. The odd chocolate bar, sweets or crisps will not harm your child (or you). A poor relationship with food is much more likely to.
- Seek help for your child or for yourself so that your own relationship with food does not play out.

CHAPTER 7

Adolescence

'Do I look fat in this?'

Women everywhere

What do you remember about your teenage years? Are your memories of fun, friendship and happiness, or angst, friend-ship ruptures, trying to fit in but feeling left out, fluctuating friendship groups, photos of fashion faux pas, terrible hairstyles and make-up, changing identities, an acne-covered face, awkward kisses, unrequited crushes, body dissatisfaction, self-loathing, anxiety and low mood? Did you enjoy those years or were you delighted to see the back of them? I doubt they were the easiest in your life – they rarely are – and however much you want to protect your children, their adolescence will be bumpy too. You cannot prevent this. You can only be there alongside them helping and supporting them navigate what is probably going to be the rockiest few years of their life so far.

By the time they emerge from it, adolescence will have taken up roughly half of your child's life. There is debate around when adolescence ends, but broadly speaking, it starts from the moment at which the hormonal and biological changes of puberty begin and ends, between 19 and 25, depending on when you entered it and which definition you use.

Your child will become a more emotional being and you may find them volatile in mood, temperament and their ability to tolerate feelings. Today, they also have to learn to manage two worlds – their real world and their online world. Although they'll often dismiss your attempts to discuss this with them, they need guidance and help balancing the two and remaining grounded in reality.

Adolescence is an amazing process: the brain spends around a decade rewiring and upgrading from a child's brain to an adult one, with one area at a time coming 'offline' to rewire, leaving the rest of the brain to do its tasks as best as possible. The body transitions from a child's to a fully developed, sexual, adult body. There are the hormonal and physical changes of puberty, growth spurts, increased appetite and caloric requirements, increased strength and weight gain, particularly in girls. The circadian rhythm alters and thus teenagers tend to want to go to sleep and wake up around two hours later than adults.

Socially, friendships are key and often fluid as young people decide who they want to be. Emotional dysregulation is standard due to the hormonal, brain and emotional changes. Psychologically, there is frequently significant angst around friendships, identity, fitting in, being included or excluded, body image, and comparisons with peers. And then there are the pressures from within school and the education system, with increased work and important exams.

Your children have no choice about when these changes happen to them or how they are impacted. Despite the universal process, each young person is uniquely affected and has different resources and coping strategies. So, brace yourself and prepare for a rollercoaster ride. Bits of it you'll need to white knuckle and others will feel calm and gentle. When you lurch from one to the other is unpredictable and the issues that arise, often unexpected.

Understanding the multitude of internal and external changes that occur during this period helps make it more manageable for both you and your teen. Apart from the changes to the body and brain, there are two primary developmental tasks of adolescence: separation and individuation. Separation involves your young person separating from you emotionally so that they can become fully independent by the time they leave school and head into the adult world. Individuation is about working out their identity and who they want to be. This facilitates your beautiful child growing into an adult who knows who they are and can tackle the world in which they live independently. Not only is it a profound period of transition for your young people, it is for you, too.

Yasmin's mum was despairing. Her beloved child with whom she had had a great relationship had disappeared. In her place was a moody, young woman who did not want to hang out with her mum. She was secretive, spent hours on Snapchat with her friends and slept all morning on the weekends. They argued frequently over these things but Yasmin irritatedly told Mum to 'chill out'. She was fine; there was 'nothing wrong'. But Mum wasn't reassured, fearing there was something seriously amiss with her daughter.

Yasmin's mum, Leila, had grown up in a family where adolescence was not recognised or understood. She remembered her teenage years as tricky, but her parents had been strict: she was not allowed to sleep past 8am on any day of the week; she spoke to her friends on the phone outside of school, but as a family landline her parents had priority and her time was limited. Emotions were not discussed at home, conflict and disobedience were prohibited, and neither of her parents had discussed the changes that were taking place throughout Leila's adolescence. She bore her distress and worry silently and she neither had any knowledge of all of the processes involved in this amazing period of development, nor an internal model of a typical adolescence. Therefore, she didn't recognise what was happening to her daughter and was frightened.

The main intervention with Leila was to explain to her about everything that happens to a young person's brain and body in adolescence. In doing this and applying it to Yasmin, Leila was able to realise that the changes in Yasmin were normal and happening to all of her friends. As her worry decreased, she was able to interact with Yasmin in a more relaxed way and to help Yasmin understand everything that was happening for her. This facilitated more conversation between them and although there were better and worse days, both mum and daughter managed these and tolerated the worse days without too much distress. Knowing more about the process also enabled Leila to chat to her friends about it and hear that they were going through the same experience with their teenagers, providing her additional reassurance and comfort.

Neurologically, three main processes occur in adolescence. First, there is an increase in axon growth. Axons (see Figure 7.1, overleaf) connect with each other, enabling the flow of information. The more axons there are, the speedier the transmission of signals and information. Second is myelination, which is the development of fatty white matter surrounding the axons. Myelin wraps around the axons like a bandage protecting an arm and facilitates the transmission of information between neurons, and thereby around the brain and the body, like an electric cable conducting electricity. This process starts in utero, before birth, and is fundamental in child development. In adolescence, there is increased myelination as the brain rewires and upgrades. This causes a significant improvement in thinking, processing, analytical and problem-solving skills, allowing teenagers to respond to complex dilemmas[52] and process trickier information. Third is the process of synaptic pruning. It's like pruning trees, when branches that are not thriving are cut off (pruned) to enhance the growth of the stronger branches, which enables them to flourish and to continue to strengthen and develop. Lots of synapses emerge in childhood and then in adolescence. Those that are being used in particular environments remain and are strengthened through practice, and those that are not being used are pruned away and eliminated.

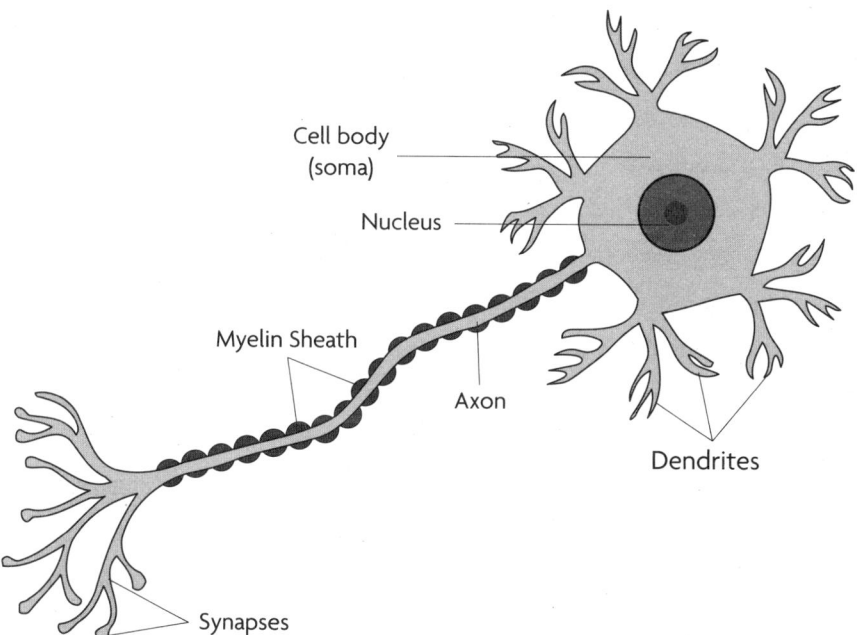

Figure 7.1. A neuron.

The way in which the brain changes and adapts to the environment is described as neuroplasticity. As the adolescent brain undergoes these profound changes, the brain is flexible and malleable (mouldable) and, as such, this period of development provides an excellent opportunity for social and educational learning and development. As we get older and move into adulthood our brain becomes less plastic, and this is why, learning a language or new skill for example, is a slower process for adults than children.

We know that during adolescence friends become the most important people to our teens and for many risk-taking behaviours increase. This happens as part of the separation process required to effectively separate from you as parents. To become a fully functional, independent adult, your young person needs to become less dependent on you emotionally and logistically; therefore, friends become their primary support. Research shows that risk-taking behaviour in adolescents is only greater when they are with their social group, not outside of it. Likewise, adolescents are highly risk-averse to anything that might be negatively judged by their peers. You are, I'm sure, familiar with teenagers dressing alike, wearing similar make-up, having similar haircuts, vaping because their group does and so on. Whilst risk-taking and risk-aversion are seemingly contradictory, both show the importance of peers in influencing each other's behaviour.

This is relevant when it comes to eating in the teenage years because it's the context of your child's life. They're going through so much change, bringing inevitable distress to them and to you. During these years they need to separate from you and develop independence, fit in with their social group(s), and work out who they want to be. They must adjust to a changing body emotionally, establish their relationship with their fuller, more sexual body and its nutritional needs. And this is before we talk about managing emotions with food, or wanting to lose weight, gain weight, bulk, shred, become vegan, cook their own meals, eat separately to the family or eat like their friends. There is also the increased academic pressure throughout secondary school with exams, increased workload and more pressure.

As each area of the brain rewires and upgrades it 'comes offline', which means that it stops doing its usual functions. Its tasks are temporarily performed by a different, incorrect, area of the brain, leading to difficulties in processing. For example, the prefrontal cortex, which is responsible for high-level cognitive functioning, including decision-making and planning, undergoes profound change during adolescence. Whilst remodelling is taking place adolescents still continue to function but notoriously struggle with decision-making and planning, because these tasks are being carried out by a different part of the brain (not the prefrontal cortex). Once the prefrontal cortex has upgraded it resumes its tasks, which explains why young adults (who have come out of adolescence) plan and make decisions better than they could a year or two earlier. In addition, during the neurological rewiring, the amygdala, which is in charge of emotions, works harder than in any other developmental stage, explaining why teenagers are so emotional and dysregulated. When you look at it like this, it's extraordinary that young people navigate it as well as they do, and mostly emerge unscathed.

Puberty

Puberty is the phase where a child's sexual development begins. It's this specific part of the transition from childhood to adulthood and as such a part of overall adolescent development. The average age of onset of puberty in girls is between the ages of 9–11 years, and in boys it's ages 11–13 years. Although all children will go through puberty, it's different in boys and girls. Boys tend to shoot up, becoming tall and lanky, before they broaden out towards the end of adolescence. They eat what seems like an inordinate amount of food without consequence other than being hungry again an hour later. Girls sometimes do this too, but unlike boys, they have to gain weight just before and at the start of puberty to ovulate and menstruate. Because body fat is essential to stimulate periods, girls need a higher percentage of body fat than boys. I loathe the phrase 'puppy fat', but I still hear it used frequently and it describes this pre-menstruation, growth-spurt weight gain. If you have daughters, know that they *must* gain weight to have periods. Gymnasts, ballet dancers and elite athletes often start periods significantly later than their non-athlete peers because they don't have enough body fat to allow ovulation. It's also why amenorrhea (no periods) comes with weight loss and anorexia, and explains why competitive female bodybuilders, gymnasts, marathon runners, etc. usually do not menstruate, regardless of their age. Body image dissatisfaction is rife during these years, and it's not only the domain of girls. Boys often dislike their changing body, with some feeling 'fat' as girls do, but many feeling that they are lanky or skinny, wanting to bulk and build muscle, leading to much gym-going.

Eating

That brings me to the place of food within adolescence. By the time your child hits adolescence, they have built a relationship with food and hopefully one that is balanced and food neutral. As they move to secondary school, they have increased independence and it's often at this point that they will pop to the shops on the way home and buy themselves snacks. Many parents find this worrying, fearing that their child will buy too much, and binge on sweets, crisps and chocolate. This is where their relationship with food comes in, because if they buy it intermittently and when they feel like it, it's all part of developing independence and nothing to fret about. If, on the other hand, there is a compulsive quality to it and they can't self-regulate, then you may need to have a conversation with them to understand what's driving the behaviour. However, going into a shop to buy themselves a treat is not only about food. It's part of becoming independent and autonomous. They have more freedom now and need to practise all of the skills involved in buying something independently: decision-making, social communication when interacting with the cashier or shopkeeper, learning about the cost of goods and the value of money; if they pay with cash, then the practical money and mathematical skills.

It's also during adolescence that most disordered eating and eating disorders emerge. I'll cover this fully in Chapter 9, but the factors that impact this are: diet culture, societal expectations, a developing body, body-image difficulties, emotional dysregulation, trying to manage feelings, friendship and relationship issues, and any trauma that may have been present in childhood or that happens in adolescence. There is no guarantee that any of these factors will lead to eating issues, but it's good to be aware of the possibility so that you can spot them and intervene as early as possible.

With all this in mind, the division of responsibility for food remains throughout your child's adolescence. Despite their increased independence, your child still needs you. They often act as if they don't need you or want your input, but your teenager depends upon you to maintain the structure of meals and to prioritise family meals. They need to connect with you and their family as much as ever, but they also sometimes want to go to friends, be out at dinner time or do their own thing. Your task is to maintain the boundaries without being too controlling, which is challenging.

Tell them when dinner is and expect them to join the family hungry and ready for the meal. You won't be able to control school lunches through these years, so you'll need to have helped them to develop autonomy in having lunch at school and eating breakfast before school. They may well want a snack when they arrive home from school, which is fine. Having a second supper an hour or two after dinner is also common, particularly with teenage boys. Continue to trust your child to know when they are hungry and full, to respect their body and don't ban any foods. As during their infancy and childhood, let your teenager find their own ways with food when they are not at home, in terms of what to eat, how much to eat and where to get food. Discuss any food management issues with them and then give them the responsibility for whatever you can so that they implement any necessary actions.

Throughout these years, help your child to learn to cook, buy food, plan meals and manage their food so that they are prepared and responsible when they go to college, university or leave home. They don't acquire these skills by magic so the more you cook and bake with them, share recipes and chat about how they will cope away from home, the better.

Body Image and Communication

With peers being so important, wanting to fit in is foremost in the minds of teens. Whether it's fitting in through wearing similar clothes, having the same hairstyle, sharing in comparisons and body disparagement, or getting very into the gym or hobbies, your teen wants to join their tribe. This is normal and only becomes a problem if it leads to concerning changes in mood, behaviour, eating or obsessive exercise, all of which need to be addressed. And then there's social media bombarding them with idealised images and messages about how they should look, what they should eat, what exercise they should do, and so much more. Judgement is rife in adolescence: from school, friends, family, members of the public, teachers, romantic interests and, most of all, themselves. And their self-judgement will be the most punitive and critical of all.

Your relationship with your teen and your relationship with food and your body determines how you fare during this tumultuous period. Remember that girls must gain weight and not doing so is concerning. If you struggle with their weight gain this is likely your issue not theirs. Don't feel bad – it's common – but own it and seek support so that you avoid communicating it to your daughter. It's very easy to give your child mixed messages around their shape, weight and eating.

Noa arrived aged 14 with eating that was disordered. She fluctuated between skipping breakfast and restricting her lunch with feeling that she binged and lost control. She was a healthy weight and there was no immediate physical risk, but her erratic eating and her thoughts were concerning. She described looking in the mirror and seeing someone overweight; she ruminated about food all day and decided whether to go out with her friends based on whether and what they'd be eating. This had started 18 months previously when her breasts began to bud and her shape changed towards more of a curvy woman's shape. Her pubertal weight gain had not been normalised and she felt out of control of her body.

Mum was frequently on a diet, trying to lose 10lbs. She would talk about what she could and couldn't eat and would try to make Noa eat breakfast whilst refusing it herself. The family ate meals together in the evening, but Mum refused the carbs. Mum told Noa that she was beautiful as she was but then complimented friends who had seemingly lost weight. Noa was angry and confused at what she saw as double standards and hypocrisy. She needed her mum to be a role model, more now than at any other time in her childhood. In addition, Mum would tell Noa to eat well but then commented when Noa ate freely, indicating that she was not really accepting or relaxed about it. Mum was clearly struggling with both her own relationship with her body and with her daughter's, and it was leaving Noa increasingly muddled, frustrated and upset.

This is not about blame. It's never about blame; only about awareness and we all need this. Without awareness of what you might be communicating you are destined to continue as you are, potentially passing messages to your teen that you'd rather not. With understanding comes choice: new avenues emerge, allowing you to choose how you eat in front of your teen, how you talk to them about your body and theirs, how you relate to yourself and so on. I can't emphasise enough how important this is: do it for your children as well as for yourself.

I truly know how distressing it can be for young people – girls and boys – to feel uncomfortable in their body, whether due to weight gain and feeling fat, or feeling they are too skinny, scrawny, gawky or underdeveloped. No sooner have they adjusted to their more developed body, it goes and changes again. It feels difficult and comes at a time in their lives when they are most vulnerable because of the issues and changes already discussed. It's also super painful for you, to watch your teenager struggle with these feelings, and it may trigger memories or challenges from your own adolescence that increase your distress. However great your child's distress, restrain yourself from joining with them by trying to help them to lose or gain weight, cut out foods or food groups, get fit, or follow a diet and workout plan. As long as they are eating properly, doing some kind of movement or exercise and there's nothing medically wrong, just be there to acknowledge their feelings and support them, but avoid jumping in with diet and exercise plans to fix.

We know that how we see ourselves in the mirror is different to what others see, due to the way visual perception and processing works.[53] To illustrate this, notice that as you walk towards and away from a mirror your height and body size seem to change. But, in reality, they don't. You don't need to be in a hall of mirrors in a fairground: even a 'normal' mirror distorts.

Perception of size is relational needing to be viewed in context rather than alone. Expectation interacts with the way we process visual images, so our expectations alter what we see in the mirror. Have you noticed that when you feel a particular way – heavier, slimmer, tired, glamorous – you see your reflection in the mirror supporting this, particularly with the more negative feelings? It's not because the way you feel is correct, or because your body or looks change radically day to day, but because of the interplay between expectation and visual perception. Help your teenager to understand this and stop them treating their reflection in the mirror as the absolute truth of how they look; it's much more valuable than finding an external fix for them.

Normalise and validate their feelings. Be there to listen and understand what it is like to be them in that moment. Be curious and compassionate, not critical or corrective. Questions and comments, such as, 'What's that like for you?', 'Oh, that's miserable', 'What made you say/think/feel that?', 'I remember feeling the same when I was your age. It was rough' help them feel that you understand them and are interested in what they're going through. Don't judge or correct by saying 'that's not right' or 'that was unkind; no wonder they don't want to be friends'. It's possible to help your teen think about the impact of what they say and do without pointing out how they've got it wrong. I've put examples in Table 7.1 below to help you walk alongside them and share their experience. If there is an opportune moment to explain to them what is happening and why, take it and help them to understand or articulate what they're experiencing.

Instead of This (Critical and Corrective)	Try This (Curious and Compassionate)
'Don't be silly, you don't need to feel like that.' 'Look on the bright side.'	'That's rough for you.' 'It's no fun feeling like that.' 'I'm sorry you're feeling this.' 'What do you think is making you feel this way?' 'What would you like to feel?' 'What might help at the moment?' 'I get that.' 'I hear you.'
'I don't think you're working hard enough.'	'How are you getting on with revision / your essay?' 'Would you like me to test you / read it?' 'Are you finding it hard to concentrate?' 'What's stopping you from doing X?' 'What are you worried about?' 'I know you get really stressed by tests – what do you need? What can I do to help?'

Instead of This (Critical and Corrective)	Try This (Curious and Compassionate)
'You're so much more capable than you're showing.'	'Tell me about X.' 'What's happening at school/college at the moment?' 'That sounds really tricky.'
'You're unkind. I'm not surprised your friends don't want to be with you.'	'What made you say that?' 'What are you feeling about that friend?' 'It sucks when friendships aren't reciprocal.'
'That was mean; no wonder your friend won't talk to you.'	'It feels awful when a friend seems to go off you.' 'It's so hurtful for you to be treated like that.' 'Feeling angry can make it hard to think.' 'That's rubbish for you.' 'You must have felt really bad to say that.' 'What do you think he felt when you said that?' 'How do you think you'd have felt if you were them?'
'You must have done something to make them say/do that.'	'What happened?' 'Tell me about it.' 'Gosh, that's tricky.' 'How did that make you feel?' 'What do you think made them react like that?' 'I'm sorry it feels so bad.'

Instead of This (Critical and Corrective)	Try This (Curious and Compassionate)
	'How do you feel about it now?' 'What would you like to do/happen now?' 'I'd feel the same way if that happened to me.'
'You're so rude/unkind/difficult.'	'What's going on?' 'You seem to be struggling, what's up?' 'You're communicating you're cross loud and clear. What's happened?' 'What's upsetting you?' 'Things are feeling tricky for you right now.' 'Are you OK, you seem upset?' 'I've noticed that you seem out of sorts recently.'

Table 7.1. Be curious and compassionate instead of critical and corrective.

Clara had always loved clothes and her mum had prided herself on being kind but honest. They often went shopping together and when Clara tried on clothes, she received feedback that she trusted. In the run-up to her school prom at the end of GCSEs, she chose a dress with her mum, who said, 'That one would look better on Fi [Clara's best friend]; she's much slighter than you.' Instantly, Clara, who had felt pretty confident in her body, heard 'you're big'. The dress was an outright no, and so were the rest of the dresses. Not only did Clara not find a new dress for her prom, but she tracked the low mood, which brought her to see me, back to that specific comment

Mum made in the fitting room: in that moment, her self-perception radically changed.

Lucy was a competitive swimmer, telling me she was 'really broad with huge shoulders'. She felt bigger than her friends and could not wear the same tops or dresses as them. Her dad, who had swum too and played rugby often, proudly commented that Lucy's build was like his, with 'good broad shoulders'. This positive attribute by which a rugby player judges himself is not the same as his teenage daughter judges herself. Lucy felt big, and different to her peers. Although she was sociable and loved going out, she would spend hours trying on numerous outfits to find the one that made her look smallest and hid her size. She knew that she was fit and athletic, and that her shape enabled her to swim competitively, but struggled to see past what she thought was her massive build. Because her dad's narrative – said with pride – was that it was his build, it was hard for her to believe that others did not see it and judge her for it too.

Alex came from a family of rugby players. His father and brother were both props in the scrum. He, however, was built differently. Tall and lithe, he was a winger. Despite being integral to the team, he felt ashamed of his body. His family teased him for being concave, having arms like twigs and legs half the size of his brother. They appreciated his talents and had no problem with his shape – it was just banter. He believed that he was scrawny and weak, and when not paying sport, always wore long sleeves and trousers, even during the summer, to hide his arms and legs. His mates teased him for this, but he didn't feel comfortable sharing his embarrassment about being skinny.

Of course, your children want to trust your opinion and they won't if you tell them that they suit every item of clothing. It can be a tricky tightrope to walk, especially as they change size and shape every few months (this is normal and healthy). Tell them that you think a different top would look better or a different style might suit them better. Say no more than that and then help them find it. Bin the observations and the comparisons.

Take a moment to remember your adolescence and how you felt in clothes. How did your mum react to what you wore? Did she comment, pull faces to show her disapproval, compare you with a sibling or friend? How did it make you feel? How about your dad? Did he get involved? Did he counterbalance your mum in some way, for better or worse? Many of us have memories from this time in our lives that make us wince, or still generate strong emotions such as embarrassment or sadness. If this is resonating with you, then you know how important it is to be mindful of what you say to your teen: directly, to someone else when they are in earshot, as banter or family humour, or in any way that could get back to them. I am not trying to make you feel anxious, just to bring awareness. Most likely, you'll say something at some point that goes down like a lead balloon or that your young person hears differently to the way that you intended. As always, you can repair. Giving them experiences of repair teaches them how to do it, which is a life skill critical to making and maintaining relationships.

Here are some examples of what you can say:

- 'That came out all wrong, I'm sorry. It sounded like I was saying X but what I meant was Y.'
- 'I noticed you looked upset when I said X. I'm sorry I hurt your feelings; it was a thoughtless thing to say.'
- 'You know when we were talking about X, I think you heard me say Y but what I was actually trying to get across was Z.'
- 'When you were trying on dresses and I said I thought it would

look better on your friend, I was anxious about how to say I didn't think it suited you well because I knew you really liked it, but by saying what I said, I made things worse. You understandably felt hurt and angry and I'm sorry; I really didn't want you to feel this. I should've just said that I thought there would be other dresses that suited you better. I should never have compared you with Fi.'

- You can also ask your child what they would like you to say, for example: 'I'm never sure how best to say I don't terribly like an item of your clothing or I don't think something suits you. Should I tell you and, if so, what's the best way for me to say it?'

A repair almost always contains an apology, because you want to heal a wound that you have played a part in causing and you need to take responsibility for that hurt. I am not apportioning any blame, but if there is a rupture, your young person will be upset about something you said or did and the wound needs to heal. Apologise to your teen and say the same as you would to anyone else where there has been a hurtful comment, row or tricky interaction that you want to make better. Ruptures are normal. They happen often in family life, particularly when people are tired, stressed, hormonal, anxious or low. They will happen to you and with your children. Their occurrence is not the issue – it's all about the repair.

If your parent(s) believed they were always right or never apologised, repairing might be difficult for you as you won't have an internal model (like a template) of how to do it, nor appreciate the power of a parent's apology. You may have learnt that being right is the only way for a parent to go, so admitting you may have caused upset might feel threatening or unavailable to you. Or you might have learnt not to express different opinions or feelings, but rather to suppress or ignore them. In these cases, I advise you to get a little help – be it from your partner, close friend or professionally: rupture and repair is vital in relationships, especially with your teen, who is at a very emotional, often dysregulated point in life. When people haven't developed the skills to repair (and it does require skills) disagreements fester and opposing positions become entrenched, leading to increasingly difficult relationships.

And finally, tell them that their body is amazing. Focus on its functions and all it does to keep them healthy and active; the lungs breathe, the heart pumps blood, the kidneys process waste and the brain thinks, controls memory, emotion, touch, motor skills, vision, breathing, temperature, hunger and every process that regulates our body. These all happen without their consciously having to do anything and irrespective of their size and weight. Helping your teen to focus on the functionality of their body will reduce their focus on its aesthetic. Tell them their body will self-regulate both weight and shape in its own time when they come to the end of puberty, and if, for some reason, it doesn't, then you can reassess.

Help your child to understand that the size of their body is not equated with their worth, value to others or lovability. Assist them in appreciating their many qualities that are not based on shape and weight. Emphasise that it's their personality that's important, those qualities that make them uniquely them. These attributes are what will draw others to them and will be what others love and value in them. Support them in thinking about their strengths: what are they good at? It doesn't have to be academics, sports, music or anything as obvious. It can be personality traits such as their sense of fun, their kindness, warmth, wit, sarcasm or general sparkle. What do they enjoy doing and with whom? This will help them to find others with shared interests who will become part of their tribe. Explore what your teen values in their friends and help them dig deeper if they say it's that they're cool or popular. What does this really mean? Broaden out and discuss what their friends value in them. I promise you, it will not be their friends' shape or size that your child truly values. It will be their humour, kindness, compassion, fun, chat, shared values and shared interests. This is the basis of true, reciprocal friendship that we all ultimately look for and that your teen and their friends will too.

If you don't fully believe this or if you want your teen to shrink their body because they've gained weight or are in a larger body then I'm afraid this is your personal issue to deal with. It's not easy and if you need some assistance managing your feelings please get help – there's nothing to be ashamed of. Your child will be getting loads of messages about their body being too large, wrong, inadequate and they need you on their side. As we discussed at the end of Chapter 6, putting children and young people on diets doesn't work and it supports the damaging and incorrect diet culture belief that thin is better and more worthy. It also leads to disordered eating, eating disorders, low self-esteem, self-loathing, anxiety, low mood, friendship issues and more often than not, increased weight gain. None of these are beneficial or better for your teen's health than being in a larger body. They may be in a larger body, but you have to ride the rollercoaster of that until they're fully out of adolescence.

Support your teen to continue listening to their body, to identify what kind of hungry they are and to then listen to their hunger and full signals. Help them to respect and fuel their body, and understand the importance of a balanced diet that includes everything. Let them know, too, that dieting won't fix their distress. Remind them as often as you need to that it causes many more problems than it solves.

It's the number one cause of bingeing, so restricting immediately increases the risk of bingeing because it triggers a sense of deprivation and activates the famine response in the brain: when food is next available, the brain thinks it needs as much as possible in case it hits a period of starvation again. Restriction also leads to disordered eating and eating disorders just like it did with Lachlan, who we meet later on in Chapter 9.

So, help your child surf their feelings and fill their lives with friends, hobbies and real-life connections rather than 'fix' their weight. I can't stress the importance of this enough. Avoid conversations about chocolate, crisps, snacks or sugar being unhealthy or bad. Your teen will know this – the messages are unavoidable – and they'll nonetheless eat them sometimes. That's OK, as at every stage of childhood. The minute you engage in a narrative centred around bad food or weight, your child will focus on food, worry about their diet, and wonder whether to eat as they wish or as you wish. They may become stuck with an inner monologue that tells them they are bad or stupid for eating certain foods, impacting their mood and social interactions. This is all more detrimental than the size of their body. The list of what not to say is long, but if you comment on their eating, shape or weight, it's likely to backfire, as we saw in the cases of Clara, Lucy and Alex earlier in this chapter.

I love working with adolescents. It's usually rubbish for them whilst they're going through it, but it's a period of the most extraordinary change, growth and development. Being able to walk alongside my kids, their friends and my clients as they navigate this thorniest time, trying to work out who they are and the young adult that they want to be, is a privilege. Don't get me wrong: I have been driven mad, had moments of intense frustration and anxiety, had to white-knuckle-ride the rollercoaster. I've dealt with issues that caught me completely by surprise. There has been many a rupture along the way, with many a repair. I've done much of what I advise against, because it's difficult – and more so with your own children because of the bonds and family dynamics. So, if you have read this thinking 'but I have done most of what she says not to' – so have I. You're human, doing your absolute best in the most difficult job out there. Only when you are aware can you choose a certain path, change your default views, notice and assess your prejudices, catch yourself saying something that might be unhelpful and learn to repair ruptures. It will make you more thoughtful and compassionate, and help you to help your kids more than you realise.

CHAPTER TAKEAWAYS

- Adolescence is a time of profound change and development for your child and you. It's also exciting and tumultuous.
- Puberty brings physical and sexual changes, transforming the body from a child's to an adult's.
- The brain rewires and upgrades over about a decade – it's a long process.
- Whilst one part of the brain is rewiring, it comes offline and its job is done by another (wrong) part of the brain, leading to less effective processing, difficulties with organisation, planning and emotional regulation.
- The two main developmental tasks are separation and individuation: your child separates from you and the family to become independent and works out who they want to be.

- The physical and neurological changes are not within your child's control. They occur when the body is ready.
- Girls *must* gain weight to be able to progress through puberty.
- Body image difficulties are common and your teens need you to walk alongside them and support them.
- Don't try and fix their distress using meal, diet or exercise plans.
- If you are struggling with their body size remember this is yours to deal with – there's no shame in getting professional help.
- Help them think about their body as functional rather than aesthetic, and their worth as being about their personality and qualities rather than their looks and size.
- You may need to work on your own issues so as not to pass them on to your teen – this is OK, and worth doing.
- Ruptures are normal, particularly in adolescence. It's all about the repair, so take time to work on this.
- Focus on being curious and compassionate, instead of critical and corrective.

CHAPTER 8

Diet Culture

'Our bodies are not the problem. Diet culture is.'

Katherine Zavodni

Imagine you're in a room where everything is red. The walls are painted red, the floor is red, the furniture, rugs, curtains are all red. Even the windows have a red hue. The books, newspapers and magazines have red pages and red text. You eat red foods and drink red fluids, and you spend your whole life in this room. Then, one day, someone tells you that the colour red exists but you can't believe it. In fact, because it's all that you have ever known, it's almost invisible to you – you can't even see it. This is diet culture. It is so pervasive that we barely notice it, and we only see it when confronted with something jarring or with which we don't agree. Even then, we catch a glimpse of it but frequently don't realise how ubiquitous it is.

Before I continue, let's clarify exactly what diet culture is. It is a system of beliefs around food weight and shape that focus on thinness as an ideal. It has a moral hierarchy of body sizes and shapes from the sought-after thin to the negatively perceived and feared fat. It labels foods as 'good' or 'bad', 'healthy' or 'unhealthy'. It equates weight loss with health, moral value and worthiness, and portrays being anything other than thin as inherently unhealthy, bad, frightening and immoral. There is, we are told, a magic number on the scale where life will become wonderful and your problems will melt away. Its primary victims are females, although it also impacts men, especially through the fitness industry.

It is so endemic that the word 'fat', which is a simple, descriptive word, has become loaded with emotion and value. It's a 'bad' word that has been villainised in the same way that 'thin' has been exalted. To be thin is lauded. It is a compliment. Yet both words are just descriptors, no different from tall, short, blond or brunette. To describe someone as being tall and brunette is just that – a description. Add fat on and suddenly it becomes derogatory and offensive. Add thin and it is complimentary and aspirational.

When you think back to your childhood, what were your associations with words such as 'fat', 'thin' and with different body shapes? Was 'fat' a bad word, associated with fear or disgust? Did you hear your mum saying she looked fat in certain outfits, or your dad saying he needed to slim down? Were you the recipient of such comments? Did the food police patrol in your home? Some people have memories of going to the GP and being weighed, or of overhearing adults talking about their shape or size in hushed tones. This is based in diet culture. We all have memories of growing up in relation to food, mealtimes and attitudes around size and weight, and our unique family and social background unavoidably influences us. Once aware, their impact can be challenged, especially in relation to how you talk to your children around size, weight, food and eating. Diet culture is inescapable. You can't avoid it. It's a struggle and the best you can do is notice it, address it and reject it, but to do this you need to understand your own baggage and feelings about it.

Diet Rules and the Food Police

Cheat days, forbidden foods, counting points, macros, calories, Syns (the Slimming World term for 'naughty treats'), meal plans, protein shakes, clean eating, intermittent fasting: these are all diet speak. Cutting carbs, increasing protein, removing the 'evil' gluten or dairy, banning all sugar, likewise. You may think they are just a lifestyle choice, getting in shape or helping your insulin levels, but they are all rules being applied to what, when, how much or at what time you eat. None are about trusting your body to let you know when you're hungry and when you're full. Or trusting yourself to listen to your body and decide what will nourish you emotionally and physically in that moment.

When you follow food rules, track your food or adhere to a plan, you communicate to yourself that you can't trust your body and need to impose external moderators or limits on your eating. This is dieting. If you follow any food rules, other than those for religious or medical reasons, such as having an allergy, you are dieting in one form or another and diet culture has got you. It's so slippery that it shapeshifts, moving stealthily from one space to the next without you noticing. The reality is that if there was a single diet that universally worked, there would be no need for new ones and the diet and fitness industries would go bust. It can be really subtle and hard to spot when advice around eating is actually a diet, but a good indication is to ask the following questions:

- Am I choosing what I eat, when I eat it, how much I eat and at what time? No – diet.

- Am I having to track what I eat? Yes – diet.
- Are there rules that I am sticking to? Yes – diet.
- Do I have any guilt or shame about what I eat? Yes – diet.
- Are there 'free' foods or 'guilt-free' foods? Yes – diet.
- Am I worried about eating any foods or food groups? Yes – diet.

Unless the reason you're eating this way is because it has been medically prescribed, the answers I've given show what constitutes a diet.

Below is a (by no means exhaustive) list of the most common diets in all forms. How many have you tried?

Atkins	Keto	Intermittent fasting (IF)
Low-carb	Low-fat	14:10
Wheat-free (if not allergic)	Detoxes	16:8
Gluten-free (if not coeliac)	Cleanses	20:4
Dairy-free (if not allergic)	Juice diet	5:2
Sugar-free	Calorie counting	Carb Cycling
Paleo	WeightWatchers: points	One meal a day (OMAD)
Clean eating	Slimming World: Syns	80/20 rule

If it fits your macros (IIFYM)	Noom	Metabolic Balance
Vegan (when not for ethical reasons)	Meal Plans	Shift, Shape, Sustain
Plant-based (if not ethical reasons)	The Fast diet	FODMAP (if not prescribed)
Health kick	Dash diet	Volumetrics
Raw food	The alkaline diet	The Mind diet

Table 8.1. Some of the most common diets.

With the rules come the enforcers. These food police can come from within, patrolling inside your head, pouncing on your every food-related thought and action, and berating you for eating something you 'shouldn't' or for having the audacity to enjoy eating. 'You can't eat that!' 'Don't you know how bad that is for you?' 'You ate that! You'll pay the price for it now.' 'OMG, you almost fell off the wagon there – you need to be more careful.' 'You ate crisps: you might as well have drunk a jug of oil.' 'A moment on the lips, a lifetime on the hips.' Are any of these familiar? Do you feel guilty for eating a slice of cake or buttery toast? Do you feel ashamed of liking certain foods and believe that you're flawed because of it?

You may also experience external food police: people in your everyday life who tell how you should eat, what the right foods are and what the wrong ones are. They may be well intentioned, and you may even ask and pay for their help, but nonetheless, they disconnect you from your body and impose external instructions on your eating.

The harshest of any critic is typically your internal one. It's often punitive and can be abusive. Usually it's an internalised voice of someone from your childhood – often a parent – from distressing experiences or just from messages that have been endlessly repeated. If you heard your parent constantly saying that they couldn't eat dessert and that fat was dangerous, for example, you may struggle with thoughts about eating pudding as being a forbidden treat – or feel that you have failed if you eat it.

Kitty had been a competitive footballer. She trained five days a week and entered puberty earlier than some of her peers in her club. One day, aged 12, the coach had pulled her aside and told her she was bulking out, looking heavy and it could slow her down. Kitty was deeply shocked. She wasn't eating any more than she had been, was training regularly and, until that moment, had not thought there was anything wrong with her body: everything changed that day. She felt anxious, body-conscious and started controlling her food intake. She stopped playing a year later, even though she was an excellent player and loved the sport. She said that she had grown and was a normal, healthy weight and size but the stress of fearing her coach would comment again was too great.

Kitty came to me as an adult because her daughter was an elite athlete, and Kitty was struggling to know how to talk to her about her diet and weight. We realised she didn't need to talk to her daughter: Kitty's own history with her sport was influencing her. The messages she wanted to give her daughter were those that had developed from the comment that her coach had made when she was 12. She needed to understand and process her own experiences. It was not her daughter's baggage to carry.

Whose voice is it in your head? When and where's it from? Is there more than one voice saying the same thing? Have you ever questioned what it's saying or have you believed it because you're so used to hearing it?

'My mum's always told me I'm big,' Maddie said, 'and it's true. I am bigger than her. When I stand in front of her, you can't see her at all.' Maddie also ate a little more than Mum and during meals her mum would often say, 'Are you sure you want more?' Or, 'Haven't you had enough?' Maddie, aged 16, was struggling with disordered eating. She was slim and a healthy weight, but she felt 'huge' and so restricted her intake, then binged and felt terrible. It had become a cycle dominating her thoughts and chipping away at her confidence and self-worth.

Maddie's mum was indeed petite, and Maddie was taller and a couple of dress sizes bigger. But to be bigger than someone five-foot tall and a size six didn't mean that she was big. She had internalised her mum's comments and had them policing everything she ate, berating her for feeling hungry and commenting on how she looked. Maddie had never challenged her mum because she believed her: objectively, she was taller and bigger, and so despite being slim and similar in size to many of her friends, she had a distorted view of herself and a critical, controlling inner voice. Had she not sought help when she did, this would have stayed with her throughout her life.

Maddie's is a common experience. As parents, it is easy to say something benign that our children internalise without us realising – even a well-meaning comment, or a joke. You don't need to censor everything that you say to your child but be aware that comments around body shape and eating can often be heard differently to the way you mean them. Should you say something that your child might dwell on, it's helpful if you notice it and then address it with them. Remember, it's not about blame or recrimination, but opportunities to repair, however tiny the error or rupture. It's natural to say the wrong thing by accident, to touch a nerve in your child that you didn't realise was sensitive or to make a joke that you think is funny in the moment but that sticks in their mind afterwards: we all do it.

It is also easy, when you have your own food police in your head, to voice those comments and unwittingly pass them on. This is intergenerational transmission. Intergenerational transmission describes how, through genetics, learned behaviour and direct and indirect communication, certain behaviours or attitudes are passed from generation to generation. Take a grandmother who suffered from severe anxiety. In bringing up her children, she communicates the world is very dangerous. She may not tell them directly, but she may be hypervigilant, only leaving the house when it's essential and always accompanied by someone else so as to manage her anxiety. Unless her children consciously realise what is happening and learn to think and act differently, they will most likely be as anxious as their mum. They will have beliefs about the world being dangerous and behaviours to manage their anxiety. Again, unless these are challenged, they will be passed to the next generation and the next, and so on.

Research shows significant intergenerational transmission of mental health disorders such as depression and anxiety.[54] The same is true of eating disorders and disordered eating, with traits, behaviours and characteristics transmitted from parents to children due to complex genetic, environmental and behavioural processes.[55] To break the cycle and avoid passing your diet culture informed beliefs to your children, you need to be aware of what you feel about food, eating, weight and shape, how you behave around it and what you communicate to your kids about it.

You may have picked up your views and any difficulties from your parents and they from theirs. This is normal and nothing to feel guilty about. Some of the mechanisms are genetic, some are not. You can't change your genes, but with an understanding of how you tick around food, you have more opportunities to influence what you might inadvertently communicate and pass on to your kids. Again, without awareness you have no chance to intervene; with it, you have some. Given our immersion in diet culture and inability to avoid its messages, this is a much bigger ask than with other mental health disorders.

Don't underestimate how difficult it can be to look inwards and explore your relationship with food, diet culture, your core beliefs, prejudices, biases, traumas, relationship or family difficulties. Food is wonderful. It's delicious, nurturing, nourishing and so much more, all of which we have discussed. But a troubled relationship with food can be like a sore that never heals, a backpack of rocks that you carry round continuously. For some, it is like a toxic relationship: you think about it multiple times a day, engage with it, love it at times, hate it at others, and fundamentally know the relationship is bad for you and needs to change, but you don't want it to. If this is you, you're not alone. Many more people feel like this than will admit it and have their lives ruled by something that they have to interact with multiple times a day. Professional help is worth your investment. The relief and freedom that comes when you find a new and better relationship with food is transformational – for you and your kids. If professional help isn't possible, there are some great books, which I've popped in the Resources and Further Reading section under Intuitive Eating & Diet Culture on page 291.

I first met Pooja just before her fourth admission for anorexia to an inpatient eating disorder unit (EDU). She had been so unwell that she had been in hospital for most of the previous three years, as she similarly was for the next two. Fast forward to five years later and she had recovered, was at university and loving life. Her recovery was remarkable and better than I, her team and her family had ever predicted. Having feared for her life for much of the five years she'd spent in hospital, her parents got in touch with me again, concerned that Pooja was 'eating badly and drinking too much beer'. 'It's unhealthy,' her mum said. 'She's eating too many burgers and chips and not doing enough exercise.' Pooja was very slim, though at a healthy weight and with regular periods. She was active, doing well academically, had good friends and, most amazingly of all, she was eating and drinking as is typical for university students: beer, the odd burger, late-night chips, a kebab on the way home from clubbing, as well as making her own nutritious meals. I was shocked and sad that after spending so many years terrified that her daughter would die of starvation, Pooja's mum, now secure in her recovery, was plagued by the fears of diet culture.

Diet Culture and Weight Loss

Diet culture is like a super-strength magnet for perfectionism, low self-esteem, anxiety and feelings of failure. This is intentional. It is the application of psychological theories to marketing[56] – find the pain point, come up with a fix, and you, the consumer, will part with your hard-earned cash to buy it. Come on – take control! Grasp the bull by the horns and make the choice to give yourself a better life: shrink your body, reduce the size of your thighs, eliminate your bingo wings, discover the willpower you lack around food, and you'll feel better.

Only the reality is that you won't. If you think back over your life, whilst feeling more comfortable in your body *might* give you a boost of confidence, it will not heal traumas, transform difficult relationships, repair past ruptures, lessen grief or create the idyllic life that diet culture propagates. You'll be hungry because you'll have to eat less than you need, you'll push yourself to get to the gym many times a week, you'll become focused on food and potentially anxious about eating out and seeing friends, or you might ruminate on forbidden foods. What starts as a desire to 'get in shape' quickly slips into an all-consuming life of watching what you eat, counting calories (counting macros, by the way, is just another way of calorie counting) cutting out foods and food groups, feeling anxious, shrinking your social life, desperately watching the numbers on the scales or tape measure, feeling good for sticking to it, then feeling shame for 'falling off the wagon'. It's exhausting and not nearly as fulfilling as you have been promised. Guilt and shame quickly envelop you as you eat something you shouldn't, beat yourself up and promise to commit even harder tomorrow. Sound familiar? This is how disordered eating and eating disorders take hold without you realising.

I am actually not anti-exercise or against eating well, though it may seem that way. However, I want you to exercise or make choices about your food because you feel better in and for yourself. Exercise because you enjoy it. Exercise to increase strength and mobility – as long as it is the right exercise for you and your body. Many advertised workout plans won't be right for your body despite the tag line, so choose wisely and take advice. Listen to your body and trust it to tell you what it can and can't do: to feel stiff after a workout is fine, but to feel pain is not.

Here's the rub. Diets don't work for a number of reasons, whether or not you need to lose weight. First, there is no 'normal' in terms of weight and shape. There are eight billion people in the world and eight billion different bodies. I'm sure you don't try to squeeze into a shoe that is too small for you, so why do we do it with clothes and our bodies? We are not meant to be clones of each other.

Second, everyone has different genetics, biology and metabolisms. Much research has discussed the concept of a weight set point, the concept that there are homeostatic forces (within the body) that keep weight stable, even when elements outside of the body (diet and exercise, for example) are adjusted.[57] This means that the body itself strives to keep to a set point of weight for each person, making it much harder to lose weight than we have been led to believe. It's like a thermostat for weight, whose job is to keep you at your natural weight – the harder you try to move away from your weight set point, the harder your thermostat will work to bring you back to it. You may think that you gain or lose weight easily and this may be true, within a certain range – usually a few kilos maximum either side of your usual weight – but to gain or lose significant amounts of weight is much more difficult. We all have a different weight set point, and even if we all ate exactly the same and exercised identically, no two people would have the same body. Despite what we have been told, our weight and body size are not completely under our control, and we can't change them and shrink them to be whatever we want. Plus, being a lower weight is not synonymous with good health and being a higher weight does not equal poor health.

Third, our appetite is also not within our control. Whilst you can override it for a short period of time, hunger triggers the brain into thinking you are going into a period of famine and the alarm system will activate. It will work to preserve energy and to make you eat. When you do eat, you will want to feast – to stock up and prepare for the next period of famine. This is one of the many reasons that dieting is so difficult and why deprivation triggers cravings. Our biology needs us to eat and our biological mechanisms make us eat. This is why restriction directly causes bingeing.

Fourth, the idea that willpower can influence eating and weight loss is, in anything other than the very short term, physiologically flawed. In her fab book, *Good Food, Bad Diet*, dietician Abby Langer explains how the two hormones that control hunger and appetite — ghrelin and leptin — work, culminating in her conclusion that 'cheating your body out of adequate calories will backfire each and every time, no matter how dedicated you are to a diet.'[58] Have you ever noticed that if you eat a bit less and move a bit more, you may lose a little weight and feel better, but actually the results aren't that great? Or that if you lose a few kilos when unwell, you will almost certainly put them back on once you recover, even if you don't want or intend to?

Obesity research supports this. It proposes that weight loss and weight maintenance are two different systems. In a meta-analysis of 29 long-term weight-loss studies, researchers found that whilst substantial weight loss was possible, long-term maintenance of weight loss was much more challenging. More than half the weight lost was regained within two years and more than 80% was regained within five years.[59] If dieting were genuinely successful, people wouldn't battle with yo-yo dieting, we'd have fewer people struggling with overweight and obesity and there'd be no need for any new diets. Yet the diet wars continue unabated.

And, finally, shame undermines compassion. Rather than helping you to adjust your diet and behaviour where necessary, it has the opposite effect: withdrawal, increased stigma, blame and self-loathing. The research on the causes of obesity directly goes against the cultural (diet culture) understanding of obesity as a moral failure and a choice. This belief leads to stigmatisation, where society discriminates against those living with overweight or obesity and views people suffering from it as a social, financial and medical burden.[60] The portrayal of people in larger bodies is often as unattractive, lazy, weak and devoid of determination and willpower. Parents of children in larger bodies are perceived as bad parents, who don't properly look after their kids. These attitudes are unforgivable, and it's unsurprising within this societal context that we fear weight gain for ourselves and our kids. The diet culture view is that you must take personal responsibility for your own weight because it's a choice that is entirely within your control. Likewise, for your kids, whose weight and size are also deemed to be entirely within your control until they are old enough to take control of it themselves. So, if you have a child in a bigger body, you're more likely than not to feel blamed and shamed for causing them to be in a bigger body and this is terrible, as well as factually incorrect. The reality is that being stigmatised for your weight can be more detrimental and pose a greater risk to your health than what you eat or what you weigh.

Let's be clear, obesity is multifactorial and the causes exceedingly complex.[61] There is a whole conversation to be had around the food industry and food marketing to kids in particular, access to fresh foods, the pricing of different foods, genetic factors, weight set points, racial and cultural factors, school meals, emotional factors, learned behaviour, illnesses, medications and more. What we know for sure is that overweight and obesity are not a choice nor within one's personal control. We know too that shame is not a successful motivating factor for weight loss. This is both obviously true and backed up by ample research showing that it does not help in the treatment or prevention of obesity.[62] People who medically need to lose weight require compassion and support. Shame renders these almost impossible.

Shame is the most difficult and damaging emotion. It is a self-related and self-evaluating emotion, with beliefs about yourself as a person, rather than your behaviour. Typical shame beliefs are 'I am bad', 'I am defective', 'I am unlovable', 'I am unworthy', 'I am not good enough'. It is awful to feel that and it makes you want to hide away. Shame causally links to depression, anxiety, withdrawal and isolation. As Brené Brown, the preeminent author on shame, in her book, *Dare to Lead,* says, 'If you put shame in a petri dish, it needs three ingredients to grow exponentially: secrecy, silence, and judgment. If you put the same amount of shame in the petri dish and douse it with empathy, it can't survive.'[63] As a society, we have lost, if we ever had, empathy for those in bigger bodies. This is highly detrimental because those suffering learn to believe they are worthy of blame, derision and stigmatisation. They internalise this, making it more likely their mental health will suffer and less likely that they'll access professional help.

Take a couple of minutes to pause here and tune into your own beliefs about weight and size. Are you frightened of weight gain? Do you believe that sugary or fatty foods are dangerous? Do you have beliefs about your self-worth that are tied to your shape or size? Do you feel inadequate because your body changed after having children and you can't 'get it back'? Maybe you feel less lovable because you've gone up a clothes size. Do you have a list of foods that you shouldn't eat and then feel guilty or ashamed when you do? Do you think children should be weighed in school and parents told if they are overweight? Do food, eating and exercise consume your thoughts? Do you think kids need to be taught about 'good' and 'bad' foods and, if so, from what age? There are so many questions to ask yourself when being curious about the impact that diet culture has on you.

Are you reading this realising that you weren't entirely sure what it was, but you knew that you were not comfortable with diet culture? That it is detrimental or even harmful? Or are you thinking you know what diet culture is and it's not that bad? Or that it's terrible? Justifiable? Not a problem? At this moment, your thoughts may feel uncomfortable to you. You may be reading this thinking 'but it's true: people who are heavier are less careful about what they eat', 'fat people choose to be fat, or at least choose not to lose weight'. If so, I challenge you to reassess. Wherever you're at with this, treat yourself with compassion and curiosity, so that you can gain an understanding of why you think and feel as you do and importantly, how it may impact your kids.

Ditch the Diets and Learn to Eat Intuitively: How to Do It Yourself

By now, I hope I've persuaded you that dieting doesn't work and the answer to the question 'which diet should I do?' is 'none'. You know best how your body is feeling. Diets and plans only teach you to trust another above yourself and it is this disconnect that has got society into such a pickle. You may need to reconnect with your body and notice its signals (see pages 162–9), but that's OK: you can do that, and once you do, you'll find a wonderful freedom with food and eating. This is the foundation of intuitive eating, which, whilst not the right approach for everyone, is an excellent aim.

A quick myth bust here: intuitive eating is not code for eat whatever you want irrespective of any consequences. It's not permission to ignore nutrition or your health. It's about finding a way of eating that is free from rules, that nurtures your mental and physical health, and that honours your body's needs and signals. I will briefly outline the principles of intuitive eating as set out by the dieticians Evelyn Tribole and Elyse Resch[64] and discuss it in the context of how to help your kids with food, but this is not an intuitive eating book. There are some great ones out there, which I've listed under Intuitive Eating & Diet Culture in Resources and Further Reading on page 291.

Reject the Diet Mentality

Bin the diet books, fitness plans and magazines that promote weight loss and the idea of a perfect body. Unfollow people on social media who are proponents of diet culture and make you feel like a failure every time your new diet stops working and you regain the weight, or for not following their fitness plan. Give up any hope that the right plan is around the corner – it prevents you from challenging your beliefs and learning to eat intuitively, and it will keep you hooked into diet culture. Reject diet culture with full force.

Honour Your Hunger

Eat. Keep yourself fed and nourished with all the food groups, including those that previously may have been deemed scary, such as fat and carbs. Don't let yourself become excessively hungry because all intentions of moderate, thoughtful eating disappear and are irrelevant: your biology won't allow it. So, honour your body by eating when you are hungry.

Make Peace with Food

Stop fighting with food. Give yourself unconditional permission to eat, and, yes – that includes foods that you have previously forbidden yourself. Denying yourself a food leads to a feeling of deprivation and increases cravings leading to bingeing. Knowing you can eat those foods whenever you want, conversely, reduces craving and the risk of bingeing.

Challenge the Food Police

Shout at them, laugh at them, stand up to them, evict them. Get the food police out of your head by refusing notions of 'good' or 'bad' food, and imposed rules that make you feel guilty and impair your life.

Discover the Satisfaction Factor

When swamped by diet culture, you miss out on the pleasure of eating and the gratification and satisfaction of eating freely. You lose the social connection that comes with eating. Allow yourself to feel content and satisfied with food and the environments in which you eat. Once you do this, you'll find it easier to decide that you have had enough.

Feel Your Fullness

Feeling full is not the enemy. In fact, it is the essential signal that you are no longer hungry. To respect it, you need to allow yourself the foods that you fancy and want to eat. Learn and observe the signs that you are comfortably full, and pause whilst eating to check in, notice how the food tastes and gauge your current hunger level.

Cope with Your Emotions with Kindness

Know that food restriction triggers a loss of control physically and mentally, which feels like emotional eating. Find kind ways to comfort and nurture yourself and resolve your difficulties. We all experience a range of emotions in life. Restricting food won't fix your feelings – you need to find alternative methods to deal with the root of the emotion. (See Chapter 3 for more.)

Respect Your Body

Accept your genetics and your natural size and shape. Stop trying to shrink yourself into a body that's smaller. It's punitive and unsustainable. If you're critical and unrealistic about your body size and shape, it's hard to reject the diet mentality. Learn to be OK with the way you're made.

Movement – Feel the Difference

Movement is extremely important for health, happiness and wellbeing. Be active and move for pleasure. Ditch the gruelling gym regimes (unless you genuinely love them) and choose to move in a way that you enjoy – walking, dancing, team sports, whatever. Focus on feeling energised and good in yourself.

Honour Your Health – Gentle Nutrition

Remember that you don't have to eat perfectly (there is no such thing as perfect eating) to be healthy and nor do your children. Ideally, teach your kids the principles of intuitive eating rather than being hoodwinked by diet culture. This gives them the best shot at having a healthy relationship with food and listening to their body. Make food choices that are both good for you and taste good. The odd snack, dessert or some chocolate doesn't make you unhealthy, just as a lack of nutrients in one meal won't harm you. Go for progress and consistency rather than perfection or all-or-nothing thinking.

Notice how reading these principles makes you feel. Do they seem doable, exciting, something you can envisage, or are they terrifying? Does it sound like the path to gaining piles of weight and feeling out of control? Do you know people who eat this way and, if so, do you wish you could do the same and be as relaxed around food as they are? Your answers give you important information about your relationship with food, diet culture and how much of an issue these are for you. The more frightening or unimaginable it is, the bigger your hurdle, the more important it is that you go for it. For you and your kids.

Helping Your Kids to Ditch the Diets

Finally, on to your kids! Given that they are growing up surrounded by diet culture, how do you minimise its impact? I am taking for granted that having read the last few pages you want to minimise its ramifications. If you are thinking that diet culture has benefits explore why you feel that and challenge it.

In early childhood and in the first few years of primary school, young children are less exposed to diet culture than teenagers because they don't have a mobile phone and social media. Unfortunately in recent years, schools in the UK have started weighing kids as part of a routine health check, to ensure they aren't overweight and to send a concerned message home if they are. Again, this is an 'anti-obesity' measure. You can refuse consent for this so that your child isn't weighed in school, and indeed this is what I have done. It doesn't matter what weight your child is, there are too many difficult and potentially damaging communications that can occur when this happens. In addition, schools teach about healthy eating often in a way that is laden with values, judgement, binary classifications and, unfortunately, diet culture. Parents have told me that their children were asked to rate foods as good or bad, healthy or unhealthy; others were asked to count calories and look at the labels on food packets over the weekend to learn about what's bad in certain foods. None of these help children develop a healthy relationship with food. They just promote fear, dieting and lay the groundwork for disordered eating. I'm not blaming teachers; they're not specialist eating disorder dietitians or psychologists and this topic has been introduced into the personal, social, health and economic (PSHE) education curriculum at a UK government level to try to curb the rise in obesity. Education is so very important that it makes sense to add all things food to the school curriculum, but teachers need to have training on how to navigate the potential pitfalls of talking about healthy eating, body image and food.

Not wanting to contradict or undermine your child's teacher makes it tricky to know what to say when your child comes home with such homework. It's OK to say that that's not the language you use when talking about food. That you don't believe in good and bad, healthy and unhealthy. Give them all the information that you want them to know that is outlined in earlier chapters.

If your child has questions based on what they have learnt in school, seen on TV, in a magazine or online, answer them factually, again staying away from emotional language or value judgements. Kids know when we're fobbing them off and not quite telling them the truth. Make it age-appropriate by adding or removing detail and nuance but be upfront. If you have to go there, and they ask about bad foods, say something like: 'Some people think foods with a lot of sugar in are bad. Because the sweetness in sugar tastes good, it can make us want to eat more of it, so some people find it harder to listen to their tummies. Also, it gives us lots of energy immediately, but the energy doesn't last very long, so we get hungry quicker than we do when we eat toast and peanut butter, or porridge, or a meal with lots of different foods, like we do at supper time.' You could also add: 'I think it's good to eat all foods,' and/or, 'There's nothing wrong with sweet food, but we need to eat other foods with it.'

When you talk to your child like this, you are modelling balance, openness, respect and a willingness to have a real conversation with them. They appreciate this and feel comfortable asking you more questions, knowing that they will be answered properly and kindly. You're also not putting anyone else down or denigrating views that might be given at school, even if you'd like to. It's hard for kids when they can't tell parents things for fear of parents becoming angry or upset and vice versa. It's an invidious position for them. Keeping an open dialogue is key, whatever your views, and if you are unhappy, have a direct conversation with the school or your child's teacher.

As your child gets older and moves towards puberty, they get a phone and social media, and boom, the influence of diet culture increases. Never have teens received so many relentless and conflicting messages about food, eating, body shape, fitness, diet and acceptance or rejection of their body. It's constant and confusing. Their exposure to this, in addition to normalising restriction and the importance of the aesthetic, hits our children when they're at their most vulnerable. Their brains are all over the place and their bodies are changing. To progress through puberty, they must do the opposite of lose weight. However they're being told that weight loss is the ideal, along with which their social worlds can be febrile, leading to friendship instability. Adolescence is a period in which they often develop habits and attitudes that have an ongoing impact on their mental and physical health. The importance of their social world makes them particularly susceptible to the guiles of diet culture and unhealthy messages about weight, food, body size and exercise.

Our kids have an online world as well as a real world with Instagram, TikTok and Snapchat – their current platforms of choice.

These contain a vast amount of diet culture-related content, from #whatieatinaday to #fitspo, #weightlossjourney and #fatloss, and the exposure is profound. One recent study looking at key themes in popular nutrition and weight-related posts on TikTok found that 11.1% of the content was generated by school-age users. Almost 44% of the videos analysed in the study contained weight-loss content, dieting as a topic was present in 14% of the videos and, worryingly if not surprisingly, only 1.4% of the content came from registered dieticians.[65] Furthermore, most posts featured weight-normative content, which means that they emphasised the importance of weight management for good health and were not weight inclusive.

There has been a significant increase in dieting amongst teenagers in the last 30 years. Comparing samples from 1986, a 2015 study found a 7% increase in the rate of dieting in teens and a 53% increase in teens using exercise to lose weight. They also found that weight-control behaviours were associated with more depressive symptoms.[66]

We know diet culture leads to low self-esteem, anxiety, depression, disordered eating and distorted views on food and exercise,[67] so how do you mitigate or minimise its impact on your kids? Talk to them about the images they see and how so many are edited or have filters. Make them aware that many influencers take hundreds of photos and choose the very 'best'. Help them to notice and reject the messages that diet culture propagates.

I hope that their real world is more interesting, engaging and rewarding than their online world. Having hobbies throughout adolescence is incredibly valuable. It allows your child to broaden their horizons away from school, helps them to find different friendships and have their time filled by an activity they enjoy, rather than having a lot of free time to spend scrolling social media. Encourage them to start a hobby if they don't have one. It doesn't matter what it is, as long as they are interested in and enjoy it. There is someone for everyone, and engaging in hobbies is a great way to find them. Having at least one outside school hobby is particularly beneficial because it creates a whole new social group and is protective if friendships become wobbly at school.

Remain curious about your child's life, their thoughts and feelings: it will open up the opportunity for conversations. You can chat to them openly about everything raised in this chapter and how it affects them. If it generates difficult feelings for you, talk to your partner, friends or a professional because your teenager needs you to tolerate hearing about their world and to have you onside to help them navigate it.

Finally, throughout these years keep eating with your kids: have family meals and continue the division of responsibility. Allow them sweets on Halloween, mince pies and chocolate at Christmas, whatever food they're offered at parties or when connecting with friends and trust them to respect their body. You want to raise intuitive eaters who trust their bodies to tell them when they are hungry, what they would like to eat (no, I don't mean 'junk food' all the time) and when they are full. This is what the model underpins, which is why I'm reminding you of it again when it may seem out of context. The research shows that intuitive eating in children and teenagers predicts better psychological health and lower use of disordered eating behaviours.[68]

And finally, if you forget all else, remember:

The more we teach our children or ourselves to restrict, the more we overeat.

The more we focus on 'right' and 'wrong', and 'good' and' bad', the more we increase anxiety.

DIET CULTURE | 239

CHAPTER TAKEAWAYS

- Diet culture is a belief system organised around thinness being the ideal.
- It places a moral value on weight and shape.
- It leads to unrealistic goals, endless dieting, disordered eating, eating disorders, shame, blame and stigma.
- Call it out for yourself and for your children and teens.
- Ditch the diets – they don't work.
- Bin the food rules (unless medical or religious) and fire the food police.
- You might need to unlearn much of what you thought you knew to be true when it comes to your beliefs about food, weight, shape and eating. Take the time to look inwards, understand your relationship with food and challenge your beliefs. I promise, it's worth it.
- Diet culture has been around for decades and is passed down through generations.
- Be interrogative about where your beliefs have come from.
- Raise intuitive eaters: intuitive eating lays the foundations for the best possible relationship with food.
- If you want to guarantee thinness, intuitive eating won't do it (that would require everything I advocate against).
- Do all you can to prevent your child dieting.
- It's more than OK for you to refuse for your child to be weighed in school.
- If you disagree with the messages school are giving your kids about all things food, go and talk to them – you can take this book to help!

- Answer your kids' questions honestly in an age-appropriate way.
- As your children get social media, they have to navigate two worlds: the real world and the virtual world. Walk alongside them, keeping the dialogue open to help them with this.
- Kids are bombarded with relentless images and messages around weight shape, diets, exercise, etc. Help them to realise that all they see online isn't true.
- Remain curious about your kids' lives, feelings, thoughts and experiences: it opens the door for conversations, particularly through their teenage years.
- Keep eating with them and modelling a good relationship with food.

CHAPTER 9

Disordered Eating and Eating Disorders

*'And I said to my body, softly: "I want to be your friend".
It took a long breath, and replied: "I have been waiting my whole life for this."'*

Nayyirah Waheed

Having specialised in eating disorders (EDs) for over 20 years, I can't write a book on how to talk to your kids about food without talking about them here. This chapter is not meant to scare you. It's here because I want you to have an easily available resource, should you need it. I am passionate about prevention where possible and otherwise early intervention, but they're only attainable if you know what you're seeing.

Children's eating patterns frequently change during childhood and adolescence. Only a few are problematic and most don't constitute an eating disorder. Many parents are concerned by their children's eating habits, but usually it's a phase that passes without need for intervention. Most toddlers, for example, go through a fussy phase, only eating a very limited range of foods. During the pre-school years and into early childhood, many children have periods of restrictive eating, where both the range and quantity of foods eaten is limited. Although kids normally need to consume a lot of calories to grow, many children thrive, despite a small and restricted intake due to fussiness or picky eating.

It's equally common for teenagers to eat vast amounts of food, moving from a large meal to a large snack an hour later, followed by another meal-sized snack and then the next meal. Their appetite for meals is unaffected by their snacks and vice versa, which is thought to be associated with their growth spurts. Adolescence is the second greatest period of growth in life, after the first year, with adolescents needing to roughly double their weight to grow taller and develop from a child into an adult. So, the ravenous teenagers who eat an entire loaf of bread and peanut butter an hour after a huge dinner are just growing. It's developmentally appropriate and they too will return to 'normal' eating.

Many parents worry about whether their child is getting 'enough' food, the 'right kind' of food, or 'proper nutritious' food. Whilst this is understandable, often children – even very young children – pick up on it and the concerns can lead to a continuation of difficulties or worrying behaviours that would otherwise have passed naturally without concern. Worrying about your child's eating is usually unnecessary, and your anxiety transfers easily, thanks to mirror neurones, causing more problems than it solves. As a general rule, if your child is growing as expected (along their growth curve), has energy, is settled and happy, then fluctuations in eating will pass without intervention.

So, when should you worry? This is a very nuanced conversation as there is no one answer to cover all scenarios. In addition, many difficulties have as much to do with self-image, self-awareness, fear and anxiety as they do with food. Dieting is a significant risk factor for developing an eating disorder, with 35% of dieting becoming obsessive and 25% of those diets turning into eating disorders, including binge eating disorder and bulimia. Dieting doesn't just lead to restrictive EDs such as orthorexia and anorexia – it provokes them all.[69]

Often, managing food is a mechanism used to cope with emotional distress. Life events, distress and trauma are common triggers of, or precursors to, eating disorders, and many children, young people and adults develop eating disorders in response to these. Practitioners have all heard stories of sexual assault leading to anorexia, bereavement leading to bingeing, and so on. Commonly, grief, shock and low mood cause a physiological loss of appetite. Stress responses frequently bring about a change in appetite with either a loss of it or never feeling full, leading to overeating or binge eating. The concept of eating your emotions comes from this: people eat to keep their emotions stuffed down and avoid feeling. But an emotional hole can never be filled by food. If you don't feel satisfied after eating, you may be eating your feelings. When you're bingeing, there is no mental space to be reflective or even to think – it's all-consuming. Feelings only cascade in once the binge has ended – and often they include shame and self-disgust about the binge, which continue to keep the underlying feelings at bay. The same is true when purging (self-induced vomiting or similar). And when starving, thoughts very quickly become about weight loss, food, routine, cooking, eating and these replace the initial feelings of distress as well.

Because everyone's different, how we respond to traumas will be different and whether and how we use food to manage their distress likewise. In this way, eating disorders are similar to other addictions or using harmful substances, such as drugs and alcohol.

The aim is to numb or get rid of the pain. Any time you see food behaviours creeping in, the most important question to ask is: 'tell me about the pain' rather than 'Tell me about your eating / dieting / bingeing / purging behaviours.' Asking about distress brings a completely different perspective and one guided by compassion, and understanding that the eating is serving a really useful function in someone's life. I'll illustrate this with examples as we go through the different disorders, but keep the questions 'tell me about what's happening for you', 'tell me about the pain/upset' in the forefront of your mind. You'll need some idea of what your child's eating behaviour is, so that you can assess what help they need, but then the focus needs to return to their distress and finding ways other than using food to manage it.

I'm frequently asked the difference between disordered eating and eating disorders (EDs). They have many of the same symptoms but to get a diagnosis of an ED, you must meet a set of diagnostic criteria – usually a specific number of symptoms in one or more categories in the manuals of psychiatric disorders: the Diagnostic and Statistical Manual of Mental Disorders (DSM) or International Classification of Diseases (ICD).[70] Disordered eating is still serious. You or your child can have extremely disordered eating but not meet criteria for a particular ED and you won't get the diagnosis. This doesn't mean that they (or you) are OK. It doesn't mean that they're not struggling or not worthy of treatment or help. It just means that they (or you) don't tick all the boxes that would lead to a formal diagnosis. To avoid onerous repetition, in this chapter I will use the concept of an eating disorder to include disordered eating.

There has been a marked increase in eating disorders since the Covid-19 pandemic. Between February and December 2022, almost 10,000 children and young people started treatment in the NHS.[71]

This is an increase of a quarter compared to the same period in 2021, up by almost two thirds since before the pandemic, and is likely a direct consequence of the pandemic and associated factors: rates of anxiety soared in the general population; many parents lost their jobs; children did remote schooling at home, with primary school children needing a huge amount of parental input, leaving parents to work, teach and provide for their children and families. The lack of play and social interaction meant that children missed a year or more of social skills development, with friendships compromised. Adolescents, for whom friendships are fundamental, were stuck at home with their families 24/7. This is not developmentally appropriate, so whilst physical development continued apace, social and emotional development was halted. The opportunities for adolescents to explore and experiment with their identity, sexuality and relationships were also greatly impeded, and their outlets for managing the tumult of adolescence significantly reduced.

There are similarities across the eating disorders. They are all serious, they all have serious effects on physical and mental health, and no one enjoys having one. They are not a choice, and they cause huge distress to the sufferer and their family and friends. Recovery is hard, but always worth it. I have never met anyone who has regretted making it through recovery.

Having a child with an eating disorder is exceptionally stressful and often traumatic. The worry is considerable and treatment usually requires hefty parental input. Because the physical consequences of eating disorders are so severe and, in some cases, life-threatening, the anxiety that comes with them is profound and primal: it's about your child's survival. As parents, our primary job is to keep our child safe and alive, so when they are starving or bingeing, hiding food, vomiting or over-exercising, our amygdala is highly active, sending us constant signals about the imminent, potentially life-threatening danger to the most important people in our lives.

If you've suffered from an eating disorder yourself, you will feel anxious about your child developing one and having similar experiences to you. You might be vigilant to any sign of disordered eating, feeling the need to jump on the smallest behaviour that could indicate something amiss. Or you might create an environment at home where there is no stress attached to food and eating (great) but where there are no boundaries around meals and snacks at all (not great). Having had an ED, you might find that memories from that time in your life are triggered when your child gets to the same age, or you might find that feeding a child generates distressing memories. If this hits a nerve for you, seek support. When we have experienced something traumatic the memories get locked away once the event is over but can then be easily triggered by something reminiscent – it could be anything – later in life.

Likewise, if you're struggling with an ED or with your recovery from one your child may pick up your attitudes towards food, influencing how and what you feed them without realising. This does NOT mean that you are causing their difficulties or even contributing to them. However, as I keep saying throughout this book, until you are aware of your stuff, you can't choose how it plays out in your life.

Judy's mum did not consider herself to have disordered eating. Rather, she described herself as a very 'careful' eater. She had a long list of foods that she wouldn't eat, including sugar, desserts, wheat, red meat, snacks, dried fruit and any dairy that wasn't low-fat or no fat. Fifteen-year-old Judy came to see me on the recommendation of her school, who had noticed her weight loss. Judy said that she didn't want to lose weight and wasn't trying, but eating was stressful at home. She wasn't allowed the foods that Mum denied herself because Mum believed they were bad, and she was also not allowed second helpings or snacks between meals. In addition, she was having the same meals all the time and was bored of them. Mum had a menu of 'safe' meals that she rotated. Judy loved eating at her friends' houses, but this meant that she was even more fed up with eating at home than she had been previously, and sometimes she just didn't want to eat the meal at home.

Mum didn't think that she was doing anything unusual. She firmly believed that she was eating healthily and feeding her daughter healthily. Upon exploration, it emerged that she feared weight gain, having been a 'chubby child', and had taken control of her eating as soon as she was old enough. She didn't realise her daughter had different energy requirements and nutritional needs. Mum was unaware that she had quite severe disordered eating and beliefs about her own shape and size, or that these were manifesting in the way that she was feeding her family.

Ellie was very worried about her two children, aged nine and 11. She had a history of bulimia and was terrified her children would gain weight and become fat during adolescence, so she was restricting their intake of sweet foods, treats and carbs. This caused the kids to become hangry and tired. She was unaware of the need to gain weight during adolescence, or of the need for girls to gain body fat to ovulate and get their periods. She didn't realise that her eating disorder was impacting her ability to feed her children or that her desperation for them to avoid bulimia was increasing their risk.

Matt had grown up with a father whom he described as a 'functional anorexic'. His father had been very overweight as a teenager and lost it all in his 20s by becoming restrictive. He had remained restrictive with numerous food rules ever since, impacting his family by commenting on everyone's food, eating and weight. It was apparently given and received in reasonable humour, with them all knowing that Dad had an eating disorder. Matt, desperate for his kids to grow up in a different environment, had never limited what or when his children ate. They ate meals as a family, had a large snack cupboard and everyone could help themselves to whatever they wanted.

You can see from these case examples that there is no single way that disordered eating is passed on, but without awareness it usually impacts how we feed our kids.

Eating Disorders

When it comes to eating disorders, they're not evenly split. Although anorexia is often in the media and much talked about, it is the least common. By contrast, binge eating disorder is the most common.

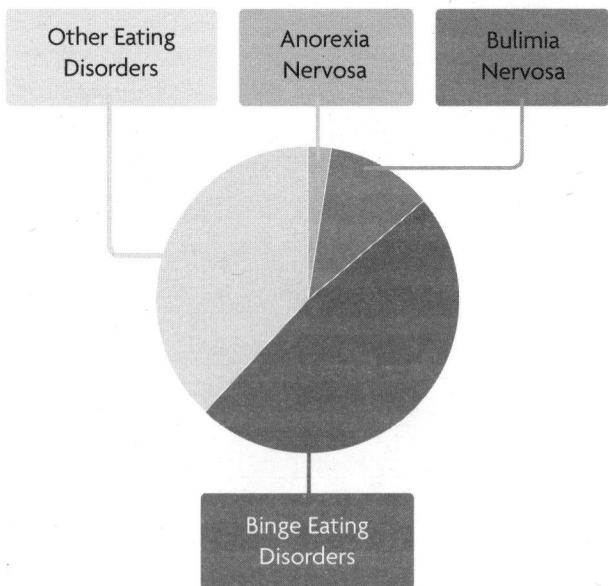

Figure 9.1. Diagram taken from the national eating disorder collaboration.[72]

Anorexia Nervosa (AN)

The Nature and Causes of AN

Anorexia nervosa – translated from the Greek to mean 'nervous loss of appetite' – is probably the most talked about and well-known eating disorder, although the least common in the UK and generally.[73] Whilst considered a modern-day illness, case reports date back to severe religious fasting in the Hellenistic era[74] and there are reports of famous historical figures including Mary Queen of Scots and Elizabeth Barrett Browning, who are believed to have suffered from it. The death of singer Karen Carpenter (half of the world-famous 1970s pop group The Carpenters) from heart failure due to complications of anorexia aged just 32 in 1983 shocked the world and prompted widespread coverage of, and research into, anorexia, eating disorders and body dysmorphia. She left a wonderful legacy of music, but the awareness of eating disorders raised by her death is also her legacy.

The loss of appetite in anorexia is misleading because sufferers consciously override their natural urges to eat and satisfy their hunger, and therefore are very hungry. Anorexia is characterised by a strong desire to lose weight, a fear of becoming fat and an overevaluation of the importance of eating, shape and weight. These drive a person to restrict food and reduce their dietary intake. Where most people are unable to do this for significant periods – it goes against our survival instinct and wiring – people with anorexia are able to override their body's increasingly strong hunger pangs.

Anorexia is an illness with several contributing factors. It usually starts with emotional issues, but once food restriction kicks in there are a multitude of neurological and physiological features that occur, taking it from being a mental health illness to one that is mixed mental and physical health. In recent years, with the emergence of fMRI (functional magnetic resonance imaging) and neuro-imaging scans, there has been a shift in understanding and anorexia is now seen – in part, at least – as a brain-based illness, with genetic and neurological influences as well as emotional, social and wider factors.

Sufferers often display high levels of perfectionism and set themselves high standards academically, within their hobbies, and with their exercise and weight-loss goals. In addition, teenagers commonly use food to manage distress and emotional dysregulation during the turbulence of adolescence as it is one of the few areas over which they can take control. Food restriction and exercise commonly bring positive feedback from others, which is gratifying and gives a feeling of success and validation.

There is significant physiology in starvation. Initially, restriction gives an emotional boost. It feels good to be in control, the plan is working, weight is dropping off, and you feel more comfortable in your body. People experience starvation highs, which are similar to the endorphin hit after exercise. But within around 10–14 days, starvation cognitions emerge, including constant thoughts about food and eating, planning of meals in detail, and rumination around how to eat less. Mood deteriorates and depression, social withdrawal and anxiety develop. Body dysmorphia follows, with negative thoughts about shape and weight, fear of eating and of social situations. Food-related behavioural changes include cutting food into small pieces, eating much slower than usual, hiding or hoarding food and lying about eating. Peoples' personalities change as sufferers become irritable, anxious, secretive, quiet and withdrawn. These symptoms are a consequence of food restriction (as well as in some, a cause) and this is how people 'slip' into anorexia in the absence of an obvious psychological trigger.

When you restrict, your brain thinks that you are in a period of famine and becomes more focused on food to help you find it. The more you restrict, the more you think about food: what you'd like to eat, what you mustn't eat, what you can cook for others, and so on. You become anxious because your thoughts are filled with food and so you tighten up your food rules. You exercise, get the endorphin hit post-workout and push your body to work in an increasingly undernourished state. It's exhausting for your body and brain to work without fuel and irritability and low mood quickly follows weight loss and hunger.

The ratio of anorexia in females to males is 10:1, with the onset often differing between genders.[75] Most often, girls start to restrict because they're unhappy with their weight or shape. This may be due to feeling uncomfortable in their changing body or to underlying factors, such as emotional distress, anxiety or friendship difficulties, that get displaced onto weight and eating. Boys and men frequently develop it through becoming obsessed by healthy eating and working out, or after a stomach bug or other illness, which has caused a limited food intake. This is an important point – food restriction, dieting, semi-starvation, whatever you want to call it – is not necessarily the consequence of anorexia nervosa. It can also be the cause, as discovered by Ancel Keys in 1945 in the famous Minnesota starvation experiment.[76] (See Appendix, pages 293–4 for a description of the study.) Restriction itself, with no precipitating psychological factors, can cause anorexia. Importantly, it is why dieting, in and of itself, is a significant risk factor for the development of an eating disorder.

There are many misconceptions about anorexia and who develops it. For example: anorexia isn't all that serious; it's a choice; it's about vanity; and it only affects wealthy, white females. These are all wrong. Boys develop it, people of all races and ethnicity suffer and it is absolutely not a choice.

Sylvie came to me aged 15. All had been well until the Covid-19 lockdown, during which she had started to follow a weight-loss and fitness plan. She was unhappy with her weight and shape and initially didn't seem to be doing anything unsafe. However, the plan taught her to weigh and measure food and within a couple of months her periods stopped. She was still following the plan, but it wasn't enough food for her body. Because she had been eating and didn't look underweight, her parents didn't realise that anorexia had stealthily snuck in. By the time they did – with the cessation of her periods – she was fully hooked and recovery took a year with the help of a specialist ED team.

Ethan, aged 16, had had a nasty bout of gastroenteritis, after which he understandably felt keen to avoid another bout and became anxious about which foods he ate. After the initial, acute infection, it took a while for his abdominal pain and inflamed oesophagus to completely subside, so by the time he was fully recovered he had lost 6kg. This, together with a smaller appetite and anxiety around getting ill again, led him to continue to undereat for his energy requirements. Without him noticing it, his thoughts became starvation thoughts, his emotions were dulled, he withdrew socially and anorexia set in. By the time I met him, he was in an in-patient eating disorder unit.

These examples illustrate how, if your child has lost their appetite or been unwell and so has been eating less than usual, it can gently nudge them into eating little and often. Instead of starting with full meals and large portions, increase snacks, smoothies and shakes and build from there. It doesn't need to be dramatic or intense, but be attentive for a while until their appetite is fully returned and they're eating normally (for them) again. For most kids, it passes naturally and they won't have the same experiences as Ethan or Sylvie, but it's worth being aware that this can happen. It's the same with dieting.

If your child has gone on a diet – which I strongly advise they don't – do make sure that they eat enough to prevent them from being hungry. It's too easy to get hooked.

Signs and Symptoms of AN

- A preoccupation with eating, shape and/or weight
- A fear of being fat
- Restricting food intake
- Cutting out foods
- Controlling what is eaten in an attempt to control weight
- Increasing or excessive exercise
- Weight loss
- Weight loss to a very low weight or to a very unhealthy weight
- A slow or irregular pulse (heartbeat)
- Low blood pressure
- Feeling cold even when it is objectively not cold
- Cold hands and feet
- Feeling dizzy or light-headed
- Feeling tired
- Being lethargic/lacking in energy
- Feeling nauseous
- Abdominal pain
- Periods getting lighter and less regular
- Periods stopping if they have already started
- Delayed puberty
- Delayed growth
- Lanugo – a fine, downy hair growing on the face and body
- Sporadic bingeing

- Laxative use
- Vomiting

Whilst all of these are signs and symptoms of anorexia not every young person will have them all, and not everyone with these symptoms has anorexia. Bingeing is common with anorexia because of the severe hunger. Often, people can't continually suppress their hunger, leading them to binge, after which they feel appalled, ashamed and commit even more rigidly to restriction going forward.

Treatment of AN

Treatment of anorexia is challenging. Starvation numbs the real thoughts and feelings and replaces them with starvation ones. When the trigger is emotional, sufferers may feel less distressed. Food restriction is so appealing because it gives people control over a tangible area of their life, when much of it feels out of control. Of course, that sense of control is deceptive as the illness takes control so fast, both physiologically and psychologically, and one is actually out of control, with anorexia in control.

In many ways, starvation is like any other addiction: drugs, alcohol, nicotine, etc. It numbs emotions, gives you an immediate coping strategy that makes you feel better and causes changes in the brain and the body. Similarly, the physiology is so powerful that the urge to continue to restrict is overwhelming and the fear associated with eating and weight gain similar. A young person's identity can easily become allied with the eating disorder too, leaving them unsure of who they are without it. The anorexia becomes like a toxic best friend who is simultaneously making you feel safe and secure whilst placing you in danger.

One of the most significant differences, however, is that in every other addiction, the addictive substance can be removed. If you are recovering from substance addiction, such as alcoholism or smoking, you remove the chemical from your body and your life and never touch it again. By contrast, in starvation, the addictive substance (food or the lack thereof) can't be removed. With eating disorders, you have to interact with the addictive element many times a day. This makes it tricky. To the extent there is a parallel to be drawn with alcoholism – an alcoholic in recovery can't even have one small drink as it can trigger a relapse – so an anorexic in recovery can't skip a meal or a snack as the pull back to restriction can just be too great.

Treatment for anorexia in young people is usually family based. This is not because the family is at fault or parents are to blame. You absolutely are not. Families are profoundly affected by having a child or sibling with anorexia, and parents are fundamental to recovery. Sufferers usually require a multidisciplinary team so that they receive therapeutic and dietetic input and medical monitoring.

The best prognostic factor for recovery is early intervention. Don't watch and wait to be sure that your child has a problem. If you're concerned, listen to your parental intuition and go to the doctor. It is never too early to seek help. As I say all the time, I would much rather someone brought their child to see me and we concluded there was nothing to worry about than that they waited until they were certain there was something wrong. To address a common concern, you are not wasting the doctor's time, the psychiatrist's time or the psychologist's time. We want you to come as early as possible and if there's no cause for concern, that's a great outcome – we'll all be delighted. And finally, if you have a child with anorexia, or any other eating disorder, it is NOT your fault. Not only is it not your fault, you will be integral to their recovery.

Bulimia Nervosa (BN)

The Nature and Causes of BN

Nervous ravenous hunger – that is the direct translation of bulimia nervosa from the Greek. Bulimia is characterised by binge eating, followed by purging to compensate for the binge. A binge is not just eating more than feels comfortable. It is consuming large amounts of food and drink within a short period of time and, most importantly, with the sense of a loss of control. One of the key questions I ask my patients is: 'Could you stop mid-binge to answer your phone or the door?' The answer is often 'no'. The foods consumed during binges tend to be foods otherwise avoided or 'forbidden'. The stricter the food rules, the more likely they are to be broken during a binge. If eating feels in one's control, then it's not a binge, it's just overeating, and overeating sometimes is normal in everyday life.

Purging behaviours include self-induced vomiting, taking laxatives or diuretics, excessive exercise, or fasting/restriction. Purging is a way of compensating or making up for the binge. Unlike with anorexia, those with bulimia are often in the normal weight range, though in very severe cases they can lose weight. As with anorexia, bulimia includes a fear of weight gain, an overestimation of shape and size and a desperate desire to lose weight.

One of the most common misperceptions about bulimia is that it's not as dangerous as anorexia. This is not true. Bulimia brings a wealth of physical health complications, as shown in Figure 9.2 overleaf, the most serious of which can be fatal.

DISORDERED EATING AND EATING DISORDERS | 257

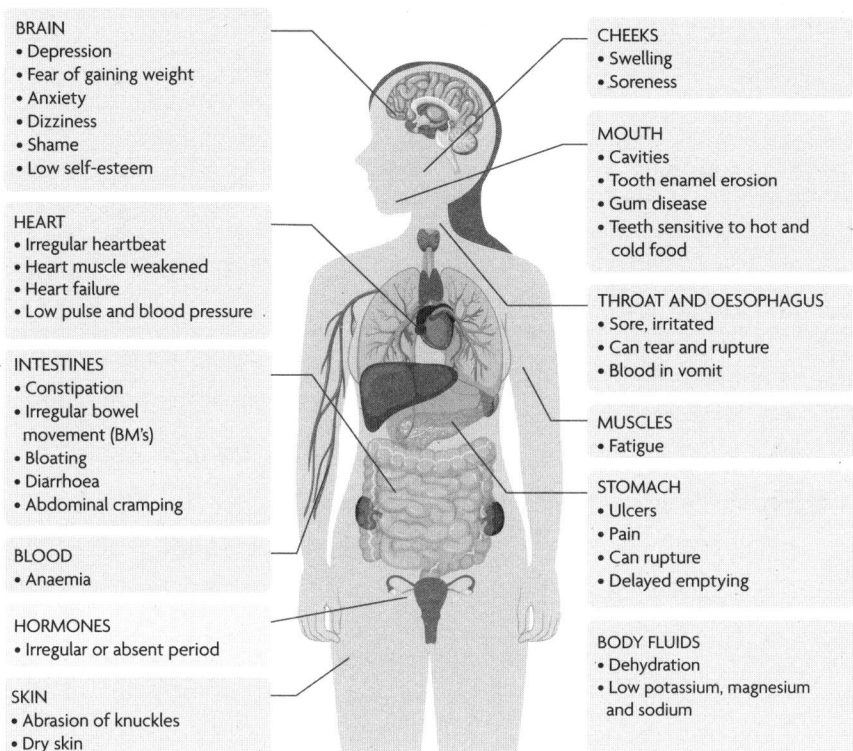

Figure 9.2. Complications of bulimia.

Bulimia is more common than anorexia, and less common than binge eating disorder, with the prevalence in Europe estimated to be 2.2% of the population and 4.6% in the US.[77] The primary cause of bingeing is hunger. It's that straightforward. When we are hungry our body communicates to us. If we ignore this, our body goes 'past' the hunger for a while, but the signals grow stronger and stronger until we have to eat. It is a survival mechanism. When treating bulimia, the first step is to eliminate hunger and regulate eating, which gets rid of the hunger-driven binges; the remaining binges are emotion-driven.

Just like anorexia, bulimia can be triggered by dieting and restricting and/or by emotional triggers. When engaged in bingeing or purging there is no mental space to think about whatever's distressing. Some people report feeling detached and out of body during their binges and purges, which takes them away from their distress even more.

Niamh's mum had died suddenly when she was 14. Her dad brought her to me a few months later because he was worried about her eating, saying that she was bingeing and restricting. He also thought she was making herself sick. He was right. Niamh said that she had had thoughts of wanting to lose a bit of weight before her mum died but hadn't done anything about it. After Mum died, she was overwhelmed by tricky and conflicting emotions, and she found that when she was bingeing she didn't think or feel.

The problem came when she felt awful post-binge and so she would purge. She didn't mind that either because, like when she was bingeing, she didn't have space to think about Mum. In her periods of restriction, she felt focused and more in control, even though she was becoming more out of control with the eating disorder taking control. At the same time, the ED thoughts became louder, distracting her from thoughts about Mum. Because she oscillated between restriction and episodes of bingeing and purging when hunger was too great, Niamh was able to keep her feelings suppressed for much of the time.

Niamh's example demonstrates that EDs have a function. There is always a function: sometimes it's easy to spot and other times it's harder. The role can also change over time, with the initial function being replaced with another, such as 'it's my identity; it's who I am'. Niamh also illustrates the interplay between restricting, bingeing and purging.

Signs and Symptoms of BN

- Eating large amounts of food – sometimes you will notice empty cupboards rather than seeing a binge in action.

DISORDERED EATING AND EATING DISORDERS | 259

- Purging with laxatives, diuretics, vomiting, exercise or restriction. You may notice:
    - Grazed knuckles caused by rubbing on the teeth when fingers are used to induce vomiting
    - Bits of sick in the toilet
    - Nasty stomach aches whilst the laxatives take effect
    - Puffiness around the eyes or under the jaw line caused by swollen salivary glands due to vomiting
    - Damage to the teeth
    - A hoarse voice
- Going to the loo shortly after eating – at home, in restaurants, wherever you are
- Secrecy about eating
- Hoarding food
- Mood swings
- Poor skin condition
- Bloating
- Stomach ache
- Constipation
- Tiredness
- Difficulty sleeping
- Blood sugar swings
- Dizziness or feeling faint
- Regular fluctuation in weight
- Preoccupation with eating, shape and weight
- Fear of weight gain
- Distress around weight
- Social withdrawal
- Anxiety

Treatment of BN

Regulating eating is the first step in treatment for bulimia but it can be very frightening because of the fears around weight gain. Ensuring that there is enough support is fundamental.

The binge-purge cycle of bulimia dominates everyday life, leaving people utterly exhausted, isolated and hopeless. Bulimia frequently causes guilt and shame, preventing sufferers from seeking help. Shame also leads to eating in secret, not wanting to eat around others and anxiety about eating with others, going out, and socialising for fear of there being food involved. As with the other EDs, changes in mood tend to come before any physical changes are noticeable. Low self-esteem, body-disparagement, low mood, irritability and anxiety are very common. Unlike with anorexia, people rarely feel good about themselves. It's not an effective weight-loss strategy — and this helps them to hide their difficulties from others — people don't get the positive feedback about looking good due to losing weight and they don't feel in control.

Treatment is most effective early in the illness. Getting treatment later is also successful, it just takes a bit longer as the bulimia is more established. It is usually an out-patient treatment and involves individual therapy and sometimes dietetic input, too.

Binge Eating Disorder (BED)

The Nature and Causes of BED

Binge Eating Disorder is the most common eating disorder. It is as it sounds: people binge on food as in bulimia but without the compensatory behaviours of BN. People suffering with BED do not 'just overeat', 'overindulge' or enjoy large portions of food as some myths would imply, nor do they enjoy binges. Like for those with bulimia, binges involve eating large quantities of food very fast, feeling out of control. Usually, sufferers binge alone and often when they're not physically hungry, finding it difficult to stop even when they want to. Binges are extremely distressing and, as with bulimia, people often report feeling disconnected from themselves during them. Some can't even remember what they have eaten during the binge.

Some binges are planned and ritualised, involving buying special food on which to binge, or they can be impulsive or spontaneous. Many describe it as being like a switch flicking: they are overtaken by the urge to binge without conscious thought or the ability to regain control and stop. Others avoid keeping much food in the house so that bingeing is not easily available but then go to the shops when the urge arrives. It is common for people to go to multiple shops to protect themselves from feeling ashamed about the quantity of food they buy. Nonetheless, shame, guilt, disgust and self-loathing pile in and the distress is significant. These emotions during a binge perpetuate the cycle. Some sufferers try fasting to limit intake post binge, but this leads to hunger and feelings of deprivation, which further strengthen the urge to binge. In rare cases, the causes of bingeing are physical, but for the vast majority, other than hunger, emotional triggers lead to bingeing.

Callum, aged ten, had suffered neglect as a young boy and was not fed sufficiently or looked after. After he was removed from his mother's care, he was placed with his uncle and aunt, who brought him into their family, loved him, nurtured him, and made sure that his emotional and physical needs were met. However, he was binge eating, gaining considerable weight and seemed unable to stop, despite ample food being available whenever he was hungry and reassurance this would continue.

It wasn't just previous food insecurity that was causing Callum to binge. He ate to fill the huge void of the loss of his mother, his childhood trauma and neglect. The function of eating was to try to quell his feeling of emotional emptiness. No matter how much he ate, he did not feel sated.

Callum's story is heartbreaking and as are those of many binge-eating disorder patients. The stigma that binge eating brings makes it worse. There is also a general belief that it's an absence of self-control or a lack of self-care. It's neither. Bingeing is horrible. It leaves people feeling physically unwell and emotionally drowning in distress. And it only numbs the pain for the immediate minutes whilst bingeing. Additionally, the concurrent weight gain and common journey into overweight, along with the societal stigma and lack of understanding about BED causes further despair. It's a psychological illness and we need to treat it with more compassion. Also remember that dieting is a risk factor for it. Not everyone with BED will be overweight – it's possible to have it and be in the healthy weight range.

Finding comfort in food is normal and there's nothing to worry about if it doesn't happen frequently or come with feelings of guilt, shame and a loss of control. A bit of comfort eating differs from BED. If you are worried about your child or yourself, don't wait to get help. The sooner you seek it the better: you have a right to it and are worthy of it.

Signs and Symptoms of BED

- Buying large quantities of food
- Hoarding food
- Organising life around food
- Eating very fast

- Eating when not hungry
- Eating beyond the point of fullness and feeling uncomfortably full
- Avoiding eating around others
- Mood swings
- Irritability
- Social withdrawal
- Feeling out of control around food and/or when eating
- Bingeing
- Feeling anxious and stressed, especially when eating around others
- Feelings of shame and guilt after bingeing
- Low self-esteem
- Anxiety, depression or other mental illnesses
- Weight gain
- Bloating
- Stomach pain
- Tiredness
- Sleep difficulties
- Poor skin quality
- Obesity
- Shoplifting or spending a lot of money on food
- Hoarding food or other unusual behaviours around food
- Physical health complications such as nausea, bloating gastrointestinal symptoms and obesity.

Treatment of BED

Therapy is the main treatment for BED, but it needs to be with someone who is a specialist ED therapist. Receiving evidence-based treatment reduces the severity, duration and impact of the illness. Dietetic input is helpful as sufferers need to learn to regulate their eating and reconnect with their body. Alongside this, they can address depression, anxiety, low self-esteem and any trauma that may be causing or contributing to the condition.

Orthorexia

Orthorexia is not actually classified as an eating disorder in the diagnostic manuals, but it is well recognised and I see it in clinic often. Orthorexia is an unhealthy obsession with healthy eating and a focus on eating 'pure' or 'very healthy' food. What food is 'pure' or 'healthy' varies from person to person, but usually leads to people cutting out many foods and food groups. Orthorexia often starts as a result of an interest in fitness, as young people want to bulk or tone up; alongside exercising and gym-going, they become attentive to what they eat. Going to the gym is often a great outlet for young people, as long as they use the equipment properly and don't lift weights that are too heavy: the exercise produces endorphins that lift mood; it's social, as boys in particular often go with friends; it helps with body image; and it gives a sense of purpose with goals. However, it can become addictive. This can lead to overexercising and injury, an obsession with eating healthily to achieve body transformation goals, and, often without realising, orthorexia.

Lachlan, aged 16, was brought to me by his mum. He was not concerned about himself, but she felt that there was a problem. Lachlan was doing PE GCSE and he had got heavily into working out, going to the gym four or five times a week and playing competitive squash three times a week for two hours at a time. He also walked everywhere, refusing lifts and avoiding public transport. He ate large amounts of protein, vegetables and fruit, and some complex carbohydrates in the form of porridge, potato, sweet potato and, occasionally, wholemeal bread. He'd cut out all sugar and processed foods, and insisted on taking a packed lunch to school rather than eating school lunches as he had previously. It sounded like he was eating well, but it wasn't enough for him and he had lost 15kg without realising. He fixated on his diet and fitness at the expense of his friendships. He couldn't hang out with his mates because he was either exercising and preparing 'healthy' food or because they would order pizza and question why he wouldn't join them in eating it. He used a lot of protein powder and insisted on going for a 30-minute walk after dinner to 'walk it off' and reduce his feeling of fullness. Without realising it, he had moved from enjoying exercise and working out to orthorexia and into anorexia.

Although his mum had noticed the changes in him, by the time he got to me, Lachlan's weight loss was significant. He had withdrawn socially, developed a fear of fatness, had a list of 'fear foods', had a distorted body image and had halted his puberty. Treatment consisted of dietetic support, therapy and a great deal of help from his parents. He did brilliantly in regaining the weight, challenging his fear foods and body image, and reintegrating with his friends. It was only once Lachlan was better that he was able to appreciate how poorly he had been and how much his life had been compromised by his illness. When he was in it, he didn't notice any of this.

There is considerable overlap between orthorexia and anorexia, and what starts as an unhealthy obsession with healthy eating frequently morphs into anorexia as it did, insidiously, with Lachlan during his GCSEs. It's easy to miss orthorexia in the early stage because it often presents as someone taking more care of themselves. In young people, it links strongly with diet culture – if your child's friends are eating more healthily, it's easy for them to do similarly, to fit in. However, the troublesome thoughts we see in anorexia and other eating disorders are also present in orthorexia. There is often an over-evaluation of eating, body shape and weight, and ruminating about food and eating consumes a huge amount of mental energy. Treatment is similar to that of anorexia – therapy and dietetic input – and like the other eating disorders, the earlier it is started, the better.

Signs and Symptoms of Orthorexia

- An obsession with a healthy (or supposedly healthy) diet or 'clean eating'
- An increased focus on food and eating, which might interfere with daily life, relationships or work
- Cutting out certain foods or food groups to eat more healthily – more and more may be cut out over time
- Taking theories on healthy eating and adapting them with their own food rules
- Judgement about what others are eating
- Poor concentration
- An obsession for over-exercising or working out
- Feeling unable to put aside food rules
- Feelings of anxiety, guilt or uncleanliness about eating 'unhealthy' food
- Mood and emotional wellbeing are dependent on food
- Weight loss
- Tiredness
- Low energy levels
- Feeling weaker
- Feeling cold

Avoidant Restrictive Food Intake Disorder (ARFID)

The Nature and Causes of ARFID

Let's start by dispelling common myths: ARFID is not just 'picky eating on steroids'. It's different. People who suffer with it are not fussy and attention-seeking. It is not a way of achieving weight loss – some may lose weight but others will gain it. Indeed, it is not about weight: what happens with a sufferer's weight is a consequence of which foods are tolerated and safe and which are avoided.

ARFID presents as your child refusing to eat certain foods or types of food with a restricted intake in terms of quantity or group of food, or both. It is more common in males and can occur at any age. Unlike other eating disorders, ARFID is not driven by concerns over, shape or size. Food restriction is not to solve body image dissatisfaction and there is no drive for thinness. ARFID is about anxiety. There are a range of contributory factors, including genetic, physical and psychological. There's also a link between ARFID and neurodivergence, such as attention deficit hyperactivity disorder (ADHD) and autism spectrum disorder (ASD). With picky eating, people may not enjoy certain foods and they won't want to eat them, but they won't be shut down by anxiety. Those with ARFID are overwhelmed by anxiety – their brains go into fight or flight and the anxiety about the feared foods is overwhelming.

There are three main subtypes of ARFID: sensory; fear about the consequences of eating; and a low interest in eating. These subtypes are not mutually exclusive, and people can have one subtype or a mix. Someone with the sensory form might be very sensitive to the taste, smell, texture, appearance, colour or even sound of certain foods. This may come from a visceral aversion or from a negative experience with a food, leading to their avoidance and restricted intake.

Ewan, aged 17, and his father travelled hundreds of miles to the eating disorder team in which I worked. He'd choked on a piece of steak a year earlier and had become frightened of it happening again. To avoid the risk, he blended his meals with gravy, water or milk (depending on the meal), and refused to eat any solid food at all. He had lost considerable weight and his physical health was suffering. He had no fear of weight gain; indeed, Ewan wanted to gain weight because he did not like looking so thin or feeling exhausted and weak. However, his terror – and it *was* terror – at the thought of choking again prevented him from eating any textured food, and he was unable to meet his nutritional requirements.

Ewan's is a classic case of ARFID based on the consequences of eating. He had choked, but for others the trigger could be vomiting, food poisoning, abdominal pain, heartburn or an allergic reaction. It can also be triggered by witnessing someone else having an adverse reaction and adopting that fear.

When there is a low interest in eating, restriction may be due solely to this. It might be that someone has a poor appetite generally, or that eating is not enjoyable or feels like a chore. With ARFID, everyone's fear and reasons for restricting and avoiding certain foods are different. Nonetheless, those with ARFID share the core features of avoidance or restriction of food intake.

Whilst ARFID stands alone as a disorder, it's also often found alongside others, most commonly anxiety disorders, ADHD, ASD and specific medical conditions. As with all EDs, ARFID can have a damaging effect on physical as well as mental health, as it did with Ewan. His was a clear and specific onset, but many cannot recall what triggered it, if anything, and some people do not remember life without it. This is very different to the other eating disorders. Some children and young people fail to gain weight and thrive, whereas others gain a lot of weight. Often, there is some malnutrition because the range of accepted foods is so limited and lacking in key nutrients.

Signs and Symptoms of ARFID

There are a variety of difficulties that contribute to the restriction or avoidance of food, so the symptoms are wide-ranging. Not everyone will have all of them, but many of the typical ones are below.[78]

- Appearing to be a picky eater
- Always having the same meals and snacks
- Always eating something different to everyone else
- Only eating foods of a similar colour (e.g. beige)
- Eating a highly limited range of foods
- Finding it difficult to recognise when they're hungry
- Eating a good range of foods but in limited amounts and less than is needed to stay healthy
- Finding meals a chore
- Taking a long time to eat
- Feeling full after only a few mouthfuls and struggling to eat more
- Being highly anxious at mealtimes, for example through chewing food carefully, or taking small bites and sips
- Avoiding situations where food would be present
- Developing nutritional deficiencies such as anaemia
- A failure to gain weight or thrive as a child or weight loss
- Weight gain due to the type of foods accepted

Treatment of ARFID

Treatment depends on the type of ARFID and the level of emotional and physical compromise. Ideally, a child or young person will work with a multidisciplinary, specialist eating disorder team with input from a paediatrician, dietician, psychologist, psychiatrist, speech and language therapist, and occupational therapist. Evidence-based treatments include family-based treatments, cognitive behavioural therapy (CBT), exposure, anxiety management, mindfulness and, sometimes, medication. Usually, like with Ewan, treatment is outpatient, but in extreme cases, an admission can be necessary. For adults with ARFID, treatment is within a multidisciplinary eating disorder service with medical input where necessary. At every age, the more support someone receives during treatment from family, friends and professionals, the better.

ARFID can be profoundly challenging, causing both significant worry and frustration. As with the other EDs, support is invaluable for you and your child, and treating them with compassion or curiosity is more effective than the critical and corrective route, however understandable. Remember, your child is not actively choosing this life, even if it seems that they are: they are scared, and that fear drives their behaviour. It's an awful feeling. Take a moment to think of something in your life that has really frightened you. Connect with that fear and notice what it does to you physically and emotionally. This is what it is like for someone with ARFID: that intensity of fear about certain foods or amounts of food is pervasive. Whilst it needs to be challenged, and treatment will do this, you will be able to see with this exercise just how difficult it is.

Please Remember

No one chooses to develop an eating disorder. No one wakes up one day thinking 'ooh, bulimia sounds fun, I'm going to try it'. Whatever the trigger for the eating disorder, it always contains distress. Eating disorders are not fun. Despite some media glamorisation, they're not sexy. They don't bring joy, success or happiness. They don't heal emotional pain, though they might momentarily numb it. They impair relationships, gnaw at self-esteem, damage friendships and spoil life. Anxiety increases, mood drops, withdrawal intensifies and despair sets in. People may want to lose weight but no one who has had an eating disorder recommends it. Recovery is long, painful and bloody hard, but it's always worth it.

I don't believe that we can ever eliminate eating disorders, but we should know the signs, notice them in our kids and friends, and intervene as early as possible. Early intervention is the best predictor of a successful recovery, so act at the first sign of one. You may worry about upsetting your child, or that you'll offend your friend, but watching and waiting ensures an ED will become entrenched.

Know this: You are not to blame. No one is to blame. It's not your fault, nor is it your child's fault. If you have a child with an ED, you are integral to their recovery – they can't do it without you. They may scream at you, tell you that they hate you, say dreadful things to you, but recognise that this is the illness speaking, not your child, and hang on to this in the darkest moments. I liken the ED to a rock climber beginning to slip down a rock face: the more they lose their footing, the tighter they cling on to save themselves. When your child is going through treatment, their anorexia or ED is the rock climber beginning to slip and they desperately cling, screaming and shouting, until they can do so no more. Expect an initial uptick in the ED voice and behaviours, and the conflict around food and getting well during recovery. It's normal, though brutal. There is support out there – get the help you need. It's the most challenging journey for you all. I have included resources and some suggested reading in the Resources and Further Reading section.

CHAPTER TAKEAWAYS

- You need to be aware of the signs and symptoms of disordered eating and eating disorders to spot them.
- Disordered eating is harmful – don't wait to get help for you or your child.
- You're worthy of help whatever struggles you're having with food.
- The three most common eating disorders are binge eating disorder, bulimia and anorexia in that order.
- Early intervention is the best prognostic factor for recovery from an eating disorder.
- Eating disorders are multifactorial – there is no single cause – but diet culture, dieting, a family history, trauma and using food to manage feelings can all contribute.
- Orthorexia, an unhealthy obsession with healthy eating, easily transitions into anorexia.
- ARFID is different from the other EDs because it does not contain a fear of gaining weight or an overestimation of shape and weight. It is much more anxiety and sensory based.
- You are not to blame for your child's eating difficulties – it is not your fault.
- You are integral to their recovery.

CHAPTER 10

Putting It All Together

'And so we beat on, boats against the current, borne back ceaselessly into the past.'

F. Scott Fitzgerald, *The Great Gatsby*

We've spent a lot of time so far talking about all things food, feeding, eating and eating disorders. You have considered the way in which food is a part of your identity and has shaped your life and your family. How you celebrate and share with it, nurture, love and connect with it and maybe how you have experienced it being used punitively. We've talked about diet culture and its pervasive nature, and I hope you agree that whatever it looks like, you have your own particular relationship with food.

Your story is unique. It comes from your upbringing, your relationships throughout your life and your struggles. Whatever your issues and relationship with food, none of it is your fault. There's no blame or shame, only an opportunity to reflect on yourself and your kids, to be compassionate and to learn that it's possible to have choices that previously you didn't know existed or felt were unavailable.

And so, to your kids and eating: the best thing you can do for them is help them create a good relationship with food. It won't prevent eating disorders and it won't prevent emotional eating, overeating or obesity – but it is protective. It gives your children a better chance of using strategies other than food and eating to manage their emotions. If you've bought in so far, let's put it all together so you recognise your baggage, know what's yours, what you bring to the table and what you want to leave behind to help your child to develop that positive relationship with food.

Whose Baggage Is It?

You are at the root of helping your kids develop a healthy relationship with all things food. You, your partner and your family. Your narratives around eating directly influence them. This might be hard to hear because it means that your baggage can become your kids' (intergenerational transmission). Once you know and accept your baggage, you become aware of what is played out with your kids and you are no longer destined to pass it on.

Imagine you're going on holiday with your extended family. You all have suitcases to carry, of differing weights and sizes. You have to carry your own case, but you don't want to carry anyone else's. Yours is cumbersome enough and you feel responsible for your own stuff; there is no need to take the responsibility for anyone's bags (young kids' aside). You help your grandma with her case, but once you have checked in, you're free of both cases. You can probably see where I'm going with this: this is how I think of emotional baggage. Often, we carry far too much of other peoples' stuff without realising. We lug around our mother's body image issues, our father's disordered eating, our grandparents' trauma, our partner's distress, and we take responsibility for these, feeling burdened but unaware that they're not ours to carry.

Your task is to work out whose baggage it is and drop it. Pretty straightforward, right? In some ways it is, but it can also prove tricky, especially if you've carried it since you were young; think about your food and eating legacy, as we explored earlier in Chapter 2. The easiest way to unite owner and luggage is to say, 'This is not my issue; I actually don't believe that carbs are bad and I'm no longer going to restrict myself because it's not my stuff.' Or, 'I like my cupboards and fridge to be well stocked. I don't want to keep them spartan. That's my mum's fear of eating playing out and I don't want to be influenced by it anymore.' Once you realise it's not your issue, you mentally return the responsibility to whomever that belief or behaviour came from. For example, 'Actually, I'm not frightened that if my child eats they'll become fat. I trust them to listen to their body. That's my dad's stuff, not mine and I'm not going to buy into it anymore'. Or 'I don't want to buy into diet culture anymore and I don't want my child to be brainwashed by it'.

Breaking the Cycle

Breaking a pattern of behaviour is challenging but doable. Changing long-held behaviours and beliefs is a process. They will have been learnt from early childhood, or they developed because they were helpful before they became unhelpful. Additionally, they'll be familiar by now and the mind loves what is familiar, associating familiarity with safety (as discussed earlier in Chapter 2). Therefore, even if you want to change, it needs to be an active and conscious process. Because if you hope for change but don't actively do things differently, your brain will return to your well-practised patterns of behaviour that feel safe despite you no longer wanting them.

Step one in the process is to understand what impacted your relationship with food and eating. By now you'll have some thoughts about which issues are and aren't yours. If you're unsure, below is an exercise that might help you.

Write down your beliefs about food, any food rules you have and the way that you interact with food. So, for example, are you a three-meals-a-day person, a grazer, a little-and-often eater, an intermittent faster, and so on? Then write down the ways that you do family meals and feed your kids. For each belief, rule, behaviour and style ask yourself the following questions:

- Where did this belief come from?
- Whose is it?
- Is it mine?
- If not, why am I still holding it? (For example, familiarity, habit, because it's your partner's and you are supporting them.)
- Do I agree with it?
- Is it consistent with my values?
- What impact is it having on my life?
- What impact is it having on my partner's life?
- What impact is it having on my children's lives?
- What am I communicating by holding on to it?
- What might I be transmitting (passing on) to my kids?
- Do I want to continue with it?

There are many questions here that tap into different aspects of your belief system, but for me, one of the most important is the last: do you want to continue with a belief, rule or behaviour? You may go through these questions and recognise that it's not your belief, but you value it and want to continue with it. You may realise you are carrying your partner's baggage but feel that the conflict that giving it back will cause is too great, or you want to support them, so you'll keep it. At least you'll have actively made the decision and you mustn't underestimate the importance of that.

A word of caution: if you do this exercise and choose to continue with behaviours inconsistent with your values, or that aren't really yours (but you don't want to upset anyone), I encourage you to examine this further. Similarly, if you decide that you're worried about angering your partner, children or others, this may indicate further exploration is necessary. It's difficult to live a life that is inconsistent with your beliefs and values: it leaves you feeling disempowered and without a voice, which can then cause low mood and anxiety. Many families I've worked with disagree over how to reconcile different views about their child's eating and it causes profound distress not only within the couple relationship, but for kids and the whole family. Food and eating are so emotive and loaded with nuance.

When I talk of values, I mean the overarching principles by which you want to live your life and behave as a human being, towards yourself and others. For example, to treat yourself and others with compassion, see the best in people, be honest, to have a good relationship with food. Within each value you might have goals that you set to help you live by that value.

This is an example:

Value:	Have a good relationship with food
Goal:	Honour my hunger
Belief:	I need to connect with my body's cues and listen to my hunger and full signals
Thought:	I want to do this for myself and my children

Feeling:	Trepidation, hope
Behaviour:	Eat when I am hungry

It's helpful to separate it into categories because there are so many ways of living according to your values. If you set a goal and it's not attainable, choose another goal and live consistently with your values.

Once you understand your relationship with food, consider whether you'd like it to be different or whether you're happy as it is currently. If not, work out how you'd like it to look. Use this question to help: If you could wave a magic wand and change your relationship with food and eating, how would you change it and what would your ideal relationship be? Work through each of your values, goals, beliefs, thoughts, feelings and behaviours. Don't worry about whether they are realistic at this stage. The purpose is to ascertain what your ideal would be. Write it down. Knowing this is invaluable. Even if it feels unattainable, that will give you lots of information about what's happening for you, how big a change you want and your values, with which to work. Take time over this exercise, it's the foundation for the change you want to make. It should be thought-provoking and may also be challenging.

Then, and only then, consider what's realistic and available to you. Your ideal will be available to you, but it might take a long time and a lot of work to get from where you are to where you want to be. You might embrace the challenge and go for it. Equally, you might adjust your goal and lower the bar a little so that your desired outcome is within your reach. Throughout this, be specific in analysing what you want. To say you'd like to eat more freely or have a better relationship with food is woolly. It's not measurable and it won't guide you. You won't have any idea how to get there or recognise when you've achieved it.

Break it down. Ask yourself what a better relationship with food would look like. How would you know if it improved? What would you be able to do that you can't do now? What would you no longer do that you currently do? What would feel available to you? What could you do with your kids, family and friends that you can't at the moment? What rules would you chuck in the bin? And what would others notice if your relationship with food improved? Answer these questions and you will have some clarity about how that better relationship will look and what you want. You'll also have many clues about changes you need to make to reach your goal and the steps along the way. You won't be able to do it in one go, so break down each answer into manageable and achievable chunks.

Start with small, doable steps and build on them. No step is too small. I mean it! You're much better to take more small steps that feel easy than one big step, even if that feels more appealing and more of an achievement (see Figure 10.1). For example, if you're frightened of sugar and never eat it but you want to celebrate your kids' birthdays by sharing their cakes, you'll find it very scary to go from the fear of sugar and eating none to eating a whole piece of chocolate cake. Instead, you could break it down like this:

1. Create a 'ladder' of foods with sugar from the least scary to the most (see page 280).
2. Challenge your fear cognitively. Tell yourself that most people eat sugar and nothing bad happened. You have had some sugar at some point in your life and you are fine, etc.
3. You can't get to eating birthday cake through thought alone.
4. Start with the bottom rung of your ladder and have that food for three – four days.
5. Move up to the next rung, but don't drop the least-feared food. Keep eating that too.

6. Continue all the way up to a piece of cake.
7. Tell your family what you are doing and allow them to support you.
8. Remind yourself that you want this. It's your choice and you can do hard things.
9. Visualise eating the cake on your child's birthday and how good it will feel – this is mental rehearsal and an important part of preparation.

I have put a sample ladder below to illustrate this example – you can adapt it for whatever you need.

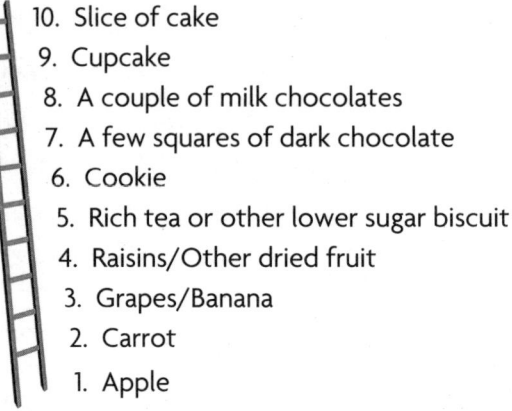

Figure 10.1. Example ladder of foods with sugar from least scary to the most.

Throughout this, be intentional about the people with whom you hang out and the content you ingest. Unsubscribe from mailing lists and unfollow social media accounts and brands who post diet culture content. Put a moratorium on diet talk with family and friends, and decline invites to events where you'll be surrounded by diet culture conversations or activities. You need as much support as possible when making significant changes to your life, but it needs to be the right support. You need people who will champion you in eating intuitively or having cake sometimes. You need to feel comfortable eating differently and clearly rejecting diet culture: you might need to be explicit about this and tell your friends and family that you're working on your relationship with food and making changes. If the friends with whom you spend the most time stick to rigid eating plans or are constantly talking about weight loss, you'll find it harder to reject this mentality, as you'll be going against the norm in your social group and may come under scrutiny about the changes you're making. It's hard to say 'I want a chocolate brownie, I'm going to have one' if those you're with look askance or say in reply 'I don't know how you can eat that, it's so fattening'. If, however, you start to socialise with intuitive eaters who take a food neutral approach with their children you'll be going with that norm and it will help you to make changes more quickly. You'll easily be able to ask for help moving towards that and will find positive reinforcement whenever you're with them.

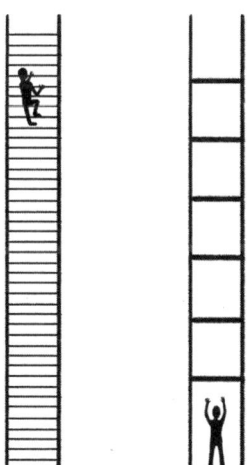

Figure 10.2. Taking small steps that may feel insignificant will get you to your goal faster than trying to take huge, ambitious steps that are appealing but likely to be too big.

When making changes to your life, it can feel like you have an insurmountable distance to travel and the end feels a long way away. Once you start to make changes, you are much better off measuring how far you have come rather than how far you have left to go. This is what is known as measuring the gain rather than the gap. The gain describes looking at where you began your journey and how far you have come. The gap starts at where you currently are and measures how far you still have left. Most people measure the gap without thinking but this is unhelpful. It reduces motivation and increases feelings of overwhelm and 'I can't do it'. You *can* do it ... Just take baby step after baby step and you will get there, as in Figure 10.1. Keep checking in to remind yourself where you started and you'll be chuffed by the progress, which is all too easy to disregard or forget otherwise.

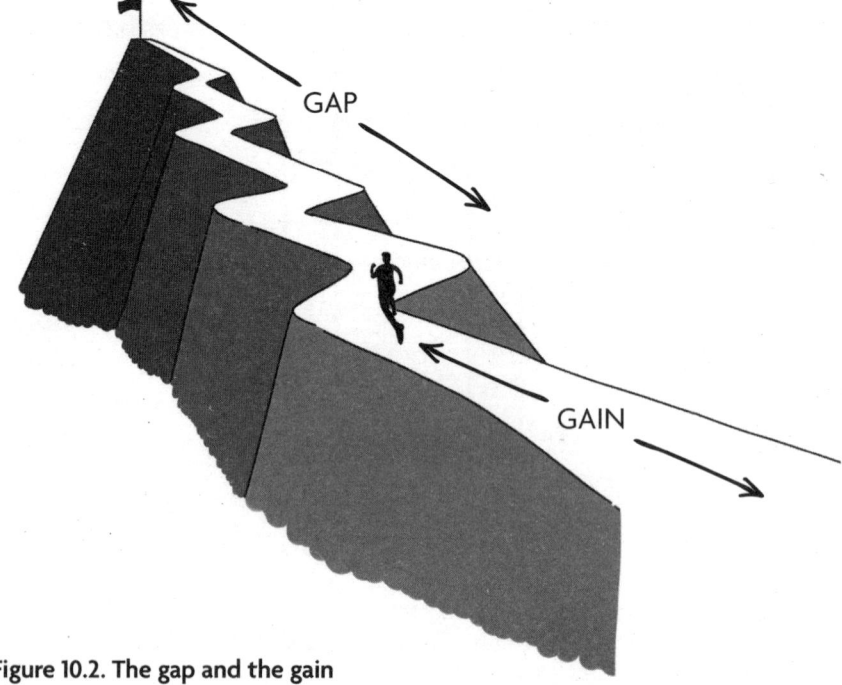

Figure 10.2. The gap and the gain

Calling out baggage that isn't yours is a vital part of the process of changing your relationship with food or teaching yourself to be different with your kids. Remember to ask yourself the questions we talked about earlier in the section on working out whose baggage it is and reject any that aren't yours and you don't want to hold.

Having thought about doing this work on yourself, it's time to return to your kids. Be responsive to their needs and cues and remember the division of responsibility in feeding. It really is deeply freeing and relieves you of so many decisions. It creates kids with the best possible relationship with food. A good relationship with food looks like eating a variety of foods, listening to your body's signals, being free from food rules, rumination and judgements about food, eating fluctuating portion sizes depending on your hunger, leaving food sometimes, overeating a little at others, enjoying a full range of foods, including the highly palatable ones, and generally being chill with all of that. One of the questions that I'm often asked in clinic is 'but what do I do when my sister talks about her newest diet in front of my kids?' or, 'how do I tell my parents not to comment on what my kids are eating?'. To help you with this I've included a table below with some ideas of how to respond. I've also added things you can say to help grandparents be more aligned with your values around food with your kids. However, grandparents are meant to indulge their grandchildren so allow for that too.

When friends or family talk about this ...	Respond with this ...
Their latest diet. Weight loss generally.	'Let's chat about this later, when the kids aren't here.' 'We're trying not to talk about diets and weight loss in front of the kids. I can hear about it, but not now.' 'We don't want the kids to hear all the diet chat as we want to protect them from the diet culture beliefs for as long as possible, so please can you not talk about this whilst they're around.' 'Can we not talk about this, there are much more interesting things to discuss.' 'We're ditching diet talk.' 'You know, your weight is the least interesting thing about you. Tell me about [insert something else about them you'd like to hear about].' If you don't want to be this direct, swiftly change the subject each time it comes up. 'Talking to kids about weight is not good for them: it leads to internalised weight bias, body dissatisfaction, disordered eating and eating disorders. Please avoid doing it.'
The dangers of sugar, ultra-processed foods (UPFs) or other foods.	'Food is really nuanced, it's not this black and white.' 'Please don't talk about sugar as poison in front of the kids, it confuses them and makes them anxious.'

When friends or family talk about this …	Respond with this …
	'UPFs can be helpful for some people sometimes.' 'Let's not demonise foods – it's unhelpful.' 'Let's not demonise foods – it's inaccurate and stresses the kids out.' 'There are important conversations to be had about food quality but not here and now.' 'All food is a source of energy.' 'All foods have value: some give us more nutrients, some give us more pleasure.' 'We're not labelling foods as good or bad, better or worse than others, so please don't say that they are with little ears around.'
They shouldn't or can't eat sweets / desserts, etc.	'The kids can be trusted to stop when they've had enough, don't worry.' 'Chocolate tastes good and is one of the foods we eat, nothing more or less than that.' 'Sometimes we need to eat for joy. It's normal human behaviour and it's fine for me / the kids to do that.' 'It's much better to focus on enjoying food than stressing about it, and I really don't want the kids to stress.' 'If you make a big deal out of sugar it'll become a big deal.' 'I'm happy for them to have it, so please don't worry.'

When friends or family talk about this ...	Respond with this ...
No pudding until they've had their veg. Rewarding with food.	'Please don't do that – it makes pudding special and we don't want it to have special status.' 'You don't have to give the kids pudding but please don't make it conditional on eating veg or a main course.' 'We're trying to keep all foods neutral with the kids, please can you help us [then if you need, explain why].' 'Please don't give the kids sweets as rewards.' 'You know, when the kids have behaved well they want praise for that. Sweets don't give them what they most want.' 'We don't want to reward or threaten with food, so instead please can you do ...' 'Bribing the kids with dessert will make them want less dinner, so please can you either offer it or not – whichever.'
When grandparents or other adults give sweets or other treats.	'The kids really love spending time with you. They come for that, not the sweets, so please don't give them so many.' 'Thanks so much for offering these to Ryan. Actually he doesn't eat them yet.' 'This is the only snack Ryan's allowed [give whatever food it is]. He's so looking forward to being with you.' 'This is Ryan's favourite snack, thanks for giving it to him later.'

To help you in this quest for your kids (and yourself), there are a few things to avoid. Don't ban or cut out foods unless they have a genuine allergy. Steer clear of making certain foods conditional on eating others. Likewise, find logical consequences for behaviours rather than rewarding and punishing with food. Rewards and punishments are contrary to food neutrality and lead to the creation of special foods and a sense of deprivation leading to cravings, rumination about the forbidden food, bingeing, secret eating and disordered eating. The same goes for dieting, so guide your children well away from it — it's a significant risk factor for eating disorders. Childhood and adolescence are two decades of profound growth and development, and kids need to be fuelled throughout. Their dietary needs and energy requirements change constantly, and they need to gain weight to mature into healthy, fully functioning adults.

Your kids will do as you do, not as you say, so remain present and aware of what you model. They are like sponges and absorb your thoughts and feelings non-verbally. Teach them to listen to and respect their bodies. Help them know and value its extraordinary functions, which allow them to live a full life. Give them as broad an emotional vocabulary as possible so they can express what they're feeling and don't have to use food. Stay curious and compassionate. It's easy to slip into being critical and corrective when you're fraught or exhausted, and at all costs, avoid getting into battles with them over food — ultimately you'll lose: they may submit and you might think you've 'won', but it damages their relationship with food, turning eating into a mode of communication. A poor relationship with food is more damaging than a point of principle, some sugar, crisps or other foods that concern you.

You might put in all the work, parent really consciously, have a food-neutral approach, model a great relationship with food to your kids and they may struggle nonetheless. It doesn't mean you've failed – you haven't. You've done nothing wrong and if you have screwed up, don't fret. You're human, we all mess up and you can always repair. It sometimes happens, just as life happens. Your kids might go through a fussy phase, or an overeating phase, or they may develop an eating disorder. Do whatever you need to do in the latter circumstance and get the right professional help as quickly as possible. Remember this: if you are supporting a child with an eating disorder, you have to ride the rollercoaster and you can't get off it until it stops. You can't fix the problem with a simple solution. It takes time, patience, boundaries, consistency, a tonne of compassion and white-knuckle riding. You are integral to your child's recovery, but that doesn't mean it'll be straightforward or have the trajectory you desire. Hiccoughs are normal. Lapses and relapses are part of the process. Bumps in the road, clashes, evenings of distress because your child has binged or not eaten enough are par for the course. None of these mean you're not doing the right thing or that you've failed. Find yourself the correct support – professional and non-professional – and buckle up for the ride!

Resources and Further Reading

Weaning
NHS – Young Children and Food: Common Questions:
https://www.nhs.uk/conditions/baby/weaning-and-feeding/young-children-and-food-common-questions

Ella's Kitchen. 2015. *The First Foods Book: The Purple One*. Hamlyn.
Gill Rapley and Tracey Murkett. 2008. *Baby-led Weaning: Helping Your Baby to Love Good Food.* London: Vermilion.
Karmel, Annabel. 2020. *Weaning Made Simple: The All-You-Need-to-Know Visual Guide to Weaning.* London: Bluebird.
Stirling-Reed, Charlotte. 2021. *How to Wean Your Baby: The step-by-step plan to help your baby love their broccoli as much as their cake.* London: Vermilion.
Wilson, Rebecca. 2020. *What Mummy Makes: Cook Just Once for You and Your Baby.* DK.

Allergies
Anaphylaxis UK: https://www.anaphylaxis.org.uk
FARE (Food Allergy Research and Education):
https://www.foodallergy.org

Spokin – 36 Skills to Teach Your Food Allergic Child:
https://www.spokin.com/skills-to-teach-your-food-allergic-child

Diabetes
Diabetes UK: https://www.diabetes.org.uk/guide-to-diabetes/your-child-and-diabetes

Religious Dietary Practices
Public Health Agency – Guidance on Foods for Religious Faiths:
https://www.publichealth.hscni.net/sites/default/files/FaithsPosterA2.pdf

Eating Disorders (General)
Beat (Beat Eating Disorders): https://www.beateatingdisorders.org.uk
Bryant-Waugh, Rachel and Bryan Lask. 2013. *Eating Disorders: A Parents' Guide*. Hove: Routledge.
Lock, James and Daniel Le Grange. 2015. *Help Your Teenager Beat an Eating Disorder*. London: The Guilford Press.
Nwuba, Chukwuemeka and Bailey Spinn, eds. 2024. *Eating Disorders Don't Discriminate*. London: Jessica Kingsley Publishers.
Smith, Jane. 2011. *The Parent's Guide to Eating Disorders*. Oxford: Lion Hudson.
Treasure, Janet, Gráinne Smith and Anna Crane. 2016. *Skills-Based Caring for a Loved One with an Eating Disorder*. Hove: Routledge.

Anorexia
I Am Ruth. Film. 2022. Director Dominic Savage. United Kingdom: Me+You Productions in association with Juggle Productions.
Brown, Harriet. 2010. *Brave Girl Eating*. London: Little, Brown.
Freeman, Hadley. 2023. *Good Girls*. London: 4th Estate.
Lynch, Evanna. 2021. *The Opposite of Butterfly Hunting*. London: Headline.
Musby, Eva. 2014. *Anorexia and Other Eating Disorders*. APRICA.

Bulimia
Freddie Flintoff: Living with Bulimia. TV documentary. 2020. Director Leo Burley. United Kingdom: South Shore Productions.

Fairburn, Christopher G. 2013. *Overcoming Binge Eating.* London: The Guilford Press.

Hansen, Kathryn. 2022. *Brain over Binge.* Florida: Camellia Publishing.

Hansen, Kathryn and Amy Johnson. 2016. *The Brain over Binge Recovery Guide.* Florida: Camellia Publishing.

Hudson-Hall, Kate. 2021. *Bulimia Sucks!* London: Kate Hudson-Hall.

Schmidt, Ulrike, Janet Treasure and June Alexander. 2015. *Getting Better Bite by Bite.* Hove: Routledge.

Feeding Your Children and Picky Eating
Kids Eat in Color: https://kidseatincolor.com

The Ellyn Satter Institute: https://www.ellynsatterinstitute.org

Cormack, Jo. *War & Peas.* 2014. Galanthus Press.

Cormack, Jo. *Helping Children Develop a Positive Relationship with Food.* 2017. London: Jessica Kingsley Publishers.

Creighton, Sarah A. *The Boy Who Loved Broccoli.* 2011. California: CreateSpace.

Potter, Claire. *Getting the Little Blighters to Eat.* 2013. London: Featherstone.

Potter, Claire and Ailie Busby. *Which Food Will You Choose?* 2021. London: Featherstone.

Health at Every Size (HAES)
Association for Size Diversity and Health: https://asdah.org

Lindo Bacon: https://lindobacon.com

Intuitive Eating & Diet Culture
Langer, Abby. *Good Food, Bad Diet.* 2021. London: Simon & Schuster.

Thomas, Laura. *Just Eat It.* 2019. London: Bluebird.

Thomas, Laura. *How to Just Eat It.* 2021. London: Bluebird.

Tribole, Evelyn and Elyse Resch. *Intuitive Eating: A Revolutionary Anti-Diet Approach*. 4th ed. 2020. New York: St. Matin's Essentials. https://www.intuitiveeating.org.

Avoidant Restrictive Food Intake Disorder (ARFID)

Rowell, Katja and Jenny McGlothlin. *Helping Your Child with Extreme Picky Eating*. 2015. Oakland, CA: New Harbinger Publications.

Beat – ARFID: What is Avoidant/Restrictive Food Intake Disorder?: https://www.beateatingdisorders.org.uk/get-information-and-support/about-eating-disorders/types/arfid

General Parenting Books (Behaviour)

Collado, Martha Deiros. *How to Be the Grown-Up*. 2024. London: Bantam.

Perry, Philippa. *The Book You Wish Your Parents Had Read*. 2019. London: Penguin Life.

Porter, Tara. *You Don't Understand Me*. 2022. London: Lagom.

Maté, Gabor, Neufeld, Gordon, et al. *Hold on to Your Kids: Why Parents Need to Matter More than Peers*. 2021. Penguin Audio.

Nicola Morgan. *Blame My Brain: The Amazing Teenage Brain Revealed*. 2013. Walker Books.

Sarah-Jayne Blakemore. *Inventing Ourselves: The Secret Life of the Teenage Brain*. 2019. Black Swan.

Siegel, Daniel J. and Payne Bryson, Dr Tina. *No-Drama Discipline: The Whole-Brain Way to Calm the Chaos and Nurture Your Child's Developing Mind*. 2014. Random House Audio.

Siegel, Dr Daniel J. and Payne Bryson, Dr Tina. *The Whole-Brain Child: 12 Proven Strategies to Nurture Your Child's Developing Mind*. 2020. Little, Brown Audio.

APPENDIX

The Minnesota Starvation Experiment

Towards the end of the Second World War, Ancel Keys, an American physiologist who studied the influence of diet on health, took a sample of fit, healthy young men with no psychiatric history and conducted the Minnesota Starvation Experiment. He and his team studied their behaviour, eating patterns and personalities during an initial period of three months, followed by a six-month period of severe restriction where their daily calorie intake was halved, and then another three months during which time they were re-fed and weight restored. The results were shocking to Keys and his team. The men lost about 25% of their body weight, but more disturbing were the changes across all domains of their lives and functioning. They became increasingly preoccupied with food and eating and unable to concentrate on more normal topics. Mealtimes became quiet as the men slowed down their eating speed, often taking an extremely long time to eat, cutting their food into tiny pieces and focusing on their food alone. Several men succumbed to binge eating during the restriction phase of the experiment and even after refeeding, a number of the men did not return to eating as they had done before the experiment.[79]

There were also social, sexual, physical, emotional and cognitive changes – the same as those that we eating disorder clinicians see in patients today. These included insomnia, irritability, anxiety, depression, withdrawal, strained relationships, reduced sexual interest, and impaired comprehension, judgement and concentration. The men suffered dizziness, headaches, were cold, tired and weak. There is a full list of attitudes and behaviours at the end of this appendix.[80] The thing is, because all the effects of starvation are physiological, including the social and emotional, they cannot be reversed without weight gain. To be clear, the only way to reverse the effects of starvation is to eat and restore weight. Talking alone will not do it.

HAES – Health at Every Size

HAES is a model that first emerged in the 1960s off the back of an article by Lew Louderback in 1967 called 'More People Should be fat!'[81] Louderback believed that the change in culture towards the pursuit of thinness was detrimental to fat people, arguing that amongst others:

- Dieting seems to unleash destructive and emotional tendencies.
- Forced changes in weight are not only likely to be temporary but also to cause physical and emotional damage.
- There are 'thin fat people' who suffer physically and emotionally from having dieted to below their natural body weight.
- The five-year cure rate for obesity is virtually zero.

- Forced changes in weight are likely to be temporary and to cause physical and emotional damage.
- It has become so 'in' to be thin that fat peoples' civil rights are repeatedly and openly violated.
- Fat people are discriminated against in education.
- The persecution of fat people is not for health reasons but for aesthetics.

Following this, the 1970s saw the constructing of feminism and a mounting pressure on women to be thinner. In her groundbreaking book, *Fat is a Feminist Issue*,[82] Susie Orbach suggested that white, middle-class women's eating issues were a result of their subordination in society and she recommended they stop dieting, start listening to hunger and full cues, and learn to use their voice rather than food and their body to express difficult feelings and ideas. From here on, questions were raised about dieting, with more literature and research emerging showing what we really ought to know by now: that dieting does not work in anything other than the short term; that bingeing is a natural response to hunger and dieting; that weight-loss efforts damage health; that eating habits are not the main or sole cause of fat; and that the health problems of fat people are not innately due to fat but to the stress, self-hatred and dieting in response to being fat.[83] It's extraordinary that almost 50 years after the HAES model emerged, these points remain so debated and little known.

Now the main components of the HAES approach are closely linked with the anti-diet movement. It is intended to be a weight-neutral approach for people of all body sizes based on the pillars of intuitive eating, body acceptance regardless of shape or size and physical activity for movement and health rather than for elite performance or to shape the body.[84] It is about taking care of your body without worrying about its size, with the focus being on health, not weight. It aims to promote a mentally healthy relationship with food, to promote body positivity and to remove stigma and fat phobia from society.[85] To believe that we should all be the same size or weight is like saying we should all be the same height or have the same shoe size. Whilst the research is relatively new, there are some promising results in terms of physical and psychological health.[86,87,88]

Effects of Semi-Starvation: A Summary

Attitudes and Behaviour Related to Eating

- Increased preoccupation with food
- Planning meals
- Tendency to hoard
- Change in speed of eating
- Increased hunger

Emotional Changes

- Depression
- Anxiety
- Irritability
- Apathy
- Neglected personal hygiene

Social and Sexual Changes

- Withdrawal
- Reduced sense of humour
- Feelings of social inadequacy

- Isolation
- Strained relationships
- Reduced sexual interest

Cognitive Changes

- Impaired:
  - Concentration
  - alertness
  - comprehension
  - judgement

Physical Changes

- Gastrointestinal discomfort
- Reduced need for sleep
- Dizziness
- Headaches
- Hypersensitivity to noise and light
- Reduced strength
- Oedema (fluid retention causing swelling)
- Hair loss
- Reduced tolerance for cold temperatures
- Abnormal tingling/pricking sensations in hands and feet

Physical Activity

- Tiredness
- Weakness
- Listlessness
- Apathy

References

Dear Reader

1   Jennifer Couturier and Mark Norris, 'The Shadow Pandemic: Eating Disorders, Youth, and COVID-19', *Journal of Adolescent Health* 72, no. 3 (March 2023): pp. 321–2, https://doi.org/10.1016/j.jadohealth.2022.12.008

Chapter 1: What Is Food?

2   Paul A.S. Breslin, 'An Evolutionary Perspective on Food and Human Taste', *Current Biology* 23, no. 9 (May 2013): R409–R418, https://doi.org/10.1016/j.cub.2013.04.010

3   Stephen P. Wooding, Vicente A. Ramirez and Maik Behrens, 'Bitter Taste Receptors: Genes, Evolution and Health', *Evolution, Medicine, and Public Health* 9, no. 1 (2021: pp. 431–47, https://doi.org/10.1093/emph/eoab031

4   'The Science of Taste', *Food Insight*, 13 March 2018, https://foodinsight.org/the-science-of-taste

Chapter 2: Your Family Food Legacy

5   Peters, S. (2012). *The Chimp Paradox*. Vermilion.

6   Claude Fischler, 'Food, Self and Identity', *Social Science Information* 27, no. 2 (1988): pp. 275–92, https://doi.org/10.1177/053901888027002005

7   Sidney W. Mintz, 'Food and Eating: Some Persisting Questions', in *Food Nations*, edited by Warren Belasco and Philip Scranton (New York: Routledge, 2014): pp. 24–32

8   Larson, N. and Story, M. (2009), 'A review of environmental influences on food choices', *Annals of Behavioral Medicine*, 38(suppl_1), s56-s73.

9   Christina Sterbenz, 'The Entire "Popeye" Franchise Is Based on Bad Science', *Business Insider*, 18 January 2014, https://www.businessinsider.com/spinach-typo-popeye-2014-1

10 Marit Pauwelyn, Petrit Krasniqi and Chloe Mclain, '"It's Like a Chronic Illness"', November 2022, https://www.childhoodtrust.org.uk/wp-content/uploads/2022/11/Food-Insecurity-2022-Report-1.pdf

11 Russell Viner, 'Food Insecurity Is Toxic for Our Children and a Threat to the Future of Our Next Generation', *The BMJ Opinion*, 18 October 2021, https://blogs.bmj.com/bmj/2021/10/18/food-insecurity-is-toxic-for-our-children-and-a-threat-to-the-future-of-the-next-generation

12 Danielle Gallegos, Areana Eivers, Peter Sondergeld and Cassandra Pattinson, 'Food Insecurity and Child Development: A State-of-the-Art Review', *International Journal of Environmental Research and Public Health* 18, no. 17 (August 2021): p. 8990, https://doi.org/10.3390/ijerph18178990

13 Brigid Francis-Devine, Xameerah Malik and Nerys Roberts, 'Food Poverty: Households, Food Banks and Free School Meals', House of Commons Library Research Briefing, 2 September 2024, https://commonslibrary.parliament.uk/research-briefings/cbp-9209

14 Patrick Butler, 'Number of UK Children in Food Poverty Nearly Doubles in a Year to 4m', *Guardian*, 1 March 2023, https://www.theguardian.com/society/2023/mar/01/number-of-uk-children-in-food-poverty-nearly-doubles-in-a-year-to-4m

15 Patrick Butler, '"Health Emergency": 15% of UK Households Went Hungry Last Month, Data Shows', *Guardian*, 27 February 2024, https://www.theguardian.com/society/2024/feb/27/health-emergency-15-of-uk-households-went-hungry-last-month-data-shows

16 Pamela Goyan Kittler, Kathryn P. Sucher and Marcia Nahikian-Nelms, *Food and Culture*, 6th ed. (Belmont, CA: Wadsworth, 2012)

17 Stevenson, R.J., Yeomans, M.R. and Francis, H.M. (2024), Human Hunger as a Memory Process', *Psychological Review*, 131(1), 174

18 Norma Baumel Joseph, 'T'beet: Situating Iraqi Jewish Identity through Food' in *Everyday Sacred: Religion in Contemporary Quebec*, edited by Hillary Kaell (Montreal: McGill-Queen's University Press, 2017), pp. 99–126, https://doi.org/10.2307/j.ctt1vjqqhp

19 Omar Jaber, 'How to Care for the Fasting Child', Baylor College of Medicine, 8 May 2018, https://blogs.bcm.edu/2018/05/08/how-to-care-for-the-fasting-child

20 Monique C Alblas et al., 'Consuming Media, Consuming Food: Investigating Concurrent TV Viewing and Eating Using a 7-D Time Use Diary Survey', *Public Health Nutrition* 26, no. 4 (2023): pp. 748–57, https://doi.org/10.1017/s1368980021002858

Chapter 3: Feelings

21 W. Kyle Simmons et al., 'Appetite Changes Reveal Depression Subgroups with Distinct Endocrine, Metabolic, and Immune States', *Molecular Psychiatry* 25 (2020):1457–68, https://doi.org/10.1038/s41380-018-0093-6

22 Plutchik, R. (1980). A general psychoevolutionary theory of emotion. *Emotion: Theory, research, and experience*, 1. Academic Press

23 'Emotion Wheel for Children', Mentally Healthy Schools, 5 July 2021, https://mentallyhealthyschools.org.uk/resources/emotion-wheel-for-children

24 'Build Mindfulness Skills with Our Emotion Wheels and Needs Wheels', Human Systems, 25 August 2020, https://humansystems.co/emotionwheels

Chapter 4: Communication Through Food

25 Qingqing Liu et al., 'Changes in the Global Burden of Depression from 1990 to 2017: Findings from the Global Burden of Disease Study', *Journal of Psychiatric Research* 126 (2020): pp. 134–40

26 Derek Summerfield, 'Depression: Epidemic or Pseudo-Epidemic?', *Journal of the Royal Society of Medicine* 99, no. 3 (March 2006): pp. 161–2, https://doi.org/10.1258/jrsm.99.3.161

27 Alan R. Teo, HwaJung Choi and Marcia Valenstein, 'Social Relationships and Depression: Ten-Year Follow-Up from a Nationally Representative Study', *PLOS One* 8, no. 4 (2013), https://doi.org/10.1371/journal.pone.0062396

28 Robert S. Wilson et al., 'Loneliness and Risk of Alzheimer Disease', *Archives of General Psychiatry* 64, no. 2 (February 2007): pp. 234–40, https://doi.org/10.1001/archpsyc.64.2.234

29 R.I.M. Dunbar, 'Breaking Bread: the Functions of Social Eating', *Adaptive Human Behaviour and Physiology* 3, no. 3 (March 2017): pp. 198–211, https://doi.org/10.1007/s40750-017-0061-4

30 Jessica Martino, Jennifer Pegg and Elizabeth Pegg Frates, 'The Connection Prescription: Using the Power of Social Interactions and the Deep Desire for Connectedness to Empower Health and Wellness', *American Journal of Lifestyle Medicine* 11, no. 6 (October 2015): pp. 466–75, https://doi.org/10.1177/1559827615608788

31 G. Di Pellegrino et al., 'Understanding Motor Events: A Neurophysiological Study', *Experimental Brain Research* 91 (1992): pp. 176–80, https://doi.org/10.1007/BF00230027

32 S. Acharya and S. Shukla, 'Mirror Neurons: Enigma of the Metaphysical Modular Brain', *Journal of Natural Science Biology and Medicine* 3, no. 2 (July 2012): pp. 118–24, https://doi.org/10.4103/0976-9668.101878

33 First observed and developed by behavioural psychologist Frank Skinner in the early 20th century.

Chapter 5: Developmental Stages with Eating

34 'Raise a Healthy Child Who Is a Joy to Feed', Ellyn Satter Institute, 23 October 2017, https://www.ellynsatterinstitute.org/how-to-feed/the-division-of-responsibility-in-feeding

35 Mariko Makino, Mitsuo Yasushi and Sueharu Tsutsui, 'The Risk of Eating Disorder Relapse During Pregnancy and After Delivery and Postpartum Depression Among Women Recovered from Eating Disorders, BMC Pregnancy and Childbirth', *BMC Pregnancy Childbirth* 20, no. 323 (May 2020), https://doi.org/10.1186/s12884-020-03006-7

36 'Feeling Depressed After Childbirth', NHS, 18 May 2023, https://www.nhs.uk/conditions/baby/support-and-services/feeling-depressed-after-childbirth

37 'Postnatal Depression in Dads and Co-Parents: 10 Things You Should Know', NCT, 22 October 2024, https://www.nct.org.uk/life-parent/emotions/postnatal-depression-dads-and-co-parents-10-things-you-should-know

38 'Developmental Stages in Infant & Toddler Feeding', Infant and Toddler Forum, 15 August 2015, https://infantandtoddlerforum.org/wp-content/uploads/2015/08/ITF_Developmental_Stages_FINAL.pdf

39 A. Brown and M. Lee, 'A Descriptive Study Investigating the Use and Nature of Baby-Led Weaning in a UK Sample of Mothers', *Maternal and Child Nutrition* 7, no. 1 (2011): pp. 34–47, https://doi.org/10.1111/j.1740-8709.2010.00243.x

40 Costa, '20 Shocking Allergy Statistics You Need to Know', London Allergy and Immunology Centre, 27 October 2021, https://www.allergycliniclondon.co.uk/20-shocking-allergy-statistics

41 'Cow's Milk Allergy', Anaphylaxis UK, 6 March 2018, https://www.anaphylaxis.org.uk/fact-sheet/cows-milk-allergy

42 James T.C. Li, 'Food Allergy vs. Food Intolerance: What's the Difference?', Mayo Clinic, 2 May 2019, https://www.mayoclinic.org/diseases-conditions/food-allergy/expert-answers/food-allergy/faq-20058538

43 'Food Allergy vs. Food Intolerance', Family Allergy and Ashma Care, 3 March 2021, https://www.faaccares.com/2021/food-allergy-vs-food-intolerance

44 'Diabetes', Royal College of Paediatrics and Child Health, 4 March 2020, https://stateofchildhealth.rcpch.ac.uk/evidence/long-term-conditions/diabetes

45 'Is Sugar More Addictive Than Cocaine?'. Conifer Park, 21 March 2024, https://www.coniferpark.com/blog/sugar-more-addictive-than-cocaine

46 Stevenson, R.J. (2024). The psychological basis of hunger and its dysfunctions. *Nutrition Reviews*, *82*(10), 1444–1454

47 https://www.coniferpark.com/blog/sugar-more-addictive-than-cocaine

Chapter 6: Childhood

48 Ellyn Satter, *Child of Mine* (Boulder, CO: Bull Publishing Company, 2000).

49 Jo Cormack, *Helping Children Develop a Positive Relationship with Food* (London: Jessica Kingsley Publishers, 2017)

50 Rachel Bryant-Waugh and Bryan Lask, *Eating Disorders: A Parents' Guide* (Hove: Routledge, 2017).

51 https://images.app.goo.gl/zaxYhFbjW1iuxHDk7

Chapter 7: Adolescence

52 Mariam Arain et al., 'Maturation of the Adolescent Brain', *Neuropsychiatric Disease and Treatment* 9 (2013): pp. 449–61, https://doi.org/10.2147/NDT.S39776

53 'Mirrors and the Mind', British Psychological Society, 10 February 2010, https://www.bps.org.uk/psychologist/mirrors-and-mind

Chapter 8: Diet Culture

54   F. Rice, 'The Intergenerational Transmission of Anxiety Disorders and Major Depression', *American Journal of Psychiatry* 179, no. 9 (2022): pp. 596–8.

55   A. Arroyo, C. Segrin and K.K. Andersen, 'Intergenerational Transmission of Disordered Eating: Direct and Indirect Maternal Communication Among Grandmothers, Mothers, and Daughters', *Body Image* 20 (2017): pp. 107–15.

56   Bob M. Fennis and Wolfgang Stroebe, *The Psychology of Advertising* (London: Routledge, 2020)

57   Venu Madhav Ganipisetti and Pratyusha Bollimunta, 'Obesity and Set-Point Theory', in *StatPearls* (Treasure Island, FL: StatPearls Publishing, 2023), https://www.ncbi.nlm.nih.gov/books/NBK592402

58   Abby Langer, *Good Food, Bad Diet* (London: Simon & Schuster, 2021)

59   James W. Anderson, Elizabeth C. Konz, Robert C. Frederich and Constance L. Wood, 'Long-Term Weight-Loss Maintenance: A Meta-Analysis of US Studies', *American Journal of Clinical Nutrition* 74, no. 5 (November 2001): pp. 579–84, https://doi.org/10.1093/ajcn/74.5.579

60   Venke Ueland, 'Stigmatisation and Shame – a Qualitative Study of Living with Obesity', *Norwegian Journal of Clinical Nursing/Sykepleien Forskning* (May 2019): e-77012, https://doi.org/10.4220/Sykepleienf.2019.77012en

61   Ellen P. Williams et al., 'Overweight and Obesity: Prevalence, Consequences, and Causes of a Growing Public Health Problem', *Current Obesity Reports* 4 2015)): pp. 70–363, https://doi.org/10.1007/s4-0169-015-13679

62   S. Westermann, W. Rief, F. Euteneuer and S. Kohlmann, 'Social Exclusion and Shame in Obesity', *Eating Behaviors* 17 (April 2015): pp. 74–6, https://doi.org/10.1016/j.eatbeh.2015.01.001

63   Brené Brown, *Dare to Lead: Brave Work. Tough Conversations. Whole Hearts.* (London: Vermilion, 2018).

64   '10 Principles of Intuitive Eating', The Original Intuitive Eating Pros, 5 April 2017, https://www.intuitiveeating.org/10-principles-of-intuitive-eating

65   Marisa Minadeo and Lizzy Pope, 'Weight-Normative Messaging Predominates on TikTok – A Qualitative Content Analysis', *PLOS ONE* 17, no. 11 (November 2022): e0267997, https://doi.org/10.1371/journal.pone.0267997

66 Francesca Solmi et al., 'Changes in the Prevalence and Correlates of Weight-Control Behaviors and Weight Perception in Adolescents in the UK, 1986-2015', *JAMA Pediatrics* 175, no. 3 (November 2020): pp. 267–75, https://doi.org/10.1001/jamapediatrics.2020.4746

67 Elena Bozzola et al., 'The Use of Social Media in Children and Adolescents: Scoping Review on the Potential Risks', *International Journal of Environmental Research and Public Health* 19, no. 16 (2022): 9960, https://doi.org/10.3390/ijerph19169960

68 Vivienne M. Hazzard et al., 'Intuitive Eating Longitudinally Predicts Better Psychological Health and Lower Use of Disordered Eating Behaviors: Findings from EAT 2010–2018', *Eating and Weight Disorders* 26 (February 2021): pp. 287–94, https://doi.org/10.1007/s40519-020-00852-4

Chapter 9: Disordered Eating and Eating Disorders

69 Shisslak, C.M., Crago, M. and Estes, L.S. (1995). 'The Spectrum of Eating Disorders', *International Journal of Eating Disorders*, 18 (3), 209–19.

70 *The Diagnostic and Statistical Manual of Mental Disorders / DSM-5-TR® Handbook of Differential Diagnosis*. American Psychiatric Pub.

The International Classification of Diseases / The ICD-10 Classification of Mental and Behavioural Disorders. World Health Organization.

71 https://www.england.nhs.uk/2022/03/nhs-treating-record-number-of-young-people-for-eating-disorders/

72 https://nedc.com.au/eating-disorders/types/binge-eating-disorder

73 https://cks.nice.org.uk/topics/eating-disorders/background-information/prevalence/

74 Pearce, J.M. and Morton, Richard, 'Origins of Anorexia Nervosa', Eur Neurol. 2004;52(4):191-2. doi: 10.1159/000082033. Epub 2004 Nov 10. PMID: 15539770.

75 van Eeden, A.E., van Hoeken, D. and Hoek, H.W., 'Incidence, Prevalence and Mortality of Anorexia Nervosa and Bulimia Nervosa', Curr Opin Psychiatry. 2021 Nov 1;34(6):515-524. doi: 10.1097/YCO.0000000000000739. PMID: 34419970; PMCID: PMC8500372.

76 Keys, A., Brožek, J., Henschel, A., Mickelsen, O. and Taylor, H.L. (1950). *The Biology of Human Starvation* (2 vols).

77 https://cks.nice.org.uk/topics/eating-disorders/background-information/prevalence/

78 https://www.beateatingdisorders.org.uk/get-information-and-support/about-eating-disorders/types/arfid/

Appendix: The Minnesota Starvation Experiment

79   Garner, D.M. and Garfinkel, P.E. (Eds.). (1997). *Handbook of Treatment for Eating Disorders.* Guilford Press.

80   Waller, G., Cordery, H., Corstorphine, E., Hinrichsen, H., Lawson, R., Mountford, V. and Russell, K. (2007). *Cognitive Behavioral Therapy for Eating Disorders: A Comprehensive Treatment Guide.* Cambridge University Press.

81   Louderback, L. (1967). 'More People Should Be Fat', *Saturday Evening Post*, 240, 10-12.

82   Orbach, S. (1998). *Fat is a Feminist Issue: The Anti-diet Guide for Women + Fat is a Feminist Issue II.* Random House.

83   https://asdah.org/history-of-the-health-at-every-size-movement-the-1970s-and-80s-part-2/

84   Bacon L. and Aphramor, L. 'Weight Science: Evaluating the Evidence for a Paradigm Shift'. Nutr J. 2011;10:9.

85   Mariana Dimitrov Ulian et al., 'Effects of a New Intervention Based on the Health at Every Size Approach for the Management of Obesity: The "Health and Wellness in Obesity" Study', *PLoS One* 13, no. 7 (2018): e0198401, https://doi.org/10.1371/journal.pone.0198401

86   Bacon, L., Stern, J.S., Van Loan, M.D. and Keim, N.L., 'Size Acceptance and Intuitive Eating Improve Health for Obese, Female Chronic Dieters', J Am Diet Assoc. 2005;105(6):929–936.

87   Gagnon-Girouard, M-P, Bégin, C., Provencher, V. et al. 'Psychological Impact of a "Health-at-every-size" Intervention on Weight-preoccupied Overweight/Obese Women', J Obes. 2010 2010:pii: 928097

88   Penney, T.L. and Kirk, S.F., 'The Health at Every Size Paradigm and Obesity: Missing Empirical Evidence May Help Push the Reframing Obesity Debate Forward. Am J Public Health. 2015 May; 105(5):e38-42. doi: 10.2105/AJPH.2015.302552. Epub 2015 Mar 19. PMID: 25790393; PMCID: PMC4386524

Acknowledgements

I've wanted to write this book for years. After my first attempt sputtered to a halt, I tucked the idea away, accepting that it wasn't meant to be. Now, to find myself here with it finished, feels surreal. Somehow, it all came together, and I'm endlessly grateful to the awesome people who helped take this from wishful thinking to a reality.

First, a massive thank you to my agent, Lou, who championed this book and was determined that I should write it. You made it happen and I'm so grateful. To Borra, who has tenaciously supported me throughout the writing process, a huge thank you. And to the whole DML Talent team for your belief and support over the years.

To the team at Bonnier Books for taking a chance on me, I'm forever grateful. Thank you for pouncing on the idea and being so fabulously excited about *How to Talk to Children About Food* from its inception. Every time I doubted myself, you reminded me of readers for whom this book could offer something helpful. Blake and Clare, thank you for your PR and marketing magic. Susan, I will be eternally grateful for your insightful copy editing.

Madiya, I couldn't have got here without you. Thank you for your patience, steadfast encouragement, thoughtful and incisive edits and reassurance. I feel extremely lucky to have had you by my side throughout.

I'm also incredibly lucky to have wonderful friends and family who, once I fessed up that I was writing a book, have been endlessly interested and supportive. Ann, a huge thank you for going above and beyond in slogging through my second draft at lightning speed: a labour of love. And Gav, this project wouldn't have been the same without you: your encouragement to write a book from before this project came to be and, of course, 'book-gate'.

Katie, for the decades of friendship, laughter, learning, case discussion, being my second brain at the drop of a whatsapp message and for Zababa. Thanks a mil.

On to the fam. Husband, my rock, my bestie and my harshest (literary) critic. Thank you for putting up with me. For giving painful feedback on this book in its many iterations; tolerating my late nights, crazy early starts and poor work-life balance. For your humour, occasional flashes of wisdom and for being unashamedly you.

And finally, my gorgeous four. You rock. You're utterly inspiring, individually and as a unit, and I'm so proud of the wonderful humans that you are. You couldn't have been more supportive, interested, or chuffed for me. Your suggestions have been a mix of helpful and hilarious. From making dinner when I've been up against a deadline to taking the mick mercilessly and, at every opportunity, pointing out things I do that this book advises against!

About the Author

Dr Anna Colton is a clinical psychologist, specialising in both adolescence and eating disorders, with over 20 years of experience. Dr Anna worked in the NHS at Great Ormond Street Hospital, Vincent Square eating disorders clinic, The Tavistock Clinic and the Priory Roehampton. She now works exclusively in private practice.

Alongside her clinical practice, Dr Anna can be seen on TV as a mental health expert and behind the camera, advising TV companies, working on reality TV shows and documentaries, supporting contributors and advising production on mental health. She has also worked with BBC Bitesize on their parents' toolkit, on their Mind Set's GCSE campaign, and their body image and social media campaigns.

Additionally, Dr Anna works with several West End stage shows, such as *Matilda*, to help children and adults who are struggling with a range of issues that are affecting their performance, including stage fright and anxiety.